Amsterdam
2009

WHAT'S NEW | WHAT'S ON | WHAT'S BEST

timeout.com/amsterdam

Contents

Published by Time Out Guides Ltd
Universal House
251 Tottenham Court Road
London W1T 7AB
Tel: + 44 (0)20 7813 3000
Fax: + 44 (0)20 7813 6001
Email: guides@timeout.com
www.timeout.com

Managing Director Peter Fiennes
Financial Director Gareth Garner
Editorial Director Ruth Jarvis
Deputy Series Editor Dominic Earle
Editorial Manager Holly Pick
Assistant Management Accountant Ija Krasnikova

Time Out Guides is a wholly owned subsidiary of Time Out Group Ltd.

© Time Out Group Ltd
Chairman Tony Elliott
Financial Director Richard Waterlow
Group General Manager/Director Nichola Coulthard
Time Out Magazine Ltd MD Richard Waterlow
Time Out Communications Ltd MD David Pepper
Time Out International Ltd MD Cathy Runciman
Production Director Mark Lamond
Group IT Director Simon Chappell
Head of Marketing Catherine Demajo

Time Out and the Time Out logo are trademarks of Time Out Group Ltd.

This edition first published in Great Britain in 2008 by Ebury Publishing
A Random House Group Company
Company information can be found on www.randomhouse.co.uk
Random House UK Limited Reg. No. 954009
10 9 8 7 6 5 4 3 2 1

Distributed in the US by Publishers Group West
Distributed in Canada by Publishers Group Canada

For further distribution details, see www.timeout.com

ISBN: 978-1-84670-097-2

A CIP catalogue record for this book is available from the British Library.

Printed and bound by Firmengruppe APPL, aprinta druck, Wemding, Germany.

The Random House Group Limited supports The Forest Stewardship Council (FSC), the
leading international forest certification organisation. All our titles that are printed on
Greenpeace approved FSC certified paper carry the FSC logo. Our paper procurement
policy can be found at www.rbooks.co.uk/environment.

Time Out carbon-offsets all its flights with Trees for Cities (www.treesforcities.org).

Amsterdam Shortlist

The **Time Out Amsterdam Shortlist 2009** is one of a new series of guides that draws on Time Out's background as a magazine publisher to keep you current with what's going on in town. As well as Amsterdam's key sights and the best of its eating, drinking and leisure options, it picks out the most exciting venues to have opened in the last year and gives a full calendar of events from September 2008 to December 2009. It also includes features on the important news, trends and openings, all compiled by locally based editors and writers. Whether you're visiting for the first time in your life or the first time this year, you'll find the *Time Out Amsterdam Shortlist* contains all you need to know, in a portable and easy-to-use format.

The guide divides central Amsterdam into seven areas, each containing listings for Sights & Museums, Eating & Drinking, Shopping, Nightlife and Arts & Leisure, and maps pinpointing their locations. At the front of the book are chapters rounding up these scenes city-wide, and giving a shortlist of our overall picks. We include itineraries for days out, plus essentials such as transport information and hotels.

Our listings give phone numbers as dialled within the city. The international code for the Netherlands is 31. To call from outside the country, follow this number with the code for Amsterdam, 020, dropping the intial '0'. Some listed numbers are mobiles, indicated as such.

We have noted price categories by using one to four € signs (€-€€€€), representing budget, moderate, expensive and luxury. Major credit cards are accepted unless otherwise stated. We also indicate when a venue is NEW, and list **Event highlights**.

All listings are double-checked, but places do sometimes close or change their hours or prices, so it's a good idea to call before visiting. While every effort has been made to ensure accuracy, the publishers cannot accept responsibility for any errors that this guide may contain.

Venues are marked on the maps using symbols numbered according to their order in the chapter and colour-coded as follows:

❶ Sights & Museums
❶ Eating & Drinking
❶ Shopping
❶ Nightlife
❶ Arts & Leisure

Map key		
Selected House Number		*463*
Major Sight or Landmark		
Hospital or College		
Pedestrianised Street		
Railway Station		
Metro Station		Ⓜ
Area Name		LEIDSEPLEIN

Time Out Amsterdam Shortlist 2009

EDITORIAL
Editor Steve Korver
Deputy Editor Simon Cropper
Copy Editor Helena Smith
Proofreader Tamsin Shelton

DESIGN
Art Director Scott Moore
Art Editor Pinelope Kourmouzoglou
Senior Designer Henry Elphick
Graphic Designers Gemma Doyle,
   Kei Ishimaru
Digital Imaging Simon Foster
Advertising Designer Jodi Sher
Picture Editor Jael Marschner
Deputy Picture Editor Katie Morris
Picture Researcher Gemma Walters
Picture Desk Assistant Marzena Zoladz

ADVERTISING
Commercial Director Mark Phillips
International Advertising Manager
   Kasimir Berger
International Sales Executive
   Charlie Sokol
Advertising Assistant Kate Staddon
Advertising Sales (Amsterdam) Tamar
   Bosschaart

MARKETING
Marketing Manager Yvonne Poon
Senior Publishing Brand Manager
   Luthfa Begum
Sales & Marketing Director,
   North America Lisa Levinson
Marketing Designers Anthony Huggins,
   Nicola Wilson

PRODUCTION
Production Manager Brendan McKeown
Production Controller Damian Bennett
Production Co-ordinator Julie Pallot

CONTRIBUTORS
This guide was researched and written by Joost Baaij, Georgina Bean, Willem de Blaauw,
Dara Colwell, Shyama Daryanani, Monique Gruter, Karina Hof, Kate Holder, Luuk van Huêt,
Cecily Layzell, Steve Korver, Steven McCarron, Kim Renfrew, Marinus de Ruiter and Mark
Wedin. The editor would like to thank Kim Renfrew, Steven McCarron and Klaas&Nel.

PHOTOGRAPHY
All photography by Anne Binckebank, except: pages 9, 20, 25, 28, 33, 52, 57, 70 (top
left and right), 73, 74, 79, 80, 86, 90, 95, 99, 102, 105, 107, 111, 112, 117, 120,
123, 126, 128, 138, 142, 147, 148, 149, 150, 152, 159 Michelle Grant; page 16 Peter
Siegel www.djventilator.nl; page 23 Abel Minnee; page 29 Francesca Patella; pages 36,
37 E. P. Kroese; pages 44, 49, 60, 66, 70 (bottom), 75, 82, 92, 109, 115, 127, 131,
133, 139, 155, 160, 167 Olivia Rutherford; page 46 Gemma Day; page 62 Rogan
Macdonald; page 106 Nederlands Uitvaart Museum Tot Zover; page 145 Photo
Art/Netherlands Bard of Tourism and Conventions.

The following images were provided by the featured establishments/artists: pages 12, 42,
48, 87, 137, 158, 165.

Cover image: Sebastiano Scattolini/4Corners Images

MAPS
JS Graphics (john@jsgraphics.co.uk).

About Time Out

Founded in 1968, Time Out has expanded from humble London beginnings into the
leading resource for those wanting to know what's happening in the world's greatest
cities. As well as our influential what's-on weeklies in London, New York and Chicago,
we publish more than a dozen other listings magazines in cities as varied as Beijing
and Mumbai. The magazines established Time Out's trademark style: sharp writing,
informed reviewing and bang up-to-date inside knowledge of every scene.

Time Out made the natural leap into travel guides in the 1980s with the City Guide
series, which now extends to over 50 destinations around the world. Written and
researched by expert local writers and generously illustrated with original photography,
the full-size guides cover a larger area than our Shortlist guides and include many more
venue reviews, along with additional background features and a full set of maps.

Throughout this rapid growth, the company has remained proudly independent, still
owned by Tony Elliott four decades after he started Time Out London as a single fold-
out sheet of A5 paper. This independence extends to the editorial content of all
our publications, this Shortlist included. No establishment has been featured because
it has advertised, and no payment has influenced any of our reviews. And, for our
critics, there's definitely no such thing as a free lunch: all restaurants and bars are
visited and reviewed anonymously, and Time Out always picks up the bill.
For more about the company, see www.timeout.com.

Don't Miss
2009

cobra museum
of modern art

amstelveen www.cobra-museum.nl

Sandbergplein 1
1181 ZX Amstelveen
T +31 (0)205475050
Tram 5, Metro 51
(Amstelveen Centrum),
Busses 142, 144, 170,
172, 300 (Amstelveen
Busstation)
Opening times
Tue to Sun 10.00-17.00
Closed Mondays

Exhibitions from the CoBrA art collection and contemporary art

The Cobra Museum of Modern Art is not far from the major art museums in Amsterdam and within easy reach by bus and tram. A visit to the museum is highly recommended. In addition to housing a unique collection of works by artists of the 20th-century CoBrA movement, the museum is a leading venue for exhibitions of contemporary art.

The collection consists of major works representing the international avant-garde art movement CoBrA, which heralded a breakthrough in the development of Dutch modern art.

Alongside displays from the permanent collection, the museum organises several major exhibitions of contemporary art each year.

De Waag

Sights & Museums

If you're looking for the unholy trinity of sex, drugs and rock 'n' roll, you'll find everything you need in Amsterdam without even the slightest bit of preparation: whatever you're after will leap out at you. But this town is also dense with pursuits of the higher, nobler and brainier sort. And although it manages to pack the cultural punch of a metropolis, Amsterdam is a remarkably convenient size: most of the attractions are within half an hour's walk away from each other, and the excellent network of trams provides backup for those who are low on energy. You can also slipstream the locals and saddle up on a bike (though do beware of trams and cycle thieves); better still, beg or borrow a boat to appreciate the city at the best of all angles – looking upwards at the gabled buildings from a canal.

In the city centre are Amsterdam's old port (and rapidly developing waterfront, p209), its medieval buildings, the red lights that denote the central business district of the world's oldest trade, the grand 17th-century merchants' houses, the high spires of ancient religious institutions, the earliest and prettiest canals and also many of its most famous sights. Except to stroll to Museumplein, with its three most famous art museums and world-class concert hall, few visitors to the city go beyond the confines of *grachtengordel*, that calming concentric belt of Golden Age canals – likened by Albert

Time Out Travel Guides

Worldwide

All our guides are written by a team of **local experts** with a unique and stylish insider perspective. We offer essential tips, trusted advice and honest reviews for everything you need to know in the city.

Over 50 destinations available at all good bookshops and at timeout.com/shop

Time Out Guides

Camus, in his novel *La Chute*, to the circles of Hell – that ensnare the fascinating and historic Old Centre. Be sure not to make that mistake: although they're largely residential, the Jordaan and the Pijp are hugely attractive places.

Changes, what changes?

Although Amsterdam remains a city in flux – especially with the building of the Noord-Zuidlijn metro line (see box p112) and the massive building projects around Centraal Station and directly across the IJ in Amsterdam Noord – a big part of the city's charm lies in how little it has changed. Most of the more appealing sights have been around for many decades or, more usually, centuries. You should, however, be aware that two of the city's most prominent museums are in the midst of major change. The Stedelijk Museum of Modern Art (p124) is currently homeless while its usual home on Museumplein is massively renovated, but it plans to share its collections and get out and about. Until summer 2008 it was housed in Post CS near Centraal Station – something of a blessing in disguise, since its temporary location seems to have breathed new life into the ageing institution, placing it in a building filled with smaller galleries, young creative industries and studios.

The second major museum renovation, at the Rijksmuseum – home to Rembrandt's *Night Watch* – is also a blessing of sorts: its notoriously massive collection is so overwhelming that the present exhibition of its top 100 pieces (located in the Philips Wing) is actually all one can really expect to absorb in the course of a single visit.

SHORTLIST

Classic art
- Rijksmuseum (p125)

Cutting-edge art & photography
- Foam (p91)
- Jordaan (p117)

Entering the past
- Amsterdams Historisch Museum (p72)
- City Archives (p89)
- Concertgebouw (p130)
- Hermitage aan de Amstel (p100)
- Museum Amstelkring (p56)
- Verzetsmuseum (p103)

Back to the future
- Eastern docklands (p109)
- Nemo (p111)

Religious experiences
- Joods Historisch Museum (p100)
- Nieuwe Kerk (p56)
- Oude Kerk (p56)
- Portuguese Synagogue (p102)

Cheerful Dutch clichés
- Bloemenmarkt (p95)
- Brouwerij 't IJ (next to a windmill; p102)

Sex & drugs
- Erotic Museum (p53)
- Red Light District (p59)

Longest queues in town
- Anne Frankhuis (p85)
- Van Gogh Museum (p126)

Most scenic canals
- Leliegracht (p82)
- Prinsengracht (p82)

Getaways
- Artis (p100)
- Hortus Botanicus (p102)
- Vondelpark (p126)

Power houses
- Huis Marseille (p85)

Museum hopping

Most Amsterdam museums charge for admission, but prices are reasonable: rarely more than €10. However, if you're thinking of taking in a few, the Museumkaart (Museum Card) is a steal: €35 for adults and €17.50 for under-25s (plus a €4.95 administration fee for first-timers). The card brings free or discounted admission to over 400 attractions in the Netherlands, and is valid for a year from the date of purchase; discounted or free entry offered to holders of the card is denoted in the listings of this guide by 'MK'. You can buy the card at all participating museums.

The Amsterdam Tourist Board (p177) also sells a savings pass, the I amsterdam Card, which gives you free entry to major museums, free public transport and a free canal trip, along with a hefty 25 per cent discount at participating tourist attractions and restaurants. It costs €33 for 24 hours, €43 for 48 hours and €53 for 72 hours. Log on to www. amsterdammuseums.nl for a list of all major museums across the city and their programmes.

Sights unseen

Much of Amsterdam's charm comes from what remains hidden from the untutored view. For instance, there's an awful lot more to absorb than just sex and drugs in the Red Light District. A mix of prostitutes, clerics, schoolkids, junkies, carpenters and cops all interact with a strange brand of social cosiness, with tourists as mere voyeurs. It's all pretty harmless, as long as you remember that window girls don't like having their pictures taken, and that the drug dealers react to eye contact like dogs to bones.

Nemo

Then there are the local *hofjes*, or almshouses, many of which are pretty and deliciously peaceful, the most famous being the Begijnhof. Most are concentrated in the Jordaan. The best known are the Venetiae (Elandsstraat 106-136), the Sint Andrieshofje (Egelantiersgracht 107-114), the Karthuizerhof (Karthuizerstraat 21-31), the Suyckerhofje (Lindengracht 149-163), the Claes Claesz Hofje (1e Egelantiersdwarsstraat 3), the Raepenhofje (Palmgracht 28-38) and, oldest by far, the Lindenhofje (Lindengracht 94-112). *Hofje* hopping is always a gamble, as entrances are sometimes locked in deference to the residents; but take a chance and you may get lucky.

Meanwhile, the major canals and their radial streets are where the real Amsterdam is. What they lack in sights, they make up for as a place for scenic coffee slurping, quirky shopping, aimless walks and meditative gable-gazing.

Neighbourhood hopping

Amsterdam's notorious ground zero of consumerism, vice, entertainment and history is the Old Centre, bounded by Prins Hendrikkade to the north, Oudeschans and Zwanenburgwal to the east, the Amstel to the south and Singel to the west.

Within these borders, the Old Centre is split into the New Side (west of Damrak and Rokin) and the Old Side (east of Damrak and Rokin). Within the famous Old Side – roughly in the triangle formed by Centraal Station, the Nieuwmarkt and the Dam – is the famed Red Light District. But the area is also home to the epic Oude Kerk (p56) and the menacing De Waag (p53).

The New Side, however, acts as the Old Side's kinder, gentler twin, its history tied to the city's intelligentsia, thanks to its many bookshops, 'brown' cafés and the buildings of the University of Amsterdam, which has just opened its 'Special Collections' (p68) of printed matter to the general public.

The *grachtengordel* ('girdle of canals') that guards the Old Centre is pleasant, idyllic and uniquely Amsterdam. It boasts the two most interesting arrivals on the local sightseeing scene: the Tassenmuseum (p90) and the City Archives (p89). It's also home to the Anne Frank House (p85), the Westerkerk (p86) and two intriguing photography museums: Foam (p91) and Huis Marseille (p85). For ease of use, we've split the canals in half: Western Canal Belt denotes the canals to the west and north of Leidsegracht,

and Southern Canal Belt covers the area east of here, thus taking in Leidseplein and Rembrandtplein.

The area around Waterlooplein, just east of the Old Centre, was settled by Jews four centuries ago, and so took its name – Jodenbuurt – from them. The Plantage, lying east and southeast of Waterlooplein, holds many delights, among them the Hortus Botanicus and Artis. Further east – or Oost – lies the Tropenmuseum, before the city opens up and stretches out towards another quirky newcomer: the 'Death Museum' (see box p106).

Once the gateway to prosperity, Amsterdam's Waterfront is now the setting for one of Europe's most inspired architectural developments. Traditional sights may be few, but the eastern stretch is home to thousands of new residents, and is developing as a strong arts and nightlife boulevard.

Over in the other direction, the Westelijke Eilanden link up nicely with the Jordaan, bordered by Brouwersgracht, Prinsengracht, Leidsegracht and Lijnbaansgracht, arguably Amsterdam's most charming neighbourhood. Working-class stalwarts rub shoulders with affluent newcomers in an area that, although lacking the grandiose architecture of the canals, wants for nothing in terms of character.

With world-class museums and stupendously posh fashion emporia, Amsterdam's Museum Quarter is a mix of culture (Museumplein) and couture (PC Hooftstraat). Its two newish museums – of diamonds (Paulus Potterstraat 8, 305 5300/ www.diamantmuseum.nl) and booze (p123) – aren't that inspiring.

Against the odds, the Pijp has managed to remain a wonderful cultural melting pot, even though gentrification has been in full swing for several years.

LOS PILONES
CANTINA MEXICO

enjoy the authentic mex-mex cuisine, atmosphere, cocktails and a great tequila collection

Kerkstraat 63
1017 GC Amsterdam
Tel.: (020) – 320 4651
open from 16:00 – 24:00

1e Anjeliersdwarsstraat 6
1015 NR Amsterdam – Jordaan
(020) – 620 03 23
open from 16:00 – 24:00

www.LosPilones.com

Westergas Terras p122

WHAT'S BEST
Eating, Drinking & Smoking

Although many restaurants continue to fall like flies into pea soup, there has been a stream of new – and often daring – ventures to replace them. Many offer diners the chance to sample culinary delight in some wacky locations: De Kas (p104), for instance, in a greenhouse; Hotel de Goudfazant (p111), in a vast warehouse; Dauphine (p104), in a former car showroom; Pont 13 (p111), in a retired ferry. And for all we know, Ctaste (p94) also has a special location – but since its concept is 'dining in the dark', it's hard to be sure.

All this action makes one forget that the term 'Dutch cuisine' used to inspire only peals of laughter; but well-travelled chefs have come home to apply their lessons to fresh local (often organic) ingredients – you can even source your own at Noordermarkt's Saturday organic market (p121). Transcending a soil type best suited to spuds, cabbages, carrots and cows, the Dutch nation is now using its greenhouses to grow a startling array of great ingredients.

Fish, gruel and beer formed the trinity of the medieval diet. (Yes, Homer: beer! Would *you* want to drink the canal water?) During the

Open! p114

Golden Age, the rich chomped through hogs and pheasants – though only after having their table-straining meals painted for posterity, as various pictures in the Rijksmuseum collection clearly attest. But it was during Napoleonic rule at the dawn of the 19th century that the middle classes were seduced by innovations like herbs, spices and the radical concept that overcooking is bad. Alas, a century later it all went badly wrong (see box p131); still, there's nothing quite like a hotchpotch of potato, hot, crispy bacon and still-crunchy greens, all diligently dammed to hold a pool of gravy. Traditional Dutch food can still hit the mark, and frequently does.

Rich, spicy food from Indonesia re-eroticised the Dutch palate after World War II, when the colony was granted its independence and the Netherlands took in Indonesian immigrants. Take your pick from the various cheap Surinamese-Indonesian-Chinese snack bars, or visit the purveyors of the *rijsttafel* ('rice table'), where every known fish, meat and vegetable is worked into a filling extravaganza. Along with the fondue – a 'national' dish shamelessly stolen from the Swiss, because its shared pot appealed to the Dutch sense of the democratic – Indo is the style of choice for any celebratory meals.

Go to the Pijp if you crave econo-ethnic. Cruise the eateries of Haarlemmerstraat, Utrechtsestraat, Nieuwmarkt, the 'Nine Streets' area and Reguliersdwarsstraat if you want something posher; and only surrender to Leidseplein if you don't mind being gravely overcharged for a cardboard steak and day-old sushi (although we do note some worthy exceptions). Also, check out the web: local foodies weigh in at www.iens.nl and www.specialbite.nl, the latter being a real winner that reliably offers the scoop on all the latest – not to mention the most trendy – restaurant openings.

Sure, check out the posh places, but remember that good, cheap snack opportunities can be had in the form of fish – raw herring, smoked eel – from the ubiquitous fishstalls, in rolled 'pizzas' from Turkish bakeries, in Dutch *broodjes* (sandwiches) from local bakers and butchers, and in more spicy Surinamese *broodjes* from 'Suri-Indo-Chin' snack bars. And you really should visit an Albert Heijn supermarket to get an insight into Dutch eating habits. You can sometimes find yourself having some of your best meals in the comfort of a quiet canalside bench.

Drinking

The café (or bar – the line between the two is blurred) is central to Dutch social life, variously serving as a home-from-home, community centre and nightlife hub at all hours (most cafés open in the morning and don't shut until 1am, or between 3am to 4am at weekends). As a result, the drinking scene in Amsterdam offers oodles of choice. One thing it certainly isn't is dynamic – few people here will be lured into the grim trap of Toblerone mojitos – but that still doesn't mean that Amsterdam drinking isn't a wildly intoxicating experience. In fact, it's one of the most satisfying places in Europe to get plastered in, and one with a

SHORTLIST

Best newcomer
- Open (p114)

Sybaritic sipping
- Bubbles and Wines (p58)
- Harry's Bar (p74)
- Onassis (p114)

Outdoor drinking
- Amstelhaven (p103)
- 't Blauwe Theehuis (p126)
- 't Smalle (p119)

Made for music lovers
- Bitterzoet (p81)
- Kamer 401 (p94)
- Vaaghuyzen (p75)

A taste of the old school
- Twee Zwaantjes (p88)
- Wynand Fockink (p63)

Beers of distinction
- 't Arendsnest (p88)
- Gollem (p136)

Lush lunches
- De Bakkerswinkel (p57)
- Latei (p61)
- Small World Catering (p119)

Vegetarian delights
- Green Planet (p74)
- De Peper (p128)

Traditional eating for cheap
- Hap Hmm (p94)

Posh and proud
- De Kas (p104)
- La Rive (p94)

Dining on a ship's deck
- Pont 13 (p110)

Spice of life
- Tempo Doeloe (p95)

Best for beach bums
- Blijburg (p110)

real sense of continuity. If many bars in town look as if they've been around forever, that's because they have: take Café Chris (p119) and Wynand Fockink (p63), which vie for the title of Amsterdam's longest-serving bar.

Not that old always means fusty. For the last couple of years, Korte Leidsedwarsstraat is where glammed-up drinkers come to sip appletinis. A more dressed-down (but just as cool), music-loving bunch gathers in and around nearby Kamer 401 (p94). A short hop in the other direction brings you to Reguliersdwarsstraat, the preened heart of the gay scene. Amsterdam's newest and best gay bar, Prik (p75) – everyone's new favourite bubbly, prosecco, is on tap – is just outside the gay village, over on Spuistraat.

Away from the neon, the Jordaan is awash with *bruin* cafés, so called because they've been stained brown by decades of smoke. Befitting the area's gentrified status, many, like Café Thijssen (Brouwersgracht 107, 623 8994), are teeming with wealthy nouveau residents; nearby bars, though, will be filled with the last vestiges of the local working-class population. A similar scene is to be found in the equally poshed-up Pijp, a great place to wander around between trendy drinking spots and more homely salt-of-the-earth watering holes. Nearby is Westergasfabriek (p122), with several appealing drinking spots, including WestergasTerras (p122).

Apart from the basic international brands, spirits drinkers can opt for the gin-like jenever, drunk neat from a tiny glass. Jong is lighter and more refreshing, oud darker and mellower. It comes in a wide range of fruit-infused varieties.

Wine buffs are likely to be underwhelmed: if you're horrified by the prospect of a beaker of unspecified red or white, make for Bubbles and Wines (p58) or Vyne (p89), both part of a new breed of bar pairing posh nosh with fine wine. But there's no getting away from it: the local drink of choice is beer. In most places the pils is Heineken or Amstel, but every bar will offer a good-to-brilliant range of potent Belgian brews, and there are several specialist Belgian bars, like Gollem (p136). For a proper taste of all NL has to offer, 't Arendsnest (p88) has a huge range of tasty native brews – around 500, to be precise.

Smoking

Heart it or hate it, Amsterdam's unique selling point is the fact that you can walk into a café and buy drugs. You can also get a coffee and munchies-abating snacks, but you've not been allowed to have a beer with your spliff since 1st April 2007, when booze was banned from the city's coffeeshops – part of the creeping resistance movement against lax marijuana laws. And from July 2008, you might not even be allowed to smoke in coffeeshops (see box p76). The power of the antis means that there have been no new coffeeshops for years, but trends still develop: you won't get very far without stumbling across organic (bio) highs, which don't pack quite the same serious punch as genetically modified (and often terrifyingly potent) hydroponic skunk. That said, Dutch weed is still known the world over for its unprecedented quality and supreme strength, so if you're a beginner or used to less powerful dope (Brits, take note), go easy – and be sure to brush up on your coffeeshop etiquette (see box p76).

Noordermarkt p117

Shopping

Shopping in the Netherlands presents what at first appears to be an oxymoronic conundrum. On the one hand, you have a nation spiritually shaped by Calvinism, which makes for parsimony and unwillingness to abandon oneself to excess, consumerist or otherwise. On another, you have a wealthy country (seventh in the EU's rich list) that was founded on the practice of buying and selling.

What this translates into for the visitor – who doesn't need to feel a guilty twinge every time cash is parted with – is a rather satisfying shopping experience. Lack of excess means no horrible hypermarkets or megamalls: consumerism is still very much a localised, town-centre activity. Apart from one or two rare exceptions like IKEA and the huge Villa ArenA furniture 'village' over in Duivendrecht, the out-of-town shop experience never caught on here and probably never will – not least because the requisite vast swathes of land simply aren't available in this overpopulated, small, watery country. Add to this the fact that the natives love to wander between different vendors while sniffing out a special offer, and the business of shuttling between bakers, cheesemongers and fishmongers looks set to stay.

Market forces

The place where you can really see people in their natural shopping state is, of course, the market. For a small city, Amsterdam is rather well provided with them, markets being among the few places where the town's ethnic groups actually meet and mingle. The most famous is Albert Cuypmarkt (p143), Europe's longest, snaking through the heart of the Pijp: all Dutch life is here, from smoked eel to Surinamese sherbets to buckets and mops. Most neighbourhoods have their own version: Oost's Dappermarkt and Jordaan's Lindenmarkt are the least untouristy. Also in the Jordaan is Saturday's Noordermarkt (p117), the place at which to buy organic farmers' produce among well-heeled shoppers. The same crowd returns on Monday mornings to pick through bric-a-brac and antiques, at a smaller (but infinitely superior) variation on Waterlooplein's tourist trap (p104).

A passion for fashion

Take a glance at the average burgher, and you'll notice that sartorial matters aren't a top priority. Nevertheless, a fair few designers have struggled against the odds, and the country can certainly hold its head high in the catwalk stakes – after all, it produced avant darlings Viktor & Rolf, whose headquarters are on Museumplein. And a couple of Dutch brands have made maximum impact on street style: Gsus and G-Star Raw. The former, which works with the Fair Wear Foundation to fight sweatshop production, is available at De Bijenkorf (p77). Meanwhile, new stores like Patta Exclusive Sneakers (p78) and quirky Concrete (p78) do their bit to keep street styles real.

The fashion map of the city is divided along clear lines: go to PC Hooftstraat for top-whack designer duds; go to the Kalverstraat area for high street stalwarts like HEMA – it has

SHORTLIST

Best newcomers
- Concrete (p78)
- For Our Friends (p130)
- Vlaamsch Broodhuis (p122)

Fancy pants
- Paars (p78)

Kiddy winkels
- Joe's Vliegerwinkel (p66)
- 't Klompenhuisje (p66)

Grown-up pleasures
- Absolute Danny (p63)
- De Bierkoning (p77)
- Dampkring (p78)

Gifts for granny
- Geels & Co (p65)

Prettiest interiors
- Jacob Hooy & Co (p66)
- Lairesse Apotheek (p130)

Unmissable markets
- Albert Cuypmarkt (p136)
- Bloemenmarkt (p95)

Blocks of chocs
- Puccini Bomboni (p67)
- Unlimited Delicious (p122)

Cheesy pleasers
- Boerenmarkt (p95)
- De Kaaskamer (p89)

Pre-owned treasures
- Brilmuseum/ Brillenwinkel (p89)
- Nic Nic (p90)
- Ree-member (p90)

Best for bibliophiles
- American Book Center (p77)
- Waterstone's (p81)

Teenage kicks
- Reprezent (p121)
- Patta Sneakers (p78)
- Tom's Skate Shop (p67)

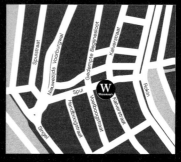

countless branches in Amsterdam – and Zara, which continues to offer catwalk fashions at cut-down prices. One thing the city does lack, alas, is an abundance of good boutiques; wander around the Jordaan, the Nine Streets and Damstraat areas to find outlets offering quirkier and home-grown labels, or try one of Blue Blood Jeans' new outlets For Our Friends (p130), located near the museums.

Design driven

Although fashion sense eludes the bulk of the populace, in terms of design the Dutch lead the world: think of Tord Boontje's Garland shade and the notorious Droog Design collective's innovations – shown at its outlet gallery in the Old Centre (p65). There's also the new Wella Warehouse (p90), its mission to present the playful products of younger Dutch designers. And to be amazed by design of all kinds, from serious high-end homeware to swanky jewellery, sniff out Utrechtsestraat; Overtoom and Rozengracht are coveted furnishing destinations.

Culture vultures

Dutch people are truly mad about reading. Bookworms should make straight for Spui, marked at one end by a mighty Waterstone's store (p81), and by the American Book Center (p77) at the other – both of them multi-storey giants of English language lit. Smaller-scale reading pleasures can be found on the shelves of multilingual Atheneum (p77), a veritable treasure trove of magazines in all languages, and in Friday's second-hand book market.

Incredible edibles

Although the Dutch tend not to be so famed for culinary finesse (though that is changing), they are renowned for hearty appetites,

which means that food is available pretty much at every step. You're spoiled for choicewhen it comes to edible souvenirs; steer towards De Kaaskamer (p89) and you'll also be spoiled for cheese – there are more than 200 types, and plenty of local specialities. For fishy dishes, pick up smoked eel, herring or tiny North Sea shrimps from the stalls dotted around town. Try Holtkamp (see box p131) for an array of cakes in a beautiful interior, and to see how they have turned the humble *kroket* into a gourmet bite by adding truffles and foie gras.

Talking shop

In general, local shops open from 1pm to 6pm on Monday (if they open at all), from 10am to 6pm Tuesday to Friday (many until 9pm on Thursday), and from 9am to 5pm on Saturday. Amsterdam is the only city in the Netherlands that boasts regular Sunday shopping, with stores usually open between noon and 5pm. Smaller shops are more erratic. Credit card payment is not universally accepted, so be sure to take cash.

Patta Exclusive Sneakers p78

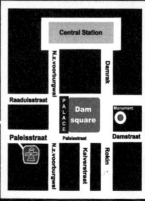

Bimhuis p114

WHAT'S BEST
Nightlife

This is a city with sound at its fingertips: you'll never have to wander far in Amsterdam to soothe your soul with melody – or with dissonant noise, if that's your bag. Even if the list of Dutch musical icons fails to trip off your tongue, the musical prowess of this city should never be underestimated.

Ever cruised down the road humming the now classic bassline to Golden Earring's rock standard 'Radar Love'? Or danced an entire night away to Tiesto or Junkie XL? Ever settled down for an evening in with a Mahler symphony performed by the Royal Concertgebouw Orchestra? Or been awe-struck by the classy jazz moves of talents like Misha Mengelberg or Han Bennink?

Throw in more eclectic and less mainstream musical genres like drum 'n' bass, heavy metal, art rock, hip hop and Frisian fado, and you start to grasp the length of the list of Dutch musical innovators.

On top of all that, there are international acts aplenty. With Amsterdam firmly established as one of the world's most important ports of call for visiting musicians, thanks to such iconic venues as Paradiso (p96) and Melkweg (p96), it's apparent that whatever you're after, it'll be readily available within close proximity of the canal ring. And that's just the tip of the iceberg; keep your eyes and ears peeled, and you may find that a gig by your favourite band or DJ is but a train ride away.

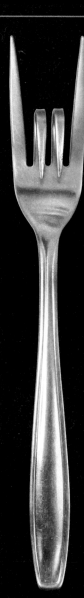

ROCK 'N' ROLL WILL NEVER DIET

AMSTERDAM
MAX EUWEPLEIN 57-61
+31 (0) 20 523 ROCK • HARDROCK.COM
THE OFFICIAL FOOD OF ROCK

Clubland Amsterdam

Since it opened three years ago, Sugar Factory (p96) has set itself up as one of the most happening clubs in town, offering a genuine alternative to the standard dance scene. It also hosts live shows, along with theatre acts, dance, left-field performance art and plain, old-fashioned craziness: WickedJazzSounds every Sunday, for example, provides a raw mix of old vinyl and live band sets. With other relative newcomers like Studio 80 (p98), Bitterzoet (p81) and Flexbar (p122), it's safe to say that local clubs have become more homely, less pretentious and more attractive. And don't forget the clutch of smaller, DJ bars along Nieuwezijds Voorburgwal, between the Dam and Spui square. There are more beyond the inner circle: Canvas club at the 'breeding ground' atop Volkskrantgebouw (see box, p69), and festival-like Studio K (see p108).

All venues in Amsterdam have bouncers, few being susceptible to bribery; you're better off showing up on time and with a mixed boy/girl group. Almost no one goes clubbing before midnight, and few venues offer discount prices if you show up before a particular time.

Storing your coat in a cloakroom sets you back €1, but tipping is far from mandatory; toilets cost between €0.50 and €1, though in many clubs outside the city centre they're free. Dutch people as a rule are far from being great tippers at the bar: a 15 per cent tip is usually considered huge.

Once inside the club, don't be afraid to strike up conversations with fellow clubbers – practically all natives speak fluent English. One topic has been swept away by a recent repressive wave, though: drugs. Although weed and hash

SHORTLIST

Best newcomer
- Studio K (p108)

Full-on cultural experiences
- Nachttheater Sugar Factory (p96)

Superclubs to the rescue
- Jimmy Woo's (p96)
- Melkweg (p96)
- Panama (p116)
- Paradiso (p96)

Cosier clubbing
- Flexbar (p122)
- Bitterzoet (p81)
- Studio 80 (p98)

Live music on tap
- Melkweg (p96)
- Paradiso (p96)

Big bands on a budget
- Club 3voor12 (p107)

Weird and wild venues
- Skek (p61)
- Winston (p67)

Jazz hand-clapping
- Badcuyp (p138)
- Bimhuis (p114)

Bustling neighbourhoods
- Leidseplein (p91)
- Nieuwezijds Voorburgwal (p71)
- Rembrandtplein (p91)

Best one-off parties
- NDSM (p111)
- Westergasfabriek (p122)

Where life's a beach party
- Blijburg (p111)

Gays of glory
- Getto (p58)
- Prik (p75)

DON'T MISS: 2009

are fine, it's unwise to solicit for anything stronger, as undercover cops have started trawling techno parties. And a word of warning for groups of men: if you must have your stag night here, don't expect to get into hipper venues without some women in tow.

Gay capital

After a couple of years of serious hand-wringing about whether or not Amsterdam still deserves the Gay Capital crown – the confusion largely inspired by a sad spate of homophobic incidents – the city seems to be back on track. Local political parties have made a real effort to make Amsterdam gay-friendly for residents and visitors; the council even promotes the pinkness of the city on the web (www.amsterdam4gays.nl). And Amsterdam Pride (see box p87) has gone the way of many other events by cosying up to corporate

sponsors; some major companies even have their own floats.

Although gays and lesbians enjoy a range of venues, the scenes are still quite separate except for special occasions like Queen's Day and Pride, or during one-off parties like the mighty Love Dance.

On the upside, clubland has been reinvigorated by young talent: clubs like Club Roque (p96) and bars like Prik (p75) have opened, and several new one-off parties are going strong. Bear in mind, though, that free condoms aren't universal, and STDs – including HIV – are on the up, with barebacking as popular here as in other big cities.

Finger on the pulse

The city's main ticket retailer is the Amsterdam Uitburo (AUB), which operates an elaborate online database and sales point for events at www.aub.nl, as well as a counter service at the AUB Ticketshop in Leidseplein, open from 10am to 7.30pm daily, except Sundays when it opens at noon. It also sells tickets by phone, though commission is even higher and you'll be paying premium phone rates at 0900 0191 (+31 20 621 1288 from abroad); lines are open 9am to 8pm daily.

Before you buy, pick up the English-language listings mag *Amsterdam Weekly* (www. amsterdamweekly.nl) or AUB's free monthly magazine *Uitkrant* (pronounced 'out-krant'), both available in theatres, bars, bookshops and the AUB Ticketshop, which is also a great place at which to browse flyers and other listings magazines. This is also home to the Last Minute Ticket Shop (www.lastminuteticketshop.nl), which sells tickets at half their face value for same-day musical and theatrical events, from noon every day of the week.

Nachttheater Sugar Factory p96

Bimhuis p114

Arts & Leisure

The Dutch are a cultured lot,
and their capital bristles with
world-class venues for every form
of artistic expression. Add to this
an active underground scene of
free-thinking old hippies and ex-
squatters, and you have lively
cultural events at every level.

The breadth and quality of
the Amsterdam arts experience
are due, partly at least, to
enlightened funding from
government and city, supporting
many of the city's festivals, and
new buildings like Muziekgebouw
(p116); such forward thinking also
helps connect the work of diverse
groups and venues. In the case of
Leidseplein, the connection

will be real: work is being done
to link the Melkweg (p94) to
the Stadsschouwburg (p98), due
for completion some time in 2009.

The art scene

Amsterdam has no shortage
of squat nostalgists weeping
for the 1980s and '90s salad
days, when cultural squats
provided the coolest, edgiest
and most frolicsome places in
town. But although a vacuum
did appear as many of the larger
squats were emptied at the dawn
of the new millennium, the recent
'breeding ground' policy seems
to now be revitalising the scene
(see box p112).

Meanwhile, in the Netherlands at large, the blurring of disciplines continues. Not only do the photographers (Anton Corbijn, Rineke Dijkstra), street artists (Ottograph, Laser 3.14), cartoonists (Joost Swarte) and architects (Rem Koolhaas) easily pass themselves off as 'artists', but the inspired work of John Körmeling and Atelier van Lieshout, equal parts artistry and oddball carpentry, is a perfect fusion of function, whimsy and good, old-fashioned aesthetics. On the other hand, many people who would have called themselves artists in the past now proudly proclaim themselves designers – and have redeployed their skills for all the international-tilted ad and graphic design agencies that set up shop here in recent years.

Compared with the art factories of Paris, New York and London, Amsterdam's galleries remain adventurous and welcome up-and-comers. Even auction house Christie's is trying to erase its staid image by sponsoring some hip art shows. Still, there's also a backlash against all this cutting-edge stuff, with many artists returning to the sort of painting, drawing and sculpting that was so popular with the ancients.

The silver screen

The biggest recent event was the homecoming of Paul Verhoeven, who returned from his Hollywood hideout with *Black Book*, the most expensive film ever to be shot in the Netherlands, filled to the brim with explosions, ravishing beauties, noble Nazis and treacherous resistance fighters. His old friend Rutger Hauer is also back in the country, regularly leading acting master classes and lending his formidable skills to smaller independent film productions.

SHORTLIST

Full-on sporting excitement
- Ajax (p107)

Interdisciplinary action
- De Balie (p98)
- Frascati (p71)

Golden Age film screenings
- Nederlands Filmmuseum (p132)
- Pathe Tuschinski (p98)

World-class jazz acts
- Bimhuis (p114)

Best classical
- Concertgebouw (p130)

Best modern classical
- Muziekgebouw (p116)

Cosiest clubbing
- Bitterzoet (p81)
- Nachttheater Sugar Factory (p96)
- Studio 80 (p98)

Cutting-edge contemporary
- Gasthuis Werkplaats & Theater (p132)
- Kinetic Noord at NDSM (box p111)

Underground vibes
- NDSM (p111)
- W139 (p69)
- Westergasfabriek (p122)

Regular gallery openings
- Chiellerie (p68)

Big bands on a small scale
- Melkweg (p96)
- Paradiso (p96)

International belly laughs
- Boom Chicago (p98)
- Comedy Theatre (p68)

Non-Western theatre
- KIT Tropentheater (p108)

Most creative festivals
- Over het IJ (p37)
- De Parade (p37)

DON'T MISS: 2009

Perhaps the most 'relevant' Dutch director working today is Eddy Terstall, whose films are usually set in his home neighbourhood of the Jordaan – *Simon*, for example, his acclaimed story of the friendship between a gay dentist and a gruff pot dealer with a big heart – and promote the best of tolerant Dutch values.

Theatre & dance

Amsterdam is home to countless choreographers and companies, a relatively recent phenomenon – and again, one due to enlightened funding. The Muziektheater (p71) is home to the internationally renowned company De Nederlandse Ballet. Smaller companies who have made a name on the world stage (and who perform regularly inside the capital) include Dansgroep Krisztina de Châtel and Het Internationaal Danstheater.

The city is also well served by a truly outstanding theatre scene – Ivo van der Hove's Toneelgroep Amsterdam at Stadsschouwburg is just one of many – but if language is a barrier, the multipurpose, multimedia De Balie (p98) is worth a visit, as it often stages performances in many tongues. Alternatively, NDSM also mounts regular, site-specific pieces that transcend linguistic limitations. The Over het IJ and De Parade fests (both p37) are worthy of attention, or – if you prefer the outdoors – you can pack up a picnic basket and head for the Vondelpark's Openluchttheater (p132); then again, if apocalyptic grandeur is your thing, try the Robodock festival (p33). Newcomer the Amsterdam Fringe Festival (p38) lets loose underground companies on the main stages of more established theatres, where they rewrite the rules as they go.

Classical music

Many of the greatest orchestras from across the world perform here, and there's access for all – typically for little more than the price of the biggest rock or pop concerts, and frequently for considerably less. And thanks to official funding, you'll not only hear the classics played in the grand halls, but beside canals, in parks or even on the streets.

Of course, Amsterdam is also the home of some of the most renowned orchestras and soloists around. Led by chief conductor Mariss Jansons, the Royal Concertgebouw Orchestra is one of the world's most famous. They play at home in most weeks of the cultural season; if you get the chance, even just for a lunch concert, don't pass it up.

The sporting life

Football remains the game most alluring to many, with fans still pining for the 1970s and '80s glory days of Cruijff and Van Basten. Although plenty of young starlets like Arjen Robben and Robin van Persie have made their names and riches internationally, the magic spark is still missing from the national team, and the Dutch heart is left battered and bruised after every big failure. The same goes for local team Ajax, whose fortunes seemed set to improve when Johan Cruijff stepped up in 2008 to reshape the team – and then stepped aside again after a week, when he saw he wouldn't get total freedom. Yet the desire to be the best often pays off elsewhere, and in field hockey, ice skating, swimming, darts and cycling, Dutch stars still manage to bag medals on a regular basis, achieving the coveted status of national heroes as they do.

Queen's Day p35

Dates in bold are public holidays.

September 2008

1 Sept-22 Apr 2009 Amsterdam World Book Capital
Various locations
www.amsterdamwereldboekenstad.nl

1-7 **Gaudeamus Music Week**
Muziekgebouw (p116)
www.gaudeamus.nl
Contemporary classical music.

4-13 **Africa in the Picture**
Various locations
www.africainthepicture.nl
Features, docs and shorts from Africa.

13-14 **Open Monumentendag**
Various locations
www.openmonumentendag.nl
Free or cheap entry to historic sites.

21 Dam tot Damloop
Amsterdam to Zaandam
www.damloop.nl
Long-running mini-marathon.

24-26 **Picnic '08**
Westergasfabriek (p122)
www.crossmediaweek.org
Gathering for world creative industries.

Late Sept **Robodock**
NDSM (p111)
www.robodock.org
Spectacular theatre festival with robots and mechanical installations.

October 2008

Ongoing **Amsterdam World Book Capital** (see Sept)

3 Oct-18 Jan 2009 **125 Favourites**
Van Gogh Museum (p124)
www.vangoghmuseum.nl
Artworks from Rembrandt Society.

4-6 **International Buddhist Film Festival Europe**
Nederlands Filmmuseum (p132)
www.ibff-europe.eu
Movies either inspired by or about the Buddhist faith.

Mid Oct **Rocket Cinema Festival**
Various locations
www.rocketcinema.nl
Old movies re-scored.

17 Oct-4 Jan 2009 **Indian Miniatures**
Van Gogh Museum (p126)
www.vangoghmuseum.nl
Highlights from the Rijksmuseum.

19 **ING Amsterdam Marathon**
Various locations
www.amsterdammarathon.nl

19-26 **Cinekid Festival**
Various locations
www.cinekid.nl
Child-centred film and media festival.

23-25 **Amsterdam Dance Event**
Various locations
www.amsterdam-dance-event.nl
Dance music festival and conference.

24-26 **Bock Beer Festival**
Beurs van Berlage (p53)
www.pint.nl
Festival of seasonal beer.

November 2008

Ongoing **Amsterdam World Book Capital** (see Sept); **125 Favourites** (see Oct); **Indian Miniatures** (see Oct)

1 **Museum Night**
Various locations
www.n8.nl
Late-night opening and special events.

5-9 **Jewish Film Festival**
Het Ketelhuis
www.joodsfilmfestival.nl
Four days of Jewish movies.

14-15 **London Calling**
Various locations
www.londoncalling.nl
New rock and pop from the UK.

16 **Sinterklaas Intocht**
Prins Hendrikkade, Dam to Leidseplein
Children's Christmas parade.

19-22 **Crossing Border**
The Hague

www.crossingborder.nl
International literature and music fest.

20-30 **International Documentary Film Festival (IDFA)**
Various locations
www.idfa.nl
The mother of all documentary fests.

23-27 **High Times Cannabis Cup**
Various locations
www.cannabiscup.com
Contest promoting cannabis.

Late Nov **Shadow Festival**
Various locations
www.shadowfestival.nl
Documentary fringe festival.

December 2008

Ongoing **Amsterdam World Book Capital** (see Sept); **125 Favourites** (see Oct); **Indian Miniatures** (see Oct)

1 **Lovedance**
Paradiso (p96)
www.lovedance.nl
World AIDS Day charity gala.

Early Dec **Resfest**
Various locations
www.dnerve.com
Travelling digital media festival.

5-6 **Sinterklaas**
Various locations
Traditional gift-giving parties.

Late Dec **Roze Film Dagen**
Various locations
www.rozefilmdagen.nl
International queer film festival.

25 **Eerste Kerstdag (Christmas)**

26 **Tweede Kerstdag (Boxing Day)**

31 **Oudejaarsavond**
All over Amsterdam, including Dam and Nieuwmarkt
Plenty of excitement and fireworks.

January 2009

Ongoing **Amsterdam World Book Capital** (see Sept 2008); **125**

Favourites (see Oct 2008); **Indian Miniatures** (see Oct 2008)

1 Nieuwjaarsdag (New Year's Day)

17-25 Amsterdam International Fashion Week
Various locations
www.aifw.nl
Putting the city on the fashion map.

Late Jan/Early Feb **Chinese New Year**
Nieuwmarkt (p53)
Celebrations and fireworks.

February 2009

Ongoing **Amsterdam World Book Capital** (see Sept 2008)

March 2009

Ongoing **Amsterdam World Book Capital** (see Sept 2008)

Early Mar **Amsterdam Restaurant Week**
Various locations
www.restaurantweek.nl
Special deals on dining out in selected restaurants across the capital.

21 Stille Omgang
Spui, Red Light District
www.stille-omgang.nl
Silent procession commemorating the 14th-century Miracle of Amsterdam.

Mid Mar **Amnesty International Film Festival**
www.amnestyfilmfestival.nl
Screenings of various films on the subject of human rights.

Mid Mar **Boekenweek**
www.boekenweek.nl
Week of events promoting literature and reading throughout the city.

Late Mar **London Calling**
See November 2008.

April 2009

Ongoing **Amsterdam World Book Capital** (see Sept 2008)

Early April **CinemAsia**
Various locations
www.cinemasia.nl
Screenings of pan-Asian features and cutting-edge documentaries.

Early April **National Museum Weekend**
Various locations
www.museumweekend.nl
Free or cheap entry to the city's many museums, plus special events.

10 Goede Vrijdag (Good Friday)

12 Eerste Paasdag (Easter Sunday)

13 Tweede Paasdag (Easter Monday)

16-19 **Motel Mozaïque**
Rotterdam
www.motelmozaique.nl
Three-day music, theatre and arts fest.

29 Queen's Night
All over Amsterdam
The start of Queen's Day (see below); paint the town orange.

29 Apr-mid June **World Press Photo**
Oude Kerk (p56)
www.worldpressphoto.com

30 Queen's Day
All over Amsterdam
This epic celebration is a giant open air disco-cum-flea-market enjoyed by all, republicans included.

Late Apr **Amsterdam Fantastic Film Festival**
Various locations
www.afff.nl
Eight days of silver screen schlock, horror, splatter and trash.

Late April **Roze Wester Festival**
Homomonument (p85)
www.gala-amsterdam.nl
Lesbian and gay open-air party.

May 2009

Ongoing **Amsterdam World Book Capital** (see Sept 2008); **World Press Photo** (see April)

Fantastic Film Festival p35

4 Dodenherdenkingsdag (Memorial Day)
Dam Square
7.30pm ceremony remembering those who lost their lives in World War II.

5 Bevrijdingsdag (Liberation Day)
Various locations
www.amsterdamsbevrijdingsfestival.nl; www.oosterparkfestival.nl
Marking national liberation from Nazi occupation.

Mid May **Art Amsterdam**
Amsterdam RAI Theater (p130)
www.artamsterdam.nl
Huge, commercial, five-day exhibition.

Mid May **National Windmill Day**
Around the Netherlands
www.molens.nl
Windmills spin sails and open to the public in this quaintest of celebrations.

Mid May **Kunstvlaai**
Westergasfabriek (p122)
www.kunstvlaai.nl
Hip art for the discerning masses.

21 Hemelvaartsdag (Ascension Day)

Late May **Open Studios**
Westelijke Eilanden
www.oawe.nl
Artists open their doors to the public.

31 Eerste Pinksterdag (Pentecost)

June 2009

Ongoing **Amsterdam World Book Capital** (see Sept 2008); **World Press Photo** (see April)

1 Tweede Pinksterdag (Pentecost)

Early June **Hindustaans Film**
Nederlands Filmmuseum (p132)
www.hindustaansfilmfestival.nl
Screenings of the best of the previous year's Bollywood offerings.

Early June **Arab Film Festival**
Various locations
www.arabfilmfestival.nl
Three days of shorts, documentaries and features by Arabic film-makers.

Early June **Beeld voor Beeld**
Tropenmuseum (p103)
www.beeldvoorbeeld.nl
Cultural and anthropological documentary film festival.

Early June-mid Aug
Openluchttheather

This respected month-long international-al dance festival draws big names and bigger crowds.

Early July **Cinedans International Dance Film Festival**
Nederlands Filmmuseum (p132)
www.cinedans.nl
Eclectic dance and choreography film screenings for stage enthusiasts.

Early July **5 Days Off**
Various locations
www.5daysoff.nl
Techno, drum 'n' bass, house and mad electro mash up.

Mid July **Over het IJ**
NDSM (p111)
www.overhetij.nl
International festival of large-scale, avant-garde theatrical projects.

Mid July **North Sea Jazz**
Rotterdam
www.northseajazz.nl
Internationally renowned jazz festival.

Mid July **Amsterdam International Fashion Week**
See January.

Late July **Amsterdam Tournament**
ArenA (p107)
www.lgamsterdamtournament.com
International footie friendlies.

Late July-mid Aug **Kwakoe**
Bijlmerpark
www.kwakoe.nl
Free festie in the multicultural suburbs.

August 2009

Ongoing **Amsterdam World Book Capital** (see Sept 2008); **Openluchttheater** (see June); **Kwakoe** (see July)

Early Aug **Amsterdam Gay Pride**
Various locations
www.amsterdamgaypride.nl
See box p87. Also look out for the boat parade on Prinsengracht.

Early Aug **De Parade**
Martin Luther Kingpark
www.deparade.nl
Travelling circus-style theatre festival.

Vondelpark
www.openluchttheater.nl
Open-air stage featuring performances from classical to urban to kids' stuff.

13-20 **Amsterdam Roots**
Various locations
www.amsterdamroots.nl

Mid June **Holland Festival**
Various locations
www.holndfstvl.nl
Huge, popular and varied arts festival.

Mid June **Oerol**
Terschelling
www.oerol.nl
For a fortnight, the Frisian island of Terschelling, 120 kilometers north of town, stages 200 theatre acts.

Mid June **Open Garden Days**
Various locations
www.opentuinendagen.nl

July 2009

Ongoing **Amsterdam World Book Capital** (see Sept 2008); **Openluchttheather** (see June)

1-31 **Julidans**
Various locations
www.julidans.nl

8-15 Sweelinck Festival
Oude Kerk (p56)
www.sweelinckorgancompetition.com
Popular organ music festival held in
the atmospheric Old Church.

Mid Aug **Grachtenfestival**
Various locations
www.grachtenfestival.nl
Canalside classical music concerts.

Mid Aug **Appelsap**
Oosterpark
www.appelsap.net
Free outdoor hip hop festival.

Mid Aug **Hartjesdag**
Zeedijk
www.hartjesdagen.nl
An ancient celebration re-invented:
cross-dressing, jazz and fireworks.

Mid Aug **Open Haven Podium**
Java-eiland
www.openhavenpodium.nl
Art, music, theatre and kids' activities
out on one of Amsterdam's islands.

Mid Aug **Lowlands**
Walibi World
www.lowlands.nl
Dutch Glastonbury: the latest bands,
comedy, global food and fashion.

28-30 Uitmarkt
Various locations
www.uitmarkt.nl
Open-air preview of the coming cultural season: theatre, opera and dance.

Late Aug **Het Theaterfestival**
All over Amsterdam
www.tf-1.nl
Showcase for Dutch and Belgian theatre, plus Amsterdam Fringe Festival.

September 2009

Ongoing **Amsterdam World Book
Capital** (see Sept 2008)

Early Sept **Open Monumentendag**
See September 2008.

Early Sept **Africa in the Picture**
See September 2008.

Late Sept **Robodock**
See September 2008.

October 2009

Ongoing **Amsterdam World Book
Capital** (see Sept 2008)

Mid Oct **Rocket Cinema Festival**
See October 2008.

Mid Oct **Cinekid**
See October 2008.

Late Oct **International Buddhist
Film Festival Europe**
See October 2008.

Late Oct **Bock Beer Festival**
See October 2008

November 2009

Ongoing **Amsterdam World Book
Capital** (see Sept 2008)

Early Nov **Jewish Film Festival**
See November 2008.

Mid Nov **London Calling**
See November 2008.

Mid Nov **International
Documentary Film Festival**
See November 2008.

Mid Nov **Crossing Border**
See November 2008.

Late Nov **Shadow Festival**
See November 2008.

December 2009

Ongoing **Amsterdam World Book
Capital** (see Sept 2008)

1 Lovedance
See December 2008.

Early Dec **Resfest**
See December 2008.

5-6 Sinterklaas
See December 2008.

Late Dec **Roze Film Dagen**
See December 2008.

25 Eerste Kerstdag (Christmas)

26 Tweede Kerstdag (Boxing Day)

31 Oudejaarsavond
See December 2008.

Itineraries

NDSM p111

Creative City

It was all much simpler in the 1970s. To entice people to visit Amsterdam, all you had to do was what KLM did: put out posters cajoling its long-haired American targets to 'Sleep in Hippie Park'. Word of mouth did the rest. Before that, there was the tourist board's 'Get in touch with the Dutch' campaign of the 1960s – truly a slogan from a more innocent time. Compared to that halcyon era, the boom years of the 1990s were surely the most boring of times, if their yawn-inducing slogans ('Capital of inspiration' and 'Business gateway to Europe') are anything to go by.

But now it's all about the 'Creative city', and therefore a lot easier to sell: Amsterdam has always been a creative city – you know, home to Rembrandt and Van Gogh and that whole ilk. But now it's also a marketing campaign, backed by city money and its new 'city brand': I amsterdam.

Not only are there excellent galleries, schools and other initiatives, but also a whole slew of communications and design firms kicking ass on a global level. Meanwhile, the **Pakhuis de Zwijger** (p45) opened in 2006 as a hub for a whole gamut of cutting-edge outfits, complete with an inspiring programme of conferences and exhibitions. The same year saw the arrival of the 'cross-media week' PICNIC (www.picnicnet work.org), an immediately successful annual congress in September of shows, meetings, readings, seminars and discussions on the latest developments in media, technology, art, science and entertainment. Over at the former shipyards of **NDSM**

droog

Droog Design p43

(p111), an 'art city' of studios butts heads with the European headquarters of MTV.

Indeed, the city as a whole can be seen as one great big gallery. With a long tradition of new construction projects having to give a percentage of their costs to public art, one can hardly walk for a minute without bumping into some kind of creative endeavour – and although not all examples are successful (please, someone remove the garishly coloured geometric stacks that line the Damrak), one can't deny the intrinsic charm of Hans van Houwelingen's bronze iguanas frolicking in the grass of **Kleine Gartmanplantsoen**, the extension of Leidseplein that leads to Paradiso.

Another thing to keep your eyes peeled for is the unasked-for art. A very active street art scene fills Amsterdam with freehand graffiti, stencils, sculptures, tags and stickers. One of the more prolific practitioners is Laser 3.14, Amsterdam's own 'guerilla poet'.

His words of wisdom are dotted on building sites all over town: 'Swallowed by your own introspective vortex' and 'She fears the ghouls that reside in her shadow' are just two cryptic examples. DHM has a different approach altogether, glueing tribal tattoo-style animals all over the urban jungle. Other familiar sights are the spray-painted stereos and electricity poles, courtesy of Morcky, who, with partner Boghe, is also making a name for himself outside the street scene, creating websites for the likes of Wu Tang Clan.

The most prolific and well-known group of artists are probably The London Police (TLP). This collective of three Brits specialises in 'lads': deceptively simple black-and-white blob characters that first popped up on electricity boxes around town, but later found their way into galleries.

And there are a lot of galleries in Amsterdam – especially ones with an eye for modern design.

The history of Dutch design has always fluttered between intrinsic orderliness (reinforced by both Calvinism and De Stijl) and a strong desire for personal expression. The fact that this design is often ingeniously functional and downright witty has resulted in worldwide acclaim: so much so, that the tourist board has jumped on the bandwagon at www.coolcapitals.com.

To see how design has now infiltrated every level of Dutch life, make your first port of call a **HEMA**, the ubiquitous department store. Although HEMA remains the economical place to shop in for basics, it has also made a name for itself as a source of affordable, no-nonsense design objects. It's had products designed by bigwigs like Piet Hein Eek, Gijs Bakke and Hella Jongerius; even its sale flyers are graphics classics. If you like to shop, you're bound to love HEMA.

For a stroll into the deep heart of local design, it's best to start in the heart of Amsterdam's most iconic of design wonders: the canal girdle. **Galerie Binnen** (p89) is an industrial and interior design specialist, whereas nearby **Wella Warenhaus** (p90) goes for the new generation of Dutch designer.

From here, you may want to wiggle through the always charming and arty **Jordaan** (p117-122), and perhaps take a peek into the new studio of design wunderkind and inventor of the Knotted Chair, **Marcel Wanders** (www.marcelwanders.com): it's in a former school at Westerstraat 187.

T-shirt fanatics should certainly visit **SML.X** (Donker Curtius straat 11, Westerpark, 681 2837, www.sml-x.com), an open venue for Dutch graphic designers and graffiti artists to design and silkscreen their own shirts. And you could come here via the always art-rich grounds of **Westergasfabriek** (p122).

Backtrack into town down **Rozengracht**, which has a wide range of design and furniture stores, including upmarket yet funky **SPRMRKT** (p121). Then take a right down the north side of **Prinsengracht** to one of the city's most famed design destinations, **Frozen Fountain** (p89), a paradise for lovers of contemporary furniture and design items. Its neighbour, the former central public library, is set to become a 'breeding ground' (see box p69) for the arts in 2009.

The surrounding '**Nine Streets**' area (p85) is also a great place to wander randomly around in search of eye candy. If you end up near Spui square, you can drop into **Athenaeum Nieuwscentrum** (p77), *the* place for Amsterdam-centric design books and mags, before continuing north-east down Lange Brugsteeg and Grimburgwal to take a left down Oudezijds Achterburgwal. On the corner of Rusland, there's WonderWood (p67) whose name says it all.

Follow **Rusland**, take a right down **Kloveniersburgwal** and a left down the painfully scenic **Staalstraat**, and you come to the shop of the city's most internationally renowned design collective, **Droog Design** (p65) which can rightfully lay claim to having the wittiest selection around – although perhaps not as witty as what you stumbled on by accident on the streets outside.

But you must be gasping for refreshment by now. While you're in the area, round off the cultural tour with a refreshing beer at nearby **De Jaren** (p60) – or indulge in some appropriately arty chocs from the always charming **Puccini Bomboni** (p67).

Lloyd Hotel

On the Waterfront

Amsterdam's eastern dockland area is the city's up-and-coming eating and entertainment hotspot. But, perhaps more interestingly, it's also a fantastic showcase for the Netherlands' rather daring experiments in residential living. If you want to explore the future of Amsterdam, hop on a bike, grab a map and get moving.

START: Head north-west of **Centraal Station** to the Westelijke Eilanden (Western Islands) near the Jordaan, to get a taste of how things were when Amsterdam was the richest port in the world. These artificial islands were originally created in the 17th century for maritime activity. Although there are trendy warehouse flats and a yacht basin on Realeneiland, Prinseneiland and Bickerseiland – where one-time shipyards, tar distillers and salters and smokers of fish were based –

the area still remains the city's best setting for a scenic stroll that smacks of seafaring times, a fact aided in no small measure by the sizeable community of local artists.

Since 1876, the route to the open sea has been the North Sea Canal. Because the working docks are also to the west, there's very little activity on the IJ behind Centraal Station, other than a handful of passenger ships and the free ferries that run across the water to Amsterdam Noord – one of which will take you to the vibrant cultural 'breeding ground' that is **Kinetic Noord**, set in former shipping yard NDSM (p111). Here, vivid apocalyptic splendour, artistic endeavours and old-school squat aesthetics can be found alongside funky student container housing and the brand new MTV headquarters – the epitome of old-meets-new.

If you stay on the south side, follow the water eastward from Centraal Station before hooking up with and following **Oostelijke Handelskade** and its parallel boardwalk. First, you pass the **Muziekgebouw** (p116). This new epicentre of new music, also home to the **Bimhuis** (p114), comes appended with studios, rehearsal spaces, exhibition galleries, and a grand café and restaurant complete with a terrace overlooking the scenic waters of the IJ. Its close neighbour is the visually spectacular, wave-shaped, glass passenger terminal for luxury cruise ships (www.pta.nl lists all docking times should you want to admire them in situ).

Before proceeding further to hot club **Panama** (p116), restaurant Odessa (p114) and the erstwhile youth prison turned designer accommodation **Lloyd Hotel** (p165), take the airy street Jan Schaeferbrug to the left that begins by going through the **Pakhuis de Zwijger** (www.dezwijger.nl), an old warehouse that has recently been reinvented as a new media centre; the more culturally curious may also want to pop in for a drink at its charming café.

The bridge will take you to the tip of **Java-eiland**, although if you don't feel energetic, you can travel on the free ferry that departs every 20 minutes from directly behind Centraal Station. At first glance, Java-eiland may look like a dense, designer prison, but it's not hard to be charmed on the island's dividing pedestrian street, which will have you crossing canals on funky bridges and passing a startling variety of architecture. At Azartplein, the island suddenly changes its name to **KNSM-eiland**, named after the Royal Dutch Steam Company that was once based here.

Now veer north and follow **Surinamekade**, with houseboats on one side and the visible interiors of artist studios on the other. Pass 'Black Widow' tower – you'll know it when you see it – and then loop around the island's tip and back along **KNSM-laan**, taking a left into **Barcelonaplein**, and then a right when you pass through the abstract (but strangely suggestive) sculpted steel archway. You may also want to make some time for refreshment at one of the waterside bars and restaurants, or invest in an art coffin at the alternative burial store **De Ode**; either way, linger and look at the imposing residential **Piraeus** building by German architect Hans Kollhoff, if only for its eye-twisting inner court.

The two peninsulas to the south are Borneo and Sporenburg, the work of urban planning and landscape architecture outfit West 8. The plots are all differently sized, to encourage the many architects involved – a veritable Who's Who of international stars – to come up with creative low-rise living. Cross over to **Sporenburg** via the **Verbindingsdam** to the building that has probably already caught your eye: the mighty silver **Whale** residential complex, designed by architect Frits van Dongen, over on Baron GA Tindalplein. In folky contrast, a floating Styrofoam park produced by erstwhile Provo Robert Jasper Grootveld has been set in front of it on Panamakade.

From here, cross over to **Borneo** on the swooping red bridge. Turn left up **Stuurmankade** – past a still more violently undulating pedestrian bridge – and enjoy the view at the end (and imagine an even better one enjoyed by the residents of the blue and green glass cubes that jut out of the buildings). Then return west on **Scheepstimmermanstraat**, easily Amsterdam's most eccentric architectural street, where every single façade on show – from twisting steel to haphazard plywood – manages to be more bizarre than the next.

Where **Panamalaan** meets **Piet Heinkade**, you may opt to take the IJtram from CS to IJburg (the stop is right by the stack of giant tables with beehives underneath), although more energetic types might prefer to take a 20-minute bike ride to IJburg, heading south via **C van Eesterenlaan** and **Veelaan**, then left down **Zeeburgerdijk**. This in turn connects up with **Zuiderzeeweg**, which then turns into a bridge that ends at a set of traffic lights. Here, follow the cycle path to the right, which takes you to **IJburg**. When finally completed in 2012, the seven islands here will be home to 45,000 people in over 18,000 units, many of which will float on the water. It will also be a showcase for Dutch landscape and residential architecture, with houses that combine thrilling aesthetic forms with cutting-edge, environmentally friendly mod-cons. That said, there's already plenty to look at, with funky beach **Blijburg** (p111) the clear highlight.

On the way back to town, be sure to explore the south end of the eastern half of **Zeeburg** island, one of the few 'free' places where squatters and artists are still allowed to make their ramshackle homes from trailers and boats, and where they throw some of the city's more eccentric parties – despite governmental efforts in recent years to clamp down on them. In fact, the vibe that permeates Zeeburg once defined the whole area before the yuppies came to town a few years ago, and thus inspires a fair amount of nostalgia. Granted, the overall atmosphere may not be half as lively as it once was; but the architecture, as you'll have seen on your trip, is a vast improvement. For more detailed information on architectural tours of these areas, contact **ARCAM** (www.arcam.nl).

Sights & Sore Eyes

It's all about balance here in old Amsterdam. People do work, but at the first sign of spring, the economy grinds to a halt for a few days, as everyone rushes to the nearest terrace.

For visitors, it's always a good idea to slow down and smell the tulips. For example, you must visit the **Van Gogh Museum** (p126) – but it's important to remember that Vincent was just one artist; master forger Geert Jan Jansen was several. So after staring at some authentic sunflowers and potato eaters, why not visit Jansen's new gallery, **Galerie Geert Jan Jansen** (see box p95)?

Or if you found the **Heineken Experience** (p135) just a little too slick, head to the Dirk van den Broek supermarket behind it, buy some Grolsch *beugeltjes* (the classic bottle with the reusable pop-up top), and find a bench by the Amstel river or in the Sarphatipark. Or if you're burned out by the hot new architecture along the harbour (see itinerary p44), make for the **Byzantium** building just to the right of the main entrance of **Vondelpark** (p132). It's an early work, and dark secret, by superstar architect Rem Koolhaas: it's the one with the spaceship on top, and so ugly it's actually pretty cool. Or if you leave Madame Tussaud's **Scenerama** on Dam Square with a renewed respect for wax, buy religious candles at **Abdijwinkel van Egmond** (Nieuwezijds Voorburgwal 361, 623 5911).

The Heineken Experience p47

Get the idea? You need to balance heaviness with the light. **Anne Frank Huis** (p85) is, of course, an essential place to visit; it's a full-on experience and tells a story from one of the darkest chapters in the city's history. Afterwards, head to **Café Chris** (Bloemstraat 42, 624 5942), an ancient 'brown' café with a loo so small that the flusher is outside the door – so wait for your friends to settle in, and flush away. It's said that the bar originally opened as the local for the workers building **Westerkerk** (p86), whose bells are described by Anne Frank in her diary; the church can be spotted as you leave the café.

Built between 1602 and 1631 by Hendrick de Keyser, and thought to be the last resting place of Rembrandt (who lived up the road

at **Rozengracht 188** during his later, washed-up years), the Dutch Renaissance Westerkerk was the largest Protestant church in the world until Christopher Wren came along with St Paul's Cathedral in London. Westerkerk's tower – endlessly mentioned in Jordaan songs – is topped by a rather tacky copy of the crown of Habsburg emperor Maximilian I. Maximilian gave Amsterdam the right to use his royal insignia in 1489, in gratitude for help from the city in his struggle for control of the Low Countries, and the crown's 'XXX' represents the traits of valiance, resolution and mercifulness. This marking was quickly exploited by the city's merchants as a visiting card of quality; later they were also used by 20th-century porn film exporters as a mark of another sort of quality – and there you have the origin of the term 'triple X-rated'.

Counter the blasphemy with a visit to the **Bible Museum** (p85), with its ceilings of frolicking cherubs; then catch a tram to **Rembrandtsplein**. Around the corner of the Amstel river, you can see the bizarre graffiti on the façade of **Amstel 216**. This 'House with the Bloodstains' was home to former major Coenraad van Beuningen (1622-93), whose brilliance was eclipsed by insanity. After seeing visions of fireballs and fluorescent coffins above **Reguliersgracht**, he scrawled sailing ships, stars, strange symbols and his and his wife's name, all with his own blood. Attempts to scrub the stains off have proved futile.

On entering the Plantage and the Jewish neighbourhood, find peace at the lovely lush **Hortus Botanicus** (p100) – a little oasis for a cup of coffee. Add historical resonance to your sipping with the knowledge that the Hortus harbours the descendants of the first coffee plants of Europe. A Dutch merchant stole one of the plants from Ethiopia and presented it to the Hortus in 1706, which in turn sent a clipping to a botanist in France, who sent more to Brazil, where an industry was born.

Continue up the road and turn left to get to the **Resistance Museum** (p103), across from Artis Zoo. The suspenseful story of the Dutch resistance to the occupying Nazi forces during World War II is all set out here. The highlights are the ingenious gadgets, including the bicycle-powered printing presses that pumped out fake ID papers and underground newspapers.

By way of contrast, ponder the much more prevalent idea of collaboration at the monument of former deportation point **Hollandse Schouwburg** (p100). Between 1892 and 1941, this was the venue for Dutch theatrical performances; then the Nazis deemed it a Jewish-only theatre, before deciding in 1942 to use it as a gathering point for the deportation of the city's Jews, first to the national clearing house of Westerbork, and from there to concentration camps in Germany. By the end, somewhere between 60,000 and 80,000 people passed through here. In 1993, the **Jewish Historical Museum** (p102) renovated it to include a memorial room displaying the 6,700 family names of the 104,000 Dutch Jews deported and murdered; an upstairs exhibition room tells the story of the occupation through documents, photographs and videos.

Take another break at **Café Eik en Linde** (Plantage Middenlaan 22, 622 5716), an archetypical, brown-walled drinking hole. The perfect end to a contrast-filled day.

Van Gogh Museum p47

Amsterdam by Area

De Waag

The Old Centre

AMSTERDAM BY AREA

One side embraces shopping and pursuits of the mind; the other sex and religion. The compelling Old Centre (aka Oud Centrum) surfs on a wave of contradiction.

Marked off by Centraal Station, Singel and Zwanenburgwal, the area is bisected by **Damrak**, which turns into Rokin south of Dam Square. Within the Old Centre, the saucier area to the east is the ancient **Old Side** (Oude Zijde), while the gentler area to the west – whose most notable landmark is Spui square – is the far-from-new **New Side** (Nieuwe Zijde).

The Old Side

Straight up from Centraal Station, just beyond touristy Damrak and the **Beurs van Berlage**, lies Dam square, the heart of the city since the first dam was built across the Amstel here in 1270. Once a hub of social and political activities, today it's a convenient meeting point for tourists, the majority of whom convene under the mildly phallic Nationaal Monument, a 22-metre (70-foot) white obelisk dedicated to the Dutch servicemen who died in World War II. The west side of the square is flanked by the **Koninklijk Paleis** (Royal Palace); next to it is the 600-year-old **Nieuwe Kerk**.

The nearby Red Light District is at the root of Amsterdam's infamy. Although sex is the main hook upon which the area hangs its reputation, it's actually secondary to window-shopping. People do buy here – it's estimated to be a €500-million-per-year trade

– but mostly they wander around, gawping at the live exhibits and ducking in and out of the **Erotic Museum** or Hash Marihuana Hemp Museum. The **Oude Kerk**, Amsterdam's oldest building, is literally in the centre of the sleazy action. The equally pious **Museum Amstelkring** is also nearby.

At the bottom of Zeedijk is the castle-like De Waag, or 'Weigh House'. It stands in the centre of terrace-rich Nieuwmarkt and dates from 1488, when it was built as a gatehouse and was later home to an Anatomical Theatre (where Rembrandt painted his *Anatomy Lesson of Dr Nicolaes Tulp*). Yet more relative tranquillity exists on the Nes, home to many of the city's theatres and several charming cafés. When you reach the end of Nes, take a turn left to cross a bridge and hunt down the **Oudemanhuis Book Market**. This is where Van Gogh once bought prints to decorate his room – a high-calibre recommendation if ever there was one.

Sights & museums

Allard Pierson Museum

Oude Turfmarkt 127 (525 2556/www.allardpiersonmuseum.nl). Tram 4, 9, 14, 16, 24, 25. **Open** 10am-5pm Tue-Fri; 1-5pm Sat, Sun. **Admission** €5; €2.50 4-15s; free under-4s, MK. No credit cards. **Map** p55 D5 ❶
Established in Amsterdam in 1934, the Allard Pierson claims to hold one of the world's richest university collections of archaeological exhibits, gathered from ancient Egypt, Greece, Rome and the Near East. However, if you didn't spend several years at university studying stuff like this, you'll probably be bored witless. Many of the exhibits (statues, sculptures, ceramics etc) are unimaginatively presented, as if aimed solely at scholars. Some items are instantly accessible and interesting

– the full-size sarcophagi, the model of a Greek chariot – but otherwise this is a frustrating experience.

Beurs van Berlage

Damrak 277, entrance at Beursplein 1 (530 4141/Artiflex tours 620 8112/www.beursvanberlage.nl). Tram 4, 9, 14, 16, 24, 25. **Open** 10am-10pm daily for exhibitions. Admission varies. No credit cards. **Map** p55 D2 ❷
Designed in 1896 by Hendrik Berlage as the city's stock exchange, the palatial Beurs paved the way for the Amsterdam School. Although some jaded critics thought it 'a big block with a cigar box on top', it's now considered one the country's most important pieces of architecture. It's also a socialist statement: much of its interior artwork warns against capitalism, and each of the nine million bricks was intended by Berlage to represent the individual. The Beurs is now a concert hall, exhibition space and media centre. It also has a café (10am-6pm daily).

Erotic Museum

Oudezijds Achterburgwal 54 (624 7303). Tram 4, 9, 16, 24, 25/Metro Nieuwmarkt. **Open** 11am-1am Mon-Thur, Sun; 11am-2am Fri, Sat. **Admission** €5. No credit cards. **Map** p55 D2 ❸
The Erotic Museum may be appropriately located in the middle of the Red Light District, but it's none the more authentic or interesting for that. Its prize exhibits include an odd bicycle-powered dildo and a few of John Lennon's erotic drawings, while lovers of Bettie Page will enjoy the original photos of the S&M muse on display. In general though, despite best efforts, the museum's as unsexy as can be.

Koninklijk Paleis (Royal Palace)

Dam (information 620 4060/tours 624 8698/www.koninklijkhuis.nl). Tram 1, 2, 4, 5, 9, 13, 14, 16, 17, 24, 25. **Open** *July, Aug* 11am-5pm daily. *Sept-June* times vary. **Admission** €4.50; €3.60 5-16s, seniors; free under-6s. No credit cards. **Map** p54 C3/4 ❹

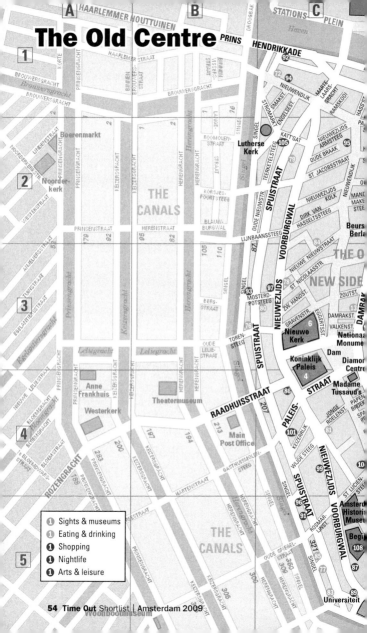

The Old Centre

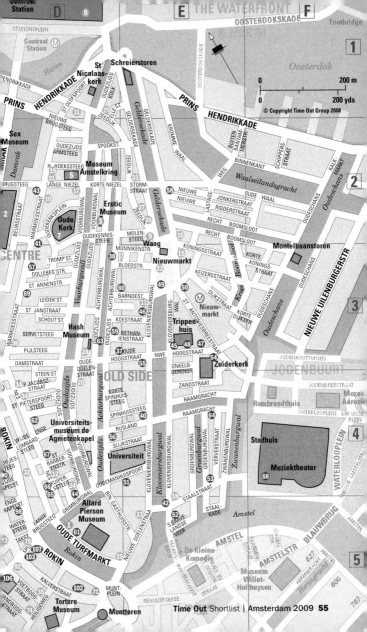

The Royal Palace, designed along classical lines by Jacob van Campen in the 17th century, has been closed for renovation until early 2009 – and we're damned lucky to have the doors reopening. It's even grander inside than out: the Citizen's Hall, with its Baroque decoration in grand marble and bronze that depicts a miniature universe (with Amsterdam as its obvious centre), is meant to make you feel about as worthy as the rats seen carved into the stone over the door of the Bankruptcy Chamber. Gentler displays of creativity can be seen in the chimney pieces, painted by the likes of Ferdinand Bol and Govert Flinck, both pupils of Rembrandt (who had his own sketches rejected). The city hall was transformed into a royal palace in 1808, after Napoleon had made his brother, Louis, King of the Netherlands, and a fine collection of furniture from this period can be viewed inside.

Museum Amstelkring

Oudezijds Voorburgwal 40 (624 6604/ www.museumamstelkring.nl). Tram 4, 9, 14, 16, 24. **Open** 10am-5pm Mon-Sat; 1-5pm Sun. **Admission** €7; €5 students, seniors; €1 5-18s; free under-5s, MK. No credit cards. **Map** p55 D2 ❺

The Museum Amstelkring is one of Amsterdam's best-kept secrets. The main attraction is upstairs, and goes by the name of Ons' Lieve Heer op Solder, or 'Our Sweet Lord in the Attic'. Built in 1663, this attic church was used by Catholics during the 17th century when they were banned from worshipping after the Alteration. It's been beautifully preserved, and the altarpiece features a painting by the noted 18th-century artist Jacob de Wit.

Nieuwe Kerk (New Church)

Dam (626 8168/recorded information 638 6909/www.nieuwekerk.nl). Tram 1, 2, 4, 5, 9, 13, 14, 16, 17, 24, 25. **Open** 10am-6pm daily. **Admission** varies. No credit cards. **Map** p54 C3 ❻

The sprightly Nieuwe Kerk dates from 1408, although the sundial on its tower was used to set all of the city's clocks until as recently as 1890. In 1645, the building was gutted by the Great Fire; the ornate oak pulpit and great organ (the latter designed by Jacob van Campen) are thought to have been constructed shortly after the blaze. Behind the black marble tomb of naval hero Admiral de Ruyter (1607-76) is a white marble relief depicting the sea battle in which he died. Poets and Amsterdam natives including PC Hooft and Joost van den Vondel are also buried here.

Oude Kerk

Oudekerksplein 1 (625 8284/www. oudekerk.nl). Tram 4, 9, 16, 24, 25, 26. **Open** 11am-5pm Mon-Sat; 1-5pm Sun. **Admission** €5; €4 seniors, students; free under-12s, MK. No credit cards. **Map** p55 D2 ❼

Originally built in 1306 as a simple wooden chapel, the Oude Kerk is the city's oldest and most interesting church. One can only imagine the Sunday Mass chaos during its heyday of the mid 1500s, when it had 38 altars each with its own guild-sponsored priest. Keep your eyes peeled for the Gothic and Renaissance façade above the northern portal, and the stained-glass windows, parts of which date from the 16th and 17th centuries. Rembrandt's wife Saskia, who died in 1642, is buried here. If you want to be semi-shocked, check out the carvings in the choir benches of men evacuating their bowels – apparently they tell a moralistic tale. Occasional art shows exhibit a range of fascinating subjects from contemporary Aboriginal art to photographs documenting the realities of life in modern Africa.

Eating & drinking

1e Klas

Line 2B, Centraal Station (625 0131). Tram 1, 2, 4, 5, 6, 9, 13, 16, 17, 24, 25. **Open** 8.30am-11pm daily. €€€. **Café.** **Map** p55 D1 ❽

This former brasserie for first-class commuters is now open to anyone who wants to kill some time in style – with a

Nieuwe Kerk

full meal or just a snack – while waiting for their train. The delightful art nouveau interior will whisk visitors straight back to the 1890s.

A Fusion

Zeedijk 130 (330 4068). Tram 4, 9, 14, 16, 24, 25/Metro Nieuwmarkt. **Open** noon-11pm daily. **€€€**. **Chinese**. Map p55 E2 ⑨

This laid back, loungey affair has obviously been taking notes from the hipper, more happening side of NYC's Chinatown. The dark and inviting interior harbours big screens playing Hong Kong music videos, bubble teas (lychee!), and some of the tastiest pan-Asian dishes in town.

De Bakkerswinkel

Warmoesstraat 69 (489 8000/www. bakkerswinkel.nl). Tram 1, 2, 4, 5, 9, 13, 14, 16, 17, 24, 25. **Open** 8am-6pm Tue-Fri; 8am-5pm Sat 10am-5pm Sun. **Café**. **Map** p55 D2 ⑩

De Bakkerswinkel is a fantastic little bakery and tearoom where you can indulge lunchtime hunger pangs with lovingly prepared sandwiches, hearty soups and the most divine slabs of quiche you've ever tasted.

De Bekeerde Suster

Kloveniersburgwal 6-8 (423 0112/www. beiaardgroep.nl). Tram 4, 9, 14, 16, 24, 25. **Open** 3pm-1am Mon-Fri; noon-1am Sat, Sun. **Bar**. **Map** p55 E3 ⑪

Those shiny copper vats and elaborate gleaming pipes aren't just for looking pretty: the Amsterdam Steambrewery Company has been making beer onsite since 2002. Home brews include refreshing white Witte Ros and seasonal bocks, as well as a list of international beer that leans heavily towards Belgium.

Brasserie Harkema

Nes 67 (428 2222/www.brasserie harkema.nl). Tram 4, 9, 14, 16, 24, 25. **Open** 11am-1am daily. **€€€**. **French**. **Map** p55 D4 ⑫

This former tobacco factory has titillated the local scene with its sense of designer space, excellent wines and a kitchen that stays open late pumping out reasonably priced French food.

Brasserie De Roode Leeuw

Damrak 93-94 (555 0666/www. restaurantderoodeleeuw.com). Tram 4, 9, 14, 16, 24, 25. **Open** 7am-11.30pm daily. **€€€€**. **Dutch**. **Map** p54 C3 ⑬

This brasserie is housed in the oldest covered terrace in Amsterdam. As you might guess, it harks back to classier times, but what's more surprising is its embrace of the digital age as a Wi-Fi point. It specialises in pricey Dutch fare, and also boasts a wide range of Dutch wines.

Bubbles and Wines

W Nes 37 (422 3318/www.bubbles andwines.com). Tram 4, 9, 14, 16, 24, 25. **Open** 3.30pm-1am Mon-Sat. **Bar**. **Map** p55 D4 ⑭

A long, low-ceilinged room with the feel of a wine cellar, one with mood lighting and banquettes. There are more than 50 wines by the glass and 180 by the bottle; posh nosh includes Osetra caviar, truffle cheese and foie gras. The final bill is unlikely to suit the faint-hearted or light of wallet.

Café Bern

Nieuwmarkt 9 (622 0034). Tram 4, 9, 14, 16, 24, 25/Metro Nieuwmarkt. **Open** 4pm-1am daily. **€€**. No credit cards. **Dutch**. **Map** p55 E3 ⑮

Despite its Swiss origins, the Dutch adopted the cheese fondue as a noted 'national dish' long ago. Sample its culinary conviviality at this suitably cosy bar that was established – oddly enough – by a nuclear physicist.

Café Stevens

Gelderskade 123 (620 6970). Tram 4, 9/Metro Nieuwmarkt. **Open** 10am-1am Mon-Thur, Sun; 10am-3am Fri, Sat. No credit cards. **Bar**. **Map** p55 E2 ⑯

With a living-room feel, plenty of seats and views over De Waag, this is a perfect spot to while away a day. The patrons are mainly locals, with a good number of tourists and students drinking in the view and sinking a few with sandwiches and (excellent) thick chips.

Centra

Lange Niezel 29 (622 3050). Tram 4, 9, 14, 16, 24, 25. **Open** 1.30-10.30pm daily. **€€**. No credit cards. **Spanish**. **Map** p55 D2 ⑰

Good, wholesome, homely Spanish cooking with a suitably unpretentious atmosphere to match. The tapas, lamb and fish dishes are all great, and the place gets justifiably busy as a result.

De Doelen

Kloveniersburgwal 125 (624 9023). Tram 9, 14/Metro Waterlooplein. **Open** 9am-1am Mon-Thu; 9am-3am Fri, Sat; 10am-1am Sun. No credit cards. **Bar**. **Map** p55 E4/5 ⑱

An old-fashioned drinking hole – complete with gritted floors – on one of the main tourist drags. Rough edges are smoothed by sophisticated breakfasts (fruit smoothies, muesli), international snacks (houmous, tapenade) and frosty jugs of sangria in summer.

Getto

Warmoesstraat 51 (421 5151/www.getto.nl). Tram 4, 9, 16, 24, 25. **Open** 4pm-1am Tue-Thur; 4pm-2am Fri, Sat; 4pm-midnight Sun. **€€**. **Global**. **Map** p55 D2 ⑲

Cheap and cheerful food in surprisingly plush surroundings catering to a mostly gay and lesbian crowd. On Wednesdays all burger dinners cost just €10. Combined with the popular weekday cocktail happy hours, this is the ideal place for an inexpensive date.

Greenhouse

Oudezijds Voorburgwal 191 (6271739/www.greenhouse.org). Tram 4, 9, 14, 16, 24, 25. **Open** 9am-1am daily. No credit cards. **Coffeeshop**. **Map** p55 D3 ⑳

This legendary coffeeshop tenders highly potent weed with prices to match. It's won the Cannabis Cup over 30 times and, with the Grand Hotel next door, occasional celebrities stop by to get caned. The vibe inside has grown a bit commercial, but it's still worth a peek, if only to see the beautifully handmade interior, with sunken floors, ornate mosaic stones and elaborate blown-glass lamps.

Greenhouse Effect

Warmoesstraat 53 (624 4974/www.greenhouse-effect.nl). Tram 4, 9, 16, 24, 25. **Open** 9am-1am Mon-Thur, Sun; 9am-3am Fri, Sat. No credit cards. **Coffeeshop**. **Map** p55 D2 ㉑

Red light blues

Are you a loud, obnoxious tourist prone to trawling through the **Red Light District** in a drunken pack? If so, your fun is running out. At the beginning of 2008, a plan was launched to clean up this iconic neighbourhood.

When he presented Project 1012 (named after the local area code), deputy mayor Lodewijk Asscher gave as his inspiration the clean-up of New York by Rudy Giuliani. What he didn't mention was the enormous difference between the sizes of the two cities, and all the New Yorkers who think the best city in the world is now just one big mall.

In 2007, the city began buying properties owned by 'Fat' Charles Geerts, a landlord who rented window spaces to prostitutes. New legislation has allowed the city to withdraw property rights from those suspected of criminal activities; Geerts and other brothel-keepers were suspected of money laundering and participation in the drug trade. The best-known 'gentleman's club', Yab Yum, was closed, and the city aims to continue buying up windows, change the zoning plan and replace dubious businesses, including coffeeshops, with galleries, artists' workshops, high-end bars and restaurants.

For PR value, 18 windows became 'fashion booths' as part of the Red Light Fashion initiative, where designers, such as couture talent Jan Taminiau and streetwear whizz Bas Kosters, are allocated former bordello rooms as affordable studios for a year.

But although the majority of Amsterdammers support the idea of hitting the criminal element behind the sex and drug traffic, many say the city plans will actually drive tourists away. A group of 110 business figures even formed an 'action committee', Platform 1012, to fight the plan. Others have argued that the area is already the closest thing to a happy, shiny Sex Disneyland that's safe for prostitute and user. But one thing's for sure, the area is changing. Those drunken hordes may soon be a thing of the past.

Dam Square p52

This snug shop is shaped like a long, sleek train carriage, and features a polished interior and reliably high-quality ganja. It tends to fill up fast, but there's a separate space with the same name next door where you will find a full bar as well as regular DJs. If the drink and dope combination renders you immobile, make a beeline for one of the hotel rooms upstairs. Also next door is Getto, arguably the best gay/straight friendly bar/restaurant in town, where the atmosphere is always jumping and toking is also allowed.

Hill Street Blues

*Nieuwmarkt 14 (no phone/www.
hillstreet-blues.nl). Tram 4, 9, 14, 16,
24, 25/Metro Nieuwmarkt.* **Open**
9am-1am daily. No credit cards.
Coffeeshop. **Map** p55 E3 ㉒
With comfy couches and natural lighting via well-placed windows, this cosy corner on the Nieuwmarkt is ideal for a mellow high. Delectable milkshakes, smoothies, space cookies and space truffles are also worth an indulgence. The basement has pool tables and arcade games, a back window overlooks the Damrak canal and, with a police station next door, you can

savour a legal toke near the law. How's that for ironic, Alanis? Hill Street Blues is also a favourite of Irvine Welsh.

De Jaren

*Nieuwe Doelenstraat 20-22 (625 5771/
www.cafe-de-jaren.nl). Tram 4, 9, 14,
16, 24, 25.* **Open** 10am-1am Mon-
Thur, Sun; 10am-2am Fri, Sat. **Bar**.
Map p55 E5 ㉓
An entire cross-section of Amsterdam – students, tourists, lesbigays, cinemagoers and the fashion pack – come here for lunch, coffee or something stronger all day long, making it sometimes difficult to bag a seat. Be prepared to fight for a spot on the popular Amstel-side outdoor terrace in summer.

Kapitein Zeppos

*Gebed Zonder End 5 (624 2057/www.
zeppos.nl). Tram 4, 9, 14, 16, 24, 25.*
Open 12am-1am Mon-Thur, Sun; 12am-
3am Fri, Sat. **Bar**. **Map** p55 D4 ㉔
A hidey-hole down the poetically named 'Prayer Without End' alley – a reference to the Santa Clara convent that stood here in the 17th century. Now it's a light-drenched, multi-roomed café and restaurant with an understated Belgian theme: it's named

after a 1960s Flemish TV detective, there's Belgian beer on tap and the soundtrack of choice is chanson.

Katoen

Oude Turfmarkt 153 (626 2635/www.goodfoodgroup.nl). Tram 4, 9, 14, 16, 24, 25. **Open** 9am-1am Mon-Thur; 9am-3am Fri, Sat; 10.30am-1am Sun. No credit cards. **Café. Map** p55 D5 ㉕
If shopping on Kalverstraat gets too much, run screaming across Rokin to this oasis of calm on the edge of the Old Centre. It has the stripped-down good looks of the 1950s (Formica tables, polished wood) and an inventive lunch menu of salads, rolls and wraps.

Latei

Zeedijk 143 (625 7485/www.latei.net). Tram 4, 9, 14, 16, 24, 25/Metro Nieuwmarkt. **Open** 8am-6pm Mon-Wed; 8am-10pm Thur, Fri; 9am-10pm Sat; 11am-6pm Sun. No credit cards. **Café. Map** p55 E2 ㉖
Packed with kitsch bric-a-brac and funky Finnish wallpaper – all of which, including the wallpaper, is for sale – this little café serves up healthy juices and snacks all day, plus vegetarian dinners based around its immaculately prepared speciality couscous.

Nam Kee

Zeedijk 111-113 (624 3470/www.namkee.nl). Tram 4, 9, 14, 16, 24, 25/ Metro Nieuwmarkt. **Open** noon-11pm Mon-Sat; noon-10pm Sun. **€€**. No credit cards. **Chinese. Map** p55 E2 ㉗
Cheap and terrific food has earned this Chinese joint a devoted following – the oysters in black bean sauce have achieved cult status. If it's busy, try sister operation and dim sum maestros Nam Tin nearby (Jodenbreestraat 11-13, 428 8508), or neighbour New King (Zeedijk 115-117, 625 2180).

Oriental City

Oudezijds Voorburgwal 177-179 (626 8352/www.oriental-city.nl). Tram 4, 9, 14, 16, 24, 25. **Open** 11.30am-11.30pm daily. **€€€**. **Chinese. Map** p55 D3 ㉘
The views from Oriental City are truly awesome, overlooking Damstraat, the Royal Palace and the canals, plus the dim sum is some of the best you'll find in all of Amsterdam.

Queen's Head

Zeedijk 20 (420 2475/www.queenshead.nl). Tram 4, 9, 16, 24, 25/Metro Centraal Station. **Open** 4pm-1am Mon-Thur; 4pm-3am Fri, Sat; noon-1am Sun. No credit cards. **Bar. Map** p55 D2 ㉙
The Queen's is a fun and attitude-free gay bar with a similarly minded clientele, plus a great view over a canal at the back. Tuesdays bring show night with drag acts and Thursday is the ArtLaunch café. It also hosts special parties on – not surprisingly – Queen's Day, plus skin nights, football nights (during the cup season), Eurovision Song Contest nights and so on.

Rusland

Rusland 16 (627 9468). Tram 4, 9, 14, 16, 24, 25/Metro Nieuwmarkt/ Waterlooplein. **Open** 10am-midnight Mon-Thur, Sun; 10am-1am Fri, Sat. No credit cards. **Coffeeshop. Map** p55 D4 ㉚
Well known as the longest-running coffeeshop in the city, this 'Russian' den has hardwood floors and colourful cushions that complement an efficient multi-level design. The top floor has a bar with 40 different loose teas, down below is a decent pipe display and up front is a dealer's booth providing the main attraction. It's off the tourist path, meaning cheaper prices and fewer crowds for the punter.

Skek

W Zeedijk 4-8 (427 551/www.skek.nl). Tram 4, 9, 16, 24, 25. **Open** noon-1am Mon-Thur, Sun; noon-3am Fri, Sat. **Cafe. Map** p55 D1 ㉛
This new little café-cum-music joint is already living up to its potential. Run by the student organisation that heads up the Filmtheater Kriterion, it focusses on both value and quality. While student visitors lap up the great discounts, other music-lovers will probably get more out of the regular singer/songwriter and jazz shows on offer.

Think global, snack local

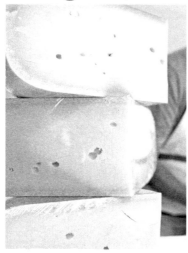

You must, yes, you simply *must* try raw herring. We don't want any excuses. The best time is between May and July when the *nieuw* (new) catch hits the stands, as they don't need any extras like onions or pickles because the flesh is at its sweetest – thanks to the high fat content the herring was set to burn off in the arduous business of breeding. There are quality fish stalls or stores on most street corners, which also offer smoked eel and other – perhaps less controversial – fish for filling sandwiches. And they're as cheap as chips (or, at the very least, a heck of a lot cheaper than sushi).

Speaking of chips, the best of these are the chunky Belgian ones (*Vlaamse*), double-fried to ensure a crispy exterior and creamy interior. Enjoy them along with your pick of toppings, such as *oorlog* (war): mayo, spicy peanut sauce and onions.

The local term for a greasy snack – *vette hap* – is translated literally as 'fat bite', which says a lot for the honesty of the Dutch when it comes to the less healthy spectrum of belly-ballast. The most iconic grease purveyor is the ubiquitous **Febo** (pronounced 'Fay-bo'), where you can put your change into a glowing *automaat* and, in return, get a dollop of grease in the form of a hot(ish) hamburger, *bamibal* (a deep-fried noodley ball of vaguely Indonesian descent), or a *kaas soufflé* (a cheese treat that, despite being unrelated to any established form of soufflé, is still surprisingly tasty if eaten when still hot). The most popular choice is the *kroket*, a native version of the croquette: a mélange of meat and potato with a crusty, deep-fried skin, best served on a bun with lots of hot mustard. The single best place to try these is **Van Dobben** (Korte Reguliersdwarsstraat 5-9, 624 4200), just off Rembrandtplein. And while this 1945-vintage late-night venue is the uncontested champion when it comes to the *kroket*, you can also find a more refined shrimp variation at nearby bakery **Holtkamp** (Vijzelgracht 15, 624 8757). Either way, it's proof that this is a great city to fill your belly without emptying your wallet.

Tara

*Rokin 85-89 (421 2654/www.thetara.
com). Tram 4, 9, 14, 16, 24, 25.* **Open**
10am-1am Mon-Thur, Sun; 10am-3am
Fri, Sat. **Bar**. **Map** p55 D4 ③②
Never overdoing the Irish theme, this
multi-roomed bar has many faces: the
Nes side is loungey, the Rokin side full
of rowdy, football-watching Brits,
while the middle is a snug conversation
pit with sofas and a roaring fire.
There's the black stuff, plus Caffrey's,
Murphys and cider. Food is always
reliable and – hallelujah! – bar snacks
include Walkers crisps.

Thaise Snackbar Bird

*Zeedijk 72 (snack bar 420 6289/
restaurant 620 1442/www.thai-bird.nl).
Tram 1, 2, 4, 5, 9, 13, 14, 16, 17, 24,
25.* **Open** *Snack bar* 2-10pm daily.
Restaurant 5-11pm daily. **€€€**. **Thai**.
Map p55 E2 ③③
Easily the most authentic Thai place in
town. No doubt because of this, it's also
the most crowded, but it's worth waiting for all the same, whether you drop
by for tom yam soup or go for a full-
blown meal. If you plan to linger, settle down in the restaurant across the
street rather than the snack bar itself.

Van Kerkwijk

*Nes 41 (620 3316). Tram 4, 9, 14, 16,
24, 25.* **Open** 11am-1am Mon-Thur,
Sun; 11am-3am Fri, Sat. No credit
cards. **Bar**. **Map** p55 D4 ③④
Far from the bustle of Dam square,
though really just a few strides away,
on one of Amsterdam's most charming
streets. Airy by day, more romantic
and candlelit at night, it's equally good
for group chats or tête-à-têtes. Lunch
brings sandwiches and the evening
more substantial food, though the
emphasis is as much on genteel drinking. Be careful of the almost vertical
stairs leading down to the toilets if you
have overindulged.

Vleminckx

*Voetboogsteeg 31 (no phone). Tram 1,
2, 5.* **Open** 11am-6pm Mon-Sat; noon-
5.30pm Sun. **€**. No credit cards. **Chips**.
Map p55 D5 ③⑤

Chunky Belgian chips served with
your choice of toppings. Go for the *oorlog* (war) variety: chips with mayo,
spicy peanut sauce and onions.

Wynand Fockink

*Pijlsteeg 31 (639 2695/www.wynand-
fockink.nl). Tram 4, 9, 14, 16, 24, 25.*
Open 3-9pm daily. No credit cards.
Bar. **Map** p55 D3 ③⑥
Tucked away in a side alley behind the
Krasnapolsky and largely unchanged
since 1679, this tasting house has been
a meeting place for Freemasons since
the year dot, with past visitors including Churchill and Chagall. The menu
of liqueurs and jenevers reads like a list
of yet-to-be-written experimental nov-
els: Parrot Soup; The Longer the Better;
Rose Without Thorns.

Shopping

2πR

*Oude Hoogstraat 10-12 (421 6329).
Tram 4, 9, 14, 16, 24, 25.* **Open**
noon-7pm Mon; 10am-7pm Tue, Wed,
Fri, Sat; 10am-9pm Thur; noon-6pm
Sun. **Map** p55 E3 ③⑦
This funky little number is just for the
boys. Two shops side by side on Oude
Hoogstraat between themselves offer
urban streetwear and killer threads
from the likes of Helmut Lang, Psycho
Cowboy and D-Squared.

Absolute Danny

*Oudezijds Achterburgwal 78 (421
0915/www.absolutedanny.com).
Tram 4, 9, 16, 24.* **Open** 11am-9pm
Mon-Thur, Sun; 11am-10pm Fri, Sat.
Map p55 D3 ③⑧
A fetish shop stocking everything from
rubber clothing to erotic toothbrushes.

Betsy Palmer

*Rokin 9-15 (422 1040/www.betsy
palmer.com). Tram 4, 9, 14, 16, 24,
25.* **Open** *Summer* noon-6pm Mon;
10am-6pm Tue-Wed, Fri, Sat; 10am-
9pm Thur; 1-6pm Sun. *Winter* 10am-
6pm Mon-Fri. **Map** p54 C4 ③⑨
Tired of seeing the same shoes in every
store, Dutch fashion buyer Gertie
Gerards put her money where her

Tunnel visions

Centraal Station

Amsterdam is being ripped apart. The redevelopment activity is an attempt to right a wrong: the building of **Centraal Station** between 1882 and 1889. Although it's now impossible to imagine Amsterdam without its 'Old Holland'-style masterpiece (or its mirror, the Rijksmuseum), the building did physically and psychologically separate the city from its harbour and Amsterdam North across the IJ river – as well as from its history as the world's richest city port during its 17th-century Golden Age.

With the completion of the Noord-Zuidlijn **metro** link in 2013, the north will be connected to the outlying south via Centraal Station, which is also undergoing total refurbishment. The station will finally be truly central, with two front sides: one facing across the waters towards a rapidly gentrifying north, and the other, traditional front side that faces the Old Centre and the radiating horseshoe of canals with their iconic gabled houses.

Work on the 9.5-kilometre (5.9-mile) Noord-Zuidlijn started in 2003 and will run at least until 2013. Most of the aldermen responsible for initiating the project are now elsewhere, leaving the city with a legacy that's at best merely too expensive, and at worst out of control. The Noord-Zuidlijn is way over its original budget – a staggering €1.8 billion – paid for by the council and the government. The whole thing will cost the council more than €600 million, and not the estimated €314 million. Part of the problem lies in the difficulties of digging under a city built on poles; new, time-consuming processes had to be invented to construct tunnels.

Still, it's hoped that the new metro line will eventually give the city an economic boost, especially in the southern area around rising business centre Zuidas, where, in anticipation of the new line, many new office blocks have been built – and are lying largely empty.

mouth was and set up shop. Betsy Palmer is her in-house label, which sits alongside a huge variety of other labels that change regularly as they sell out.

Book Exchange

Kloveniersburgwal 58 (626 6266). Tram 4, 9, 14/Metro Nieuwmarkt. **Open** 10am-6pm Mon-Fri, Sat; 11.30am-4pm Sun. No credit cards. **Map** p55 E4 ⓪

The owner of this bibliophiles' treasure trove is a shrewd buyer who's willing to do trade deals. Choose from a range of second-hand English and American titles (mainly paperbacks).

Condomerie het Gulden Vlies

Warmoesstraat 141 (627 4174/www. condomerie.com). Tram 4, 9, 14, 16, 25. **Open** 11am-6pm Mon-Sat. **Map** p55 D3 ④

An astounding variety of innovative and imaginative rubbers of the non-erasing kind, designed to wrap up trouser snakes of all shapes and sizes.

Droog Design

NEW *Staalstraat 7A/7B (523 5059/ www.droogdesign.nl). Tram 4, 9, 14, 16, 24, 25.* **Open** noon-6pm Tue-Sat; noon-5pm Sun. **Map** p55 E5 ④

This internationally acclaimed Dutch design collective has its own shop, with some of the wittiest ranges around: Marcel Wanders, Hella Jongerius, Richard Hutten and Jurgen Bey.

Geels & Co

Warmoesstraat 67 (624 0683/www. geels.nl). Tram 4, 9, 14, 16, 24, 25. **Open** *Shop* 9.30am-6pm Mon-Sat. **Map** p55 D2 ④

Here they dish out coffee beans and loose teas, in addition to a wide range of coffee-making contraptions and decorative utensils. Head upstairs and you'll find a museum of brewing equipment, open on Saturday afternoons.

Grimm Sieraden

Grimburgwal 9 (622 0501/www. grimmsieraden.nl). Tram 16, 24, 25. **Open** 11am-6pm Tue-Fri; 11am-5pm Sat. **Map** p55 D4 ④

Brasserie Harkema p57

AMSTERDAM BY AREA

Betsy Palmer p63

While Elize Lutz's shop features the most avant-garde Dutch jewellery designers, she concentrates on their most wearable and affordable pieces.

Head Shop

Kloveniersburgwal 39 (624 9061/ www. headshop.nl).Tram 4, 9, 14, 16, 24, 25/ Metro Nieuwmarkt. **Open** 11am-6pm Mon-Sat. **Map** p55 E3 ⑮
Land at the Head Shop and you'll think Jimi, Janis and Jim are still on the go. Stocks pipes, bongs, jewellery, incense, books, mushrooms and spores.

Jacob Hooy & Co

Kloveniersburgwal 12 (624 3041/www .jacobhooy.nl). Tram 4, 9, 14, 16, 24, 25/Metro Nieuwmarkt. **Open** 1-6pm Mon; 10am-6pm Tue-Fri; 10am-5pm Sat. **Map** p55 E3 ⑯
Sells a huge variety of medicinal herbs, teas, homeopathic remedies and cosmetics. The untouched 18th-century interior is worth a visit in itself.

Joe's Vliegerwinkel

Nieuwe Hoogstraat 19 (625 0139/ www.joesvliegerwinkel.nl). Tram 4, 9, 16, 24, 25/Metro Nieuwmarkt. **Open** noon-6pm Tue-Fri; 12am-5pm Sat. **Map** p55 E3 ⑰

Kites, kites and yet more kites. Also a quirky array of boomerangs, yo-yos and kaleidoscopes at this wonderfully colourful shop.

't Klompenhuisje

Nieuwe Hoogstraat 9A (622 8100/ www.klompenhuisje.nl). Tram 4, 9, 14/ Metro Nieuwmarkt. **Open** 10am-6pm Mon-Sat. **Map** p55 E3 ⑱
Delightfully crafted and reasonably priced shoes, traditional clogs and hand-made leather and woollen slippers.

Nieuwmarkt Antique Market

Nieuwmarkt (no phone). Tram 9, 14/Metro Nieuwmarkt. **Open** *May-Oct* 9am-5pm Sun. **Map** p55 E3 ⑲
A few streets away from the ladies in the windows, this antiques and bric-a-brac market attracts browsers looking for other kinds of pleasures. Old books, furniture and objets d'art.

Oriental Commodities

Nieuwmarkt 27 (626 2797/www. orientalgroup.nl). Tram 4, 9, 14, 16, 24, 25/Metro Nieuwmarkt. **Open** 9am-6pm Mon-Sat; 10.30am-5pm Sun. No credit cards. **Map** p55 E3 ⑳

Visit Amsterdam's largest Chinese food emporium for the full spectrum of Asian foods and ingredients, raning from shrimp- and scallop-flavoured egg noodles to fried tofu balls and fresh veg. You can also seek out a fine range of traditional Chinese cooking appliances and utensils.

Oudemanhuis Book Market

Oudemanhuispoort (no phone). Tram 4, 9, 14, 16, 24, 25. **Open** 9am-5pm Mon-Sat. No credit cards. **Map** p55 D4 **51**
People have been buying and selling books, prints and sheet music from this shop since the 18th century.

Palm Guitars

's Gravelandseveer 5 (422 0445/ www.palmguitars.nl). Tram 4, 9, 16, 24, 25. **Open** noon-6pm Wed-Sat. **Map** p55 E5 **52**
Palm Guitars stocks new, antique, used and rare musical instruments (and their parts). The excellent website features a calendar of upcoming local gigs, all of a worldly and rootsy nature.

Puccini Bomboni

Staalstraat 17 (626 5474/www. puccinibomboni.com). Tram 9, 14/Metro Waterlooplein. **Open** noon-6pm Mon; 9am-6pm Tue-Sat; noon-6pm Sun. **Map** p55 E4 **53**
Tamarind, thyme, lemongrass, pepper and gin are just some of the flavours of these delicious and imaginative handmade chocolates, all completely lacking in artificial ingredients. And business is going so well, it recently opened a second shop at Singel 184 (427 8341, open noon-6pm Mon, Sun; 1-6pm Tue-Sat).

Stoffen & Fournituren Winkel a Boeken

Nieuwe Hoogstraat 31 (626 7205). Tram 4, 9, 16, 24, 25. **Open** noon-6pm Mon; 10am-6pm Tue, Wed, Fri; 10am-8pm Thur; 10am-5pm Sat. **Map** p55 E3 **54**
The Boeken family has been in the rag trade hawking fabrics since 1920. Just try to find somewhere else with the

kind of variety on offer here: latex, lycra, fake fur and sequins abound.

Tom's Skate Shop

Oude Hoogstraat 35-37 (625 4922/ www.tomsskateshop.nl). Tram 4, 9, 14/Metro Nieuwmarkt. **Open** noon-6pm Mon; 10am-6pm Tue-Sat; noon-6pm Sun. **Map** p55 D3 **55**
Dual-gender gear from the likes of Nike SB, Zoo York, local label Rockwell and London label Addict. Also in stock are limited edition trainers, sunnies by Electric and plenty of skateboards.

WonderWood

NEW *Rusland 3 (625 3738/www. wonderwood.nl). Tram 6, 7, 10.* **Open** noon-6pm Wed-Sat. **Map** p55 E4 **56**
The name says it all: wonderfully sculpted wood in the form of shop-made originals, re-editions of global classics, and original plywood from the 1940s and '50s. Wonderful.

Nightlife

Winston International

Warmoesstraat 125-129 (623 1380/ www.winston.nl). Tram 1, 2, 5, 13, 14, 16, 17, 24, 25. **Open** 9pm-3am Mon-Thur, Sun; 9pm-4am Fri, Sat. No credit cards. **Map** p55 D3 **57**
An intimate venue that attracts a mixed crowd with its alternative rock and indietronica. Winston's yearly Popprijs gives hope to many student rock bands; Cheeky Mondays brings relief to yet another working week with jungle and drum 'n' bass; and other nights see live music from garage to folk to funky ska.

Arts & leisure

Amsterdam Marionetten Theater

Nieuwe Jonkerstraat 8 (620 8027/www. marionettentheater.nl). Tram 5, 9, 13, 14, 16, 17, 24, 25. **Map** p55 E2 **58**
Opera performed as you've never seen it before: put together puppets in rich velvet costumes, puppeteers and classic operas by Mozart or Offenbach, and you've got a show. One of the last

outposts of an old European tradition, the theatre also offers private lunches, dinners or high teas, consumed while the puppets perform.

Amsterdams Centrum voor Fotographie

*Bethaniënstraat 9-13 (622 4899/www.
acf-web.nl). Tram 16, 24, 25.* No credit
cards. **Map** p55 D3 ⑤⑨
Photo hounds love this sprawling space within flashing distance of the Red Light District. Besides exhibitions (also at no.39), the centre has a range of workshops and a black-and-white darkroom for hire.

Bethaniënklooster

*Barndesteeg 6B (625 0078/www.
bethanienklooster.nl). Tram 4, 9, 16,
24, 25/Metro Nieuwmarkt.* No credit
cards. **Map** p55 E3 ⑥⓪
Hidden down a small alley between Damstraat and the Nieuwmarkt, this former monastery is a wonderful stage for new talent to cut its musical teeth. In between hearing free public performances by Amsterdam's top music students, you'll also have the chance to tune into some reputable ensembles and quartets.

Bijzondere Collecties

NEW *Oude Turfmarkt 129 (525 7300/
www.uba.uva.nl/bijzondere_collecties/
overzicht.cfm). Tram 9, 14, 24.* **Open**
10.30am-5pm Mon-Fri; 1-5pm Sat, Sun.
Map p55 D5 ⑥①
They like their paper products at the University of Amsterdam's 'Special Collections': documents, prints, maps, atlases, photos and endless rows of books. The invaluable pre-1850 collection is especially strong on topics related to printing history, Hebrew and Judaica studies, Protestantism and medicine; the post-1850 collection focuses more on meritorious design, with exhibitions of anything from Linnaeus prints to book advertising of the 18th century.

De Brakke Grond

*Nes 45 (622 9014/www.brakke
grond.nl). Tram 4, 9, 14, 16, 24,
25.* No credit cards. **Map** p55 D4 ⑥②

Belgian culture does stretch beyond beer, and De Brakke Grond is here to prove it. Mind you, some good Belgian beer will go down a treat after a fix of progressive Flemish theatre, and if you're really lucky you might find an actor or two joining you at the bar of the adjoining café/restaurant.

Cannabis College

*Oudezijds Achterburgwal 124 (423
4420/www.cannabiscollege.com).
Tram 4, 9, 14, 16, 24, 25/Metro
Nieuwmarkt.* **Map** p55 D3 ⑥③
The college, occupying two floors in a 17th-century listed monument in the Red Light District, provides the public with an impressive array of information about the cannabis plant (including its medicinal uses). The place is run by volunteers and admission is free; however, staff request a €2.50 donation if you want to take a wander around the indoor garden (no prizes for guessing what's growing).

Chiellerie

*Raamgracht 58 (320 9448/www.
chiellerie.nl). Metro Nieuwmarkt.* No
credit cards. **Map** p55 E4 ⑥④
This place is home to former 'Night Mayor' Chiel van Zelst. Boasting a new exhibition every week or two culled from members of the local arts scene, the gallery feels more like a hangout than mere art hanger.

Comedy Theatre

*Nes 110 (422 2777/www.comedy
theater.nl). Tram 4, 9, 14, 16, 24,
25.* **Map** p55 D4 ⑥⑤
This old tobacco hall was reopened in April 2007 to house a new comedy theatre; it's located on the city's most venerable theatre street. Hyping itself as the 'club house' for comedians, the programming combines politically hard-hitting performers with straightforward stand up. Expect to see local legends like Javier Guzman, as well as international ones such as Tom Rhodes or Lewis Black. To make sure that at least some of the acts are English-speaking on the night, it's best to phone the venue in advance.

Squat's up, doc?

VRANKRYK

Vrankryk

This town has a lot of nostalgists weeping for the salad days of the 1980s and '90s, when **cultural squats** like Silo and Vrieshuis Amerika were the coolest cheap studio space around. Such cultural beehives were shut down by the powers-that-be, but in the last few years the city has been busy marketing itself as a 'creative city'. Now the bureaucrats, in an effort to claw back lost prestige and emigrating artists, have created less affordable non-squat squats called **broedplaatsen** (breeding grounds).

The world of Amstersquats is divided into umpteen categories. As well as *broedplaatsen*, there are proper squats, reappropriated buildings that had been left empty for more than a year; 'anti-squats', buildings with temporary residents paying no rent so squatters can't move in; and 'bought squats', old squats that were then sold cheaply by the city to their inhabitants to relieve themselves of a headache – the Vrankrijk (Spuistraat 216, www.vrankrijk. org) is the most famous example of this type.

It seems that the places that began as bona fide squats are the ones that made the crossover to *broedplaats* most efficiently: the former film academy OT301 is seriously happening, as is the former shipping yard art complex NDSM (p111). Although not a *broedplaats*, Westergasfabriek (p122) still has some street cred thanks to its industrial origins.

The homeliest of the bunch is the Chiellerie (p68). Organised by artist, old-school squatter and former 'Night Mayor' Chiel van Zelst, his gallery has a new opening almost every Friday. Its website has also become an impressive showcase for the local art scene.

Meanwhile, Volkskrantgebouw (Wibautstraat 150, www.volks krantgebouw.nl), an old newspaper building, was launched in 2007 as a new concept, a group negotiating to take over the building for seven years and fill it with artists and creative industries. It also has a great bar, which can be important when it comes to breeding.

Dampkring p72

De Engelenbak

*Nes 71 (626 3644/www.engelenbak.nl).
Tram 4, 9, 14, 16, 24, 25.* No credit
cards. **Map** p55 D4 **⑯**

Theatre productions by amateurs is
what you get at De Engelenbak. The
main draw is Open Bak, an open-stage
event (10.30pm Tue) where anything
goes: it's the longest-running theatre
programme in the country, where
everybody gets their 15 minutes of dramatic fame. Make sure you arrive half
an hour early to get a ticket (€7.50), and
bear in mind that the best groups tend
to stage performances between
Thursday and Saturday.

Frascati

*Nes 63 (751 6400/tickets 626 6866/
www.indenes.nl). Tram 4, 9, 14, 16, 24,
25.* No credit cards. **Map** p55 D4 **⑰**

A cornerstone of progressive Dutch
theatre since the 1960s, Frascati gives
promising artists the chance to stage
their productions on one of its three
stages. Their mission: to challenge the
bounds of traditional theatre by team-
ing up artists with trained back-
grounds with those from the street,
resulting in a varied selection of theatre
and dance shows featuring MCs, DJs
and VJs, like the youthful Breakin'
Walls festival. If you want to meet a
thespian rather than just see one on
stage, the adjoining café, Blincker, has
plenty of actors in permanent, loqua-
cious residence at its bar.

Muziektheater

*Amstel 3 (625 5455/www.muziek
theater.nl). Tram 9, 14/Metro
Waterlooplein.* **Map** p55 F4 **⑱**

The Muziektheater is Amsterdam at its
most ambitious. This plush, crescent-
shaped building, which opened in 1986,
has room for 1,596 people and is home
to both Dutch National Ballet and De
Nederlandse Opera, though the stage
is also used by visiting companies such
as Nederlands Dans Theater, Bill T.
Jones/Arnie Zane Dance Company and
Batsheva. On top of that, the lobby's
panoramic glass walls offer impressive
views out over the River Amstel.

W139

*Warmoesstraat 139 (622 9434/
www.w139.nl). Tram 4, 9, 14, 16, 24,
25.* No credit cards. **Map** p55 D3 **⑲**

In its two decades of existence, W139
has never lost its squat aesthetics or
sometimes overly conceptual edge,
while a recent renovation has brought
even more light and fresh inspiration.

The New Side

The Spui is the square that caps
the three main arteries that start
down near the west end of Centraal
Station: middle-of-the-road walking
and shopping street Kalverstraat
(called Nieuwendijk before it
crosses the Dam), Nieuwezijds
Voorburgwal and the Spuistraat.

   The nearby Begijnhof is a
group of houses built around a
secluded courtyard and garden.
Established in the 14th century,
it originally provided modest
homes for the Beguines, a
religious sisterhood. Nowadays,
its residents are still female and
it's the best known of the city's
many hofjes (almshouses). In the
centre is the Engelsekerk (English
Reformed Church), built around
1400 and given over to Scottish
(no, really) Presbyterians living
in the city in 1607. Also in the
courtyard is a Catholic church,
secretly converted from two
houses in 1665 following the
banning of open Catholic worship
after the Reformation. Also
close to here is one of several
entrances to the **Amsterdams
Historisch Museum**.

   The Spui square itself plays
host to many markets – the most
notable being the busy book
market held on Fridays. You
can leave Spui by going up
Kalverstraat, Amsterdam's
main shopping street, or Singel
past Leidsestraat: both routes
lead directly to the Munttoren

(Mint Tower) at Muntplein. Right across from the floating flower market, this medieval tower was once the western corner of Reguliersport, a gate in the city wall in the 1480s. The Munttoren is prettiest when it's floodlit at night, but daytime visitors may enjoy hearing its carillon ringing out at noon.

From here, walk down Nieuwe Doelenstraat past the Hôtel de l'Europe (a mock-up of which featured in Hitchcock's *Foreign Correspondent*). This street also connects with scenic Staalstraat, which is the city's most popular film location, having appeared in everything from *The Diary of Anne Frank* to *Amsterdamned*. Walk up here and you'll end up in Waterlooplein.

Sights & museums

Amsterdams Historisch Museum

Kalverstraat 92 (523 1822/www. ahm.nl). Tram 1, 2, 4, 5, 9, 14, 16, 24, 25. **Open** 10am-5pm Mon-Fri; 11am-5pm Sat, Sun. **Admission** €7; €5.25 seniors; €3.50 6-16s; free under-6s, MK. No credit cards. **Map** p54 C5 ⑩

Amsterdam's Historical Museum is a gem: illuminating, interesting and entertaining. It starts with the buildings in which it's housed – lovely 17th-century constructions built on the site of a 1414 convent – and continues with the first exhibit, a computer-generated map of the area showing how Amsterdam has changed over the last 800 years or so. It then takes a chronological trip through Amsterdam's past, using archaeological finds (love those 700-year-old shoes), works of art (by the likes of Ferdinand Bol and Jacob Corneliszoon) and plenty of quirkier displays: tone-deaf masochists may care to play the carillon in room 10A, while lesbian barflies will want to pay homage to Bet van Beeren, late owner of the infamous Het Mandje.

Orange Football Museum

Kalverstraat 236 (0900 1437 premium rate/www.supportersclub-oranje.nl). Tram 4, 9, 16, 24, 25. **Open** 11am-5pm Sat, Sun. **Admission** €5. No credit cards. **Map** p55 D5 ㉑

This enthusiastic museum has four floors of photos, art, songs and videos relating to the national football team.

Eating & drinking

Al's Plaice

Nieuwendijk 10 (427 4192). Tram 1, 2, 4, 5, 9, 14, 16, 17, 24, 25. **Open** noon-10pm daily. **€.** No credit cards. **Fish & chips. Map** p54 C1 ㉒

Visiting Brits will spot the pun from 50 paces: yep, it's an English fish 'n' chip shop with all the trimmings. Besides fish, there's a selection of pies, pasties, peas and downmarket tabloids.

Café de Dokter

Rozenboomsteeg 4 (626 4427/ www.cafe-de-dokter.nl). Tram 1, 2, 4, 5, 9, 13, 14, 16, 17, 24, 25. **Open** 4pm-1am Tue-Sat. No credit cards. **Bar. Map** p55 D5 ㉓

Officially the smallest bar in all of Amsterdam, Café de Dokter is also one of the oldest, dishing out the cure for whatever ails you since 1798. Centuries of character and all kinds of charming gewgaws are packed into the compact space, giving it a unique old-world ambience. Whisky figures large (there's a monthly special) and the range of old-school bar snacks includes the likes of smoked osseworst with gherkins.

Dampkring

Handboogstraat 29 (638 0705/www. dedampkring.nl). Tram 1, 2, 5. **Open** 10am-1am daily. No credit cards. **Coffeeshop. Map** p55 ㉔

Known for its unforgettable (even by stoner standards) interior, the visual experience acquired from Dampkring's decor could make a mushroom trip look grey. Moulded walls and sculpted ceilings are covered in deep auburns laced with caramel-coloured wooden panelling, making a perfect location for

Eddy, steady, flow

During a sojourn in the city, Hans Christian Andersen wrote, 'The view from my window, through the elms to the canal outside, is like a fairy tale.' Canals are what people imagine when they think 'Amsterdam', and they still enchant today. Like any other city built on water, Amsterdam is best seen by boat. It has 75 kilometres (47 miles) of waterways, a total of 165 canals spanned by 1,400 bridges (more than Venice): look at the bottom right corner of a bridge to see its number.

The tourist boats provide a doughty service, but they can't squeeze into the narrower waterways. Self-piloted hire boats are few and far between: in fact, there are only two such outfits, **Canal Motorboats** (Zandhoek 10A, 422 7007, www.canal motorboats. com) on Realeneiland, and **Boaty** (Jozef Israëlkade, between Ferdinand Bolstraat & 2e Van der Helststraat, 06 2714 9493, www.boaty.nl) on a dock outside Hotel Okura (p165), in the Pijp.

The boats of both companies have a capacity of six. If these don't suit, you'll just have to befriend a be-boated local or charter a tour.

Amsterdam also has its own gondola service, **Stichting Battello** (686 9868, mobile 06 474 64545, www.gondel.nl), and it's suitably unique. Not only will you glide silently and comfortably along at an angle that shows this city at its prettiest, you'll also be chauffeured by one of two Guinness World Records worthies: Hans, 'the tallest gondolier in the world', or Tirza, 'the only woman gondolier in the world'. (In Venice, the Amsterdam of the South, it would seem that gondoliering is a career open only to short men.) Best suited to lovey-dovey couples, a ride will cost a group of up to six people about €100 an hour. You can also choose to bring your own food or drink, or have them arrange it at cost price. The standard course is around the Jordaan, but you're always welcome to stipulate your own route.

AMSTERDAM BY AREA

Athenaeum Nieuwscentrum p77

the movie *Ocean's Twelve*. Monitors show the same George Clooney and Brad Pitt scene all day long.

Gartine

NEW *Taksteeg 7 (320 4132/www. gartine.nl). Tram 4, 5, 9, 14, 16, 24, 25.* **Open** 8am-6pm Wed-Sun. €€. No credit cards. **Slow food.** **Map** p55 D5 ⑯
Open only for breakfast, lunch and a full-blown high tea, Gartine is a temple to slow food, served by a friendly couple who grow veg and herbs.

Green Planet

Spuistraat 122 (625 8280/www. greenplanet.nl). Tram 1, 2, 5, 13, 17. **Open** 5.30-10.30pm Mon-Sat. €€€. No credit cards. **Vegetarian.** **Map** p54 ⑯
The city's best veggie restaurant tips organic ingredients into soups, lasagnes and stir fries. Finish with house cognac and a slice of chocolate heaven.

Harry's Bar

Spuistraat 285 (624 4384). Tram 1, 2, 5, 9, 14, 16, 17, 24, 25. **Open** 1am Mon-Thur, Sun; 5pm-3am Fri, Sat. €. **Bar.** **Map** p54 C5 ⑰
Small, dark and intimate, Harry's Bar is the perfect place to while away an afternoon lounging on a leather sofa. There's everything here to suit all manner of movers and shakers, from Cristal champagne to Montecristo cigars.

Homegrown Fantasy

Nieuwezijds Voorburgwal 87A (627 5683/www.homegrownfantasy.com). Tram 1, 2, 5, 13, 17. **Open** 10am-midnight Mon-Thur; 10am-1am Fri-Sun. No credit cards. **Coffeeshop.** **Map** p54 C3 ⑱
One of the most popular coffeeshops with visitors, this brightly lit establishment bears an ever-changing lineup of artwork, tables with chessboards and a UV light in the toilet that makes your pee a trippy colour. The ganja is all organic and Dutch-grown, including famous cheese weed, and the (non-alcoholic) drink selection is vast. Those hoping to get mashed before joining a cult (it helps, apparently) will find the Scientology HQ conveniently located right across the street.

Keuken van 1870

Spuistraat 4 (620 4018/www. keukenvan1870.nl). Tram 1, 2, 5. **Open** 5-10pm Mon-Sat. €€. No credit cards. **Dutch.** **Map** p54 C2 ⑱

Supperclub

This former soup kitchen has been renovated and reinvented but retains a menu of authentic Dutch standards and, in a homage to its roots, a set three-course menu for €7.50. Diners often end up sharing tables, so hopefully you'll enjoy rubbing shoulders with a cross-section of Dutch society.

Prik
W Spuistraat 109 (320 0002/www. prikamsterdam.nl). Tram 1, 2, 5, 13, 17. **Open** 4pm-1am Tue-Thur, Sun; 4pm-3am Fri, Sat. No credit cards. **Bar.** **Map** p54 C3 ⑩

Queer or not, Prik is hot. True to the bar's slogan, this popular addition to the gay scene succeeds in getting a diverse crowd that enjoys its movie nights, delicious snacks and very groovy sounds.

Supperclub
Jonge Roelensteeg 21 (344 6400/www. supperclub.nl). Tram 1, 2, 5, 13, 17. **Open** 7.30pm-1am Mon-Thur, Sun; 7.30pm-3am Fri, Sat. **€€€€**. **Global.** **Map** p54 C4 ㉛

With its white decor, beds for seating, irreverent food combos and wacky acts, this arty joint is casual to the point

of being narcoleptic. At the very least, we can promise that you'll remember your visit. The owners also have their own cruise ship that trawls the local waters offering dinners with a more dramatic backdrop.

Tokyo Café
Spui 15 (489 7918/www.tokyocafe.nl). Tram 1, 2, 4, 5, 9, 14, 16, 24, 25. **Open** 12am-11pm daily. **€€€**. **Japanese. Map** p55 D5 ㉜

Thought to be haunted, this Jugendstil monument now hosts its umpteenth eaterie in the form of an authentic Japanese café complete with a lovely terrace, teppanyaki pyrotechnics and a sushi and sashimi bar. High-quality dishes that may offer little protection against local ghosts, but will certainly keep hunger at bay.

Tweede Kamer
Heisteeg 6 (422 2236). Tram 1, 2, 5. **Open** 10am-1am daily. No credit cards. **Coffeeshop. Map** p54 C5 ㉝

Small and intimate, this shop embodies the refined look and feel of vintage jazz sophistication – which makes it an extremely pleasant place to get stoned. Aided by a bakery just around

Smoke-free… *coffeeshops*?

Boerenjongens Coffeeshop

On 1 July 2008, all public spaces, including bars, live music venues, restaurants and clubs, will become **smoke free** in the Netherlands. The law is set up to be flexible, in that great Dutch tradition, so people will be creative – especially in the coffeeshop sector, where there's always a lot of lateral thought floating around.

How the rule will apply to these local institutions is still the subject of much discussion. After all, not being able to smoke in a coffeeshop is rather like not being able to pee in a public convenience. The new law, drawn up to protect the health of employees, still allows separate non-service smoking areas; and besides, what happens if one just smokes the weed pure?

One coffeeshop was ahead of the curve. Boerenjongens ('Farmer Boys') – which formerly had the much snappier name Get A Life – declared itself smoke-free in February 2007; but that was a marketing ploy to get lots of free press when it rebranded itself as a sort of organic deli that only works with small growers.

The vaporiser market is now a growth industry. Vaporisers appeared about 15 years ago as home-made devices that wedded a water bong to an electric paint stripper (with much duct tape), producing a gizmo that vaporises THC at such a low temperature that the leaves remain uncombusted. The choke was finally out of the toke.

Today, they are sleekly designed devices. And a more low-tech trend is the 'blow condom', where the condoms are filled with weed smoke; you inhale from one condom and blow out in another. 'Space cuisine' is set for a renaissance – hopefully in a form other than the classic cardboard-textured brownie that leaves you excavating the hash from your teeth with the edge of a pack of rolling papers. Yes, a new Stoned Age is dawning. And coffeeshop owners don't actually have that much to lose, with 85 per cent of sales being in takeaways.

the corner, its spacecakes are delicious and hugely effective. The house hash is highly regarded, but seating inside is limited; if there's no room, walk over to nearby Dutch Flowers (Singel 387).

Vaaghuyzen

Nieuwe Nieuwstraat 17 (420 1751/ www.vaaghuyzen.net). Tram 1, 2, 5, 13, 14, 16, 24, 25. **Open** 6pm-1am Mon-Thur; 3pm-3am Fri; 6pm-3am Sat; 3pm-1am Sun. No credit cards. **Bar**. **Map** p54 C3 ❸❹
This dinky DJ bar is a great place to pick up flyers and find out what's happening in clubs all over the city centre. And there are also plenty of reasons to stay, including top-notch turntablists and interactive evenings like Singles Night, where punters play the tunes.

D'Vijff Vlieghen

Spuistraat 294-302 (530 4060/www.d-vijffvlieghen.com). Tram 1, 2, 5, 13, 17. **Open** 6-10pm daily. €€€€. **Dutch**. **Map** p54 C5 ❸❺
The Five Flies achieves a rich Golden Age vibe – it even has a Rembrandt room, with etchings – but also works as a purveyor of kitsch. The food is best described as posh Dutch. Unique, and appropriately pricey.

Shopping

Albert Heijn

Nieuwezijds Voorburgwal 226 (421 8344/www.ah.nl). Tram 1, 2, 4, 5, 9, 13, 14, 16, 17, 24, 25. **Open** 8am-10pm daily. No credit cards. **Map** p54 C4 ❸❻
This massive shop, just behind Dam Square, is one of over 40 branches of Albert Heijn in Amsterdam. It contains virtually all the household goods you could ever need, though some of the range is unnecessarily expensive.

American Book Center

Spui 12 (625 5537/www.abc.nl). Tram 1, 2, 4, 5, 9, 14, 16, 24, 25. **Open** 10am-8pm Mon-Wed, Fri, Sat; 10am-9pm Thur; 11am-6.30pm Sun. **Map** p54 C5 ❸❼
An Amsterdam institution since 1972, (though relocated a couple years back to this fancy establishment, a mere two blocks from the old shop) the American Book Center stocks a truly enormous selection of English-language books and magazines from the US and UK to a loyal core of comfortably bilingual Dutch customers. Also, check out the nearby ABC Treehouse (423 0967, Voetboogstraat 11) which regularly hosts various workshops, open-mic nights and author readings.

Artplein Spui

Spui (www.artplein-spui.nl). Tram 1, 2, 4, 5, 9, 14, 16, 24, 25. **Open** *Mar-Dec* 10am-6pm Sun. No credit cards. **Map** p54 C5 ❸❽
Oil paintings, acrylics, watercolours, graphic arts, sculpture, ceramics and jewellery are found at this small open-air (and therefore weather-dependent) Sunday arts and crafts market. There's a rotating system for the 60 or so artists, and buskers are usually on hand to lend a little atmosphere while the crowds browse wares. The perfect place to take a chilled Sunday stroll.

Athenaeum Nieuwscentrum

Spui 14-16 (bookshop 514 1460/news centre 514 1470/www.athenaeum.nl). Tram 1, 2, 5. **Open** *Bookshop* 11am-6pm Mon; 9.30am-6pm Tue, Wed, Fri, Sat; 9.30am-9pm Thur; noon-5.30pm Sun. *News centre* 8am-8pm Mon-Wed, Fri, Sat; 8am-9pm Thur; 10am-6pm Sun. **Map** p54 C5 ❸❾
This is where Amsterdam's highbrow literary browsers usually choose to hang out and chew the cultural fat. The Athenaeum Nieuwscentrum, as its name might suggest, also stocks newspapers from across the world, as well as a wide choice of magazines and periodicals in many languages.

De Bijenkorf

Dam 1 (0900 0919 premium rate/ www.bijenkorf.nl). Tram 1, 2, 4, 5, 9, 13, 14, 16, 17, 24, 25. **Open** 11am-7pm Mon; 9.30am-7pm Tue, Wed; 9.30am-9pm Thur, Fri; 9.30am-6pm Sat; noon-6pm Sun. **Map** p54 C3 ❾⓪

Amsterdam's most notable department store has a great household goods section and a decent mix of clothing (designer and own-label), kids' wear, jewellery, cosmetics, shoes and accessories. The top-floor Chill Out department caters to funky youngsters in need of streetwear, clubwear, wacky foodstuffs and kitsch accessories.

Concrete
NEW *Spuistraat 250 (0900 2662 7383 premium rate/www.concrete.nl). Tram 1, 2, 5.* **Open** noon-7pm Mon-Wed, Fri, Sat; noon-9pm Thur; 1-6pm Sun. **Map** p54 C5 **91**
This shop/gallery's concept is more loose and humorous than rigidly concrete: a cross-fertilisation of street fashion, artist-made dolls, limited-edition shoes, and exhibitions of photography and graphic design.

Dampkring
Prins Hendrikkade 10-11 (422 2137/ www.dampkringshop.com). Tram 1, 2, 4, 5, 9, 16, 17, 24, 25/Metro Centraal Station. **Open** 10am-6pm Mon-Fri; 11am-5pm Sat. **Map** p54 C1 **92**
A new member of the green-fingered Dampkring family, this delightful emporium has everything needed to set up a cannabis grow centre at home: from hydroponics and organic equipment to bio-growth books and videos.

Female & Partners
Spuistraat 100 (620 9152/www. femaleandpartners.nl). Tram 1, 2, 5, 13, 17. **Open** 1-6pm Mon, Sun; 11am-6pm Tue, Wed, Fri, Sat; 11am-9pm Thur. **Map** p54 B3 **93**
The opposite of most enterprises here, Female & Partners welcomes women (and, yes, their partners) with an array of erotic clothes, videos and toys.

Hemp Works
Nieuwendijk 13 (421 1762/www. hempworks.nl). Tram 1, 2, 5, 13, 17. **Open** 11am-7pm Mon-Wed, Sun; 11am-9pm Thur-Sat. **Map** p54 C1 **94**
One of the first shops in Amsterdam to sell hemp clothes and products, and now one of the last, Hemp Works has

had to diversify into seed sales and fresh mushrooms to keep its trade ticking over, and it's also been a notable Cannabis Cup winner for its home-grown strain of the stinky weed.

Midtown
Nieuwendijk 104 (638 4252/www.midtown.nl). Tram 1, 2, 5, 13, 17, 24, 25. **Open** noon-6pm Mon; 10am-6pm Tue, Wed, Fri, Sat; 10am-9pm Thur; noon-5pm Sun. **Map** p54 C2 **95**
Dance music galore: gabber (the store was one of the original pioneers of the hardcore hybrid), trance, mellow house and garage are among the styles on the shelves. Midtown is also a good source for getting information and tickets for hardcore parties.

Paars
Spuistraat 242 (618 2828/www.paars lingerie.nl). Tram 1, 2, 5, 13, 17. **Open** 1-7pm Mon; 11am-7pm Tue-Fri; 10am-6pm Sat; 1-6pm Sun. **Map** p54 C5 **96**
Easily the most sophisticated lingerie shop in Amsterdam right now, Paars' collections are high end and vary regularly, making it interesting for true lingerie-lovers. Galliano, Lise Charmel, Marlies Dekkers, Miss Bikini, Worth, La Perla, D&G, Malizia, Pain de Sucre and Roberto Cavalli, among others, are all on sale.

Patta Exclusive Sneakers
NEW *Nieuwezijds Voorburgwal 142 (528 5994/www.teampatta.nl). Tram 1, 2, 5, 13, 17.* **Open** noon-7pm Mon-Wed, Fri-Sat; noon-9pm Thur; 1-6pm Sun. **Map** p54 C3 **97**
Named with the Surinamese slang for shoes, this store is where street trainer fetishists come to commune: all the expected brands, from Adidas to Van, are here. Ground-floor shop Ben G provides synergy with its skateboards.

PGC Hajenius
Rokin 92-96 (623 7494/www. hajenius.com). Tram 4, 9, 14, 16, 24, 25. **Open** noon-6pm Mon; 9.30am-6pm Tue-Fri; 9.30am-6pm Sat, Sun. **Map** p55 D5 **98**

Free for all

Noordermarkt flea market

Cheapskates, take note: you don't have to spend a fortune to have fun in Amsterdam. This list of activities shows just how easily budget visitors can have fun for free across the capital.

■ The view from **Nemo**'s roof (p113).
■ Complimentary coffee at various branches of **Albert Heijn** (p77).
■ Scenic **ferry trips** from behind Centraal Station to the north (p52).
■ The **Rijksmuseum**'s garden on its west side (p129).
■ Open-air concerts and the great outdoors of **Vondelpark** (p126).
■ The **Civic Guard Gallery** at the Amsterdams Historisch Museum (p72), plus the atmospheric buildings of the **Begijnhof** (p12).
■ **Noordermarkt** flea market on Monday mornings (p117).
■ Tuesday lunchtime concerts at the **Muziektheater** (p71).
■ Wednesday lunchtime concerts at the **Concertgebouw** (p130).
■ Exploring the **hofjes** – courtyard almshouses – of the Jordaan.
■ Tasting free samples of organic foodstuffs at the Saturday **farmers' market** on Noordermarkt (p118).

■ Peering in Hendrick de Keyser's atmospheric **Zuiderkerk** (p99).
■ Smelling the flowers on sale at the floating **Bloemenmarkt** (p95).
■ Checking the biggest barometer in the Netherlands. The neon light on the **Hotel Okura Amsterdam** (p165) tells you what tomorrow's weather will be like: blue for good; green for bad; white for changeable.
■ Taking a lift to the top of **Post CS** (p109) for unsurpassed city views.
■ Picking up and having a browse through **Amsterdam Weekly**, the English-language cultural paper.
■ Lounging on a deckchair at one of the city's many **urban beaches**.
■ Attending the opening of a new exhibition, Fridays at happening art hangout **Chiellerie** (p68).
■ Going alternative queer clubbing on every first Saturday of the month at **Hot Peper**, in the fabulous De Peper café (p127).
■ Reading through countless international papers and glossy magazines at the brand new **public library** (Prinsengracht 587).
■ Seeing top-notch bands being recorded for TV at **3voor12** (p105).

PGC Hajenius p78

A smoker's paradise (tobacco, not dope) for over 250 years, Hajenius offers cigarabilia from Dutch pipes to own-brand cigars. Even non-smokers should enjoy its quaint deco interior.

Postzegelmarkt
Nieuwezijds Voorburgwal, by No.276 (no phone). Tram 1, 2, 5, 13, 17. **Open** 9am-4pm Wed, Sat. No credit cards. **Map** p54 C5 **99**
A specialist market for more avid collectors of stamps, coins, postcards and medals, with plenty of rarities.

Rituals
Kalverstraat 73 (344 9220/www. rituals.com). Tram 4, 9, 14, 16, 24, 25. **Open** noon-6pm Mon; 10am-6pm Tue, Wed, Fri; 10am-9pm Thur; 10am-6pm Sat; noon-6pm Sun. **Map** p55 D4 **100**
Cleverly integrates products for body and home. We all have to brush our teeth and do the dishes, and this store has gizmos to ritualise daily grinds.

Vrolijk
Paleisstraat 135 (623 5142/www. vrolijk.nu). Tram 1, 2, 5, 13, 14, 17. **Open** 11am-6pm Mon; 10am-6pm Tue-Fri; 10am-5pm Sat; 1-5pm Sun. **Map** p54 C4 **101**
The best selection of rose-tinted international reading – whether fiction or fact – you'll find in all of Amsterdam, in addition to a wide variety of CDs, DVDs and guides. It has a second-hand section upstairs, and also offers a range of novelty T-shirts, condoms and gifts that are always a big hit with tourists.

Vroom & Dreesmann
Kalverstraat 203 (0900 235 8363 premium rate/ www.vroomend reesmann.nl). Tram 4, 9, 14, 16, 24, 25. **Open** 11am-6.30pm Mon; 10am-6.30pm Tue, Wed, Fri; 10am-9pm Thur; 10am-6.30pm Sat; noon-6pm Sun. **Map** p55 D5 **102**
V&D means good quality products at prices that are just a small step up from those at the more ubiquitous HEMA. They stock a staggering array of toiletries, cosmetics, leather goods and watches, clothing and underwear for all the family, kitchen items, suitcases, CDs and videos. The bakery, Le Marché, sells delicious bread, quiches, shakes and sandwiches, while self-service restaurant La Place is a terrific option for a delicious and healthy lunch.

Waterstone's

Kalverstraat 152 (638 3821/www
.waterstones.com). Tram 1, 2, 4, 5, 9,
14, 16, 24, 25. **Open** 9.30am-6pm
Mon-Wed; 9.30am-9pm Thur; 9.30am-
6.30pm Fri, Sat; 11am-6pm Sun. **Map**
p55 D5 ⓵⓪③

A mighty temple to literature in an
area that's already bursting with bookshops. Thousands of books, magazines and videos, all of them in
English, are on sale in this reputable
store, and the children's section is
especially delightful.

Zara

Kalverstraat 72 (530 4050/www.zara.
com). Tram 1, 2, 4, 5, 9, 14, 16, 24,
25. **Open** 10am-6.30pm Mon-Wed, Fri-
Sun; 10am-9pm Thur. **Map** p54 C4 ⓵⓪④

Imagine that you have a lean, mean
fashion machine that can almost
instantaneously churn out approxima-
tions of the latest catwalk creations at
a fraction of the price. Now imagine
how much money you'd make. Oops!
Too late, Zara beat you to it.

Nightlife

Bitterzoet

Spuistraat 2 (521 3001/www.
bitterzoet.com). Tram 1, 2, 5. **Open**
8pm-3am Mon-Thur, Sun; 8pm-4am Fri,
Sat. No credit cards. **Map** p54 C2 ⓵⓪⑤

This busy, comfy and casual bar doubles as a venue for theatre and music.
Bands and DJs embrace jazz, world
and urban sounds, as demonstrated
by once-a-monther Crime Jazz: word-
sa and poetry and for hipper literates.

Meander

Voetboogstraat 3 (625 8430/www.
cafemeander.nl). Tram 1, 2, 4, 5, 9,
16, 24, 25. **Open** 10pm-3am Mon,
Thur; 10pm-4am Fri, Sat. No credit
cards. **Map** p55 D5 ⓵⓪⑥

Of course, the cheap beer helps this
small club bring in the student crowd;
but there's also the relaxed vibe, a
densely packed dancefloor and broad
and popular programming of DJs,
jazz, singer/songwriter and world
music nights.

Winston International p67

Arts & leisure

Arti et Amicitiae

Rokin 112 (623 3508/www.arti.nl).
Tram 4, 9, 14, 16, 24, 25. **Open**
1-6pm Tue-Sun. No credit cards.
Map p55 D5 ⓵⓪⑦

This marvellous old building houses
a private artists' society, whose initi-
ates regularly gather in the first-floor
bar. Members of the public can climb
a Berlage-designed staircase to a large
exhibition space, home to some great
temporary shows.

Engelse Kerk

Begijnhof 48 (624 9665/www.
ercadam.nl). Tram 1, 2, 4, 5, 9,
11, 14, 16, 24, 25. No credit cards.
Map p54 C5 ⓵⓪⑧

Nestled tightly within the idyllic
courtyard of Begijnhof, the English
Reformed Church has been hosting
weekly concerts of baroque and classical music here since the early 1970s.
Combined with a particular emphasis
on the use of authentic period instruments, the church's acoustics are genuinely haunting. Its healthy evening
schedule also raises funds to help
secure the building's future.

Stadsschouwburg p98

The Canals

Singel was the medieval city moat; other canals – Herengracht, Keizersgracht and Prinsengracht – that follow its line outward were part of a Golden Age renewal scheme for the rich. The connecting canals and streets, originally for workers and artisans, have the most cafés and shops, while smaller canals worth seeking out include Leliegracht, Bloemgracht, Egelantiersgracht, Spiegelgracht and Brouwersgracht.

For ease of use, we've split venues on the canals into two: the Western Canal Belt (between Singel and Prinsengracht, south of Brouwersgracht, north and west of Leidsegracht); and the Southern Canal Belt (between Singel and Prinsengracht, running from Leidsegracht south-eastward towards the Amstel).

Western Canal Belt

Cross Singel at Wijde Heisteeg, and opposite you on Herengracht is the **Bijbels Museum** (Bible Museum). A stroll south, and the Netherlands Institute of War Documentation (Herengracht 380, 523 3800, www.niod.nl) is home to Anne Frank's diary, donated by her father Otto. Head north and you'll reach an architectural gem now housing the **Theater Instituut**. For a look inside a 17th-century interior, try the **Tassenmuseum** (Herengracht 573). Hopping over to Keizersgracht, there is the equally epic home of the photography foundation, **Huis Marseille**.

Prinsengracht is easily the most charming of the canals. Pompous façades have been mellowed with shady trees, cosy cafés and some

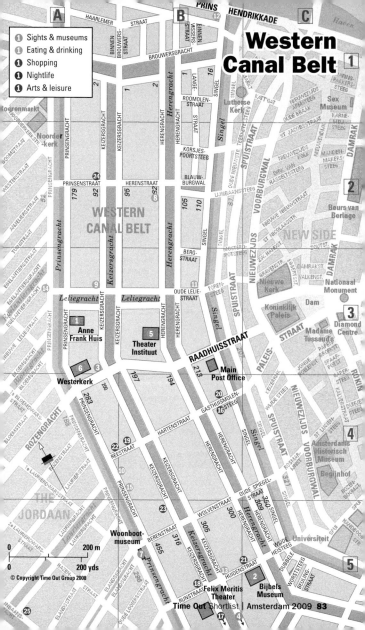

Western Canal Belt

Legend:
- ❶ Sights & museums
- ❶ Eating & drinking
- ❶ Shopping
- ❶ Nightlife
- ❶ Arts & leisure

© Copyright Time Out Group 2008

of Amsterdam's more funkadelic houseboats. There's also some good shopping to be had; further north, the smart 'Nine Streets' linking Prinsengracht, Keizersgracht and Herengracht all offer a diverse pick of speciality shops for browsing.

On your way up Prinsengracht, the tall spire of the 375-year-old **Westerkerk** should rear into view. Its tower is the tallest structure in this part of town, and if you choose to climb it you'll be able to look down upon the **Anne Frank Huis**. Meanwhile, fans of René Descartes – and if you think, you therefore probably are – can pay tribute at his house around the corner at Westermarkt 6.

Sights & museums

Anne Frank Huis

Prinsengracht 267 (556 7105/www. annefrank.nl). Tram 13, 14, 17. **Open** *Jan-Mar, Sept-Dec* 9am-7pm daily. *Apr-June* 9am-9pm Mon-Fri, Sun; 9am-10pm Sat. *July, Aug* 9am-10pm daily. **Admission** €7.50; €3.50 10-17s; free under-10s. **Map** p83 A3 ❶

It was in this 17th-century canalside house that the young Jewish diarist Anne Frank and her family hid for two years during World War II, sustained by friends who risked everything to help them. On 4 August 1944, the occupants were arrested and transported to concentration camps, where Anne died with sister Margot and their mother. Her father, Otto, survived, and decided that Anne's diary should be published. The rest, as they say, is history: tens of millions of copies have since been printed in 55 languages, and Anne's story has been written into legend. Recently, the large chestnut tree on the property, which Anne described in her diary, has been infected with several deadly fungi, and may not be standing much longer. But when it goes, it will be replaced with a sapling grafted from the original tree.

Bijbels Museum

Herengracht 366-368 (624 2436/www. bijbelsmuseum.nl). Tram 1, 2, 5. **Open** 10am-5pm Mon-Sat; 11am-5pm Sun, public holidays. **Admission** €7.50; €3.75 13-17s; free under-13s, MK. No credit cards. **Map** p83 C5 ❷

Housed in two handsome Vingboons canal houses, Amsterdam's own Bible Museum aims to illustrate life and worship in biblical times with archaeological finds from Egypt and the Middle East (including the remarkable mummy of an Israeli woman), models of ancient temples and a slideshow. There's also a splendid collection of Bibles from several centuries (including a rhyming Bible from 1271). A little dry in places, the museum attracts folk merely looking to admire the restored houses, splendid Jacob de Wit paintings and the sprawling gardens.

Homomonument

Westermarkt (www.homomonument.nl). Tram 13, 14, 17. **Map** p83 A3 ❸

Unveiled 20 years ago, Karin Daan's three-sectioned pink triangular monument to the memory of persecuted gays and lesbians was a world first. Flowers are often left on it for personal remembrance, especially during gatherings such as World AIDS Day. More info on gay and lesbian life is available from COC Amsterdam (p174).

Huis Marseille

Keizersgracht 401 (531 8989/www. huismarseille.nl). Tram 1, 2, 5. **Open** 11am-6pm Tue-Sun. **Admission** €5; €3 seniors, students; free under-17s, MK. No credit cards. **Map** p83 B5 ❹

Located in a monumental 17th-century house, the walls of this photography foundation host the latest from hotshot snappers like David Goldblatt, Valerie Belin and Jacqueline Hassink.

Theater Instituut

Herengracht 168 (551 3300/www. theaterinstituut.nl). Tram 1, 2, 5, 13, 17. **Open** 11am-5pm Mon-Fri; 1-5pm Sat, Sun. **Admission** €4.50; €2.25 students, 6-16s, over-65s; free under-6s, MK. **Map** p83 B3 ❺

Cafe Brandon p88

The ever-changing displays at the Theater Instituut are largely drawn from the institute's collection of costumes, props, posters, memorabilia and ephemera, much of which is digitally catalogued. Upstairs there is a massive library; call ahead for information on hours and prices. At the end of 2008, the museum will close permanently, and the library will reopen on Sarphatistraat 47 at a later date.

Westerkerk

Prinsengracht 277-279 (624 7766/ tower 689 2565/www.westerkerk. nl). Tram 13, 14, 17. **Open** *Tower* Apr-Oct 10am-5.30pm Mon-Sat. **Admission** *Tower* €6. No credit cards. **Map** p83 A3 ⑥

The 186-stair Westerkerk tower is a good place from which to view the surrounding city, provided that is you don't suffer from vertigo: the 85m (278ft) tower sways by 3cm (1.2in) in a good wind. It's thought that Rembrandt is buried in the church itself, though no one is sure where: Rembrandt died a pauper, and as a result of this he is commemorated inside the building with a simple plaque. Though his burial on 8 October 1669 was recorded in the church

register, the actual spot was not, but there's a pretty good chance that he shares a grave here with his son Titus who redeceased him. If queues for the tower are long, try the also excellent and expansive views at Zuidertoren or the Ouderkerkstoren, both handled by the same office (689 2565).

Woonbootmuseum

Prinsengracht, opposite no.296 (427 0750/www.houseboatmuseum. nl). Tram 13, 14, 17. **Open** *Jan, Feb, Nov, Dec* 11am-5pm Fri-Sun. *Mar-Oct* 11am-5pm Tue-Sun. Closed last 3wks Jan. **Admission** €3.25; €2.50 children under 152cm (5ft). No credit cards. **Map** p83 B5 ⑦

The Houseboat Museum is not just a museum about houseboats: it's actually on one. Aside from a few explanatory panels, the *Hendrika Maria* is laid out exactly as a houseboat would be to help visitors imagine what it's like to live on the water. It's more spacious than you might expect and does a good job of selling the lifestyle afforded by its unique comforts. Until, that is, you notice the pungent scent of urine emanating from the public toilet or 'curlie' (as they are called): it's located right by the boat itself.

Canal pride

Amsterdam Pride may be one of the lesbian and gay community's most anticipated events, but the extended weekend of crowded street parties, parades, vibrant drinking and noise draws thousands of spectators – straight and gay alike – all eager to join in.

The festival offers thousands of distractions running the A to Z of camp: androgyny, barely clad boys, flirtation, leather, lesbians, Muscle Marys, PVC poseurs, and, of course, theatrics. It's a genuinely non-stop playground.

Then there's the dizzying array of affiliated events: street parties, more street parties, singalongs, performances, and Pride's apex, the awesome Saturday afternoon Canal Parade – the world's only floating Pride, which winds along the Prinsengracht and Amstel canal between 2pm and 6pm.

The canals spill over with topless mermaids, half-naked fire fighters, Marilyn Monroe look-alikes, pole dancers, Spartans, beauty queens, angels and wrestlers all waving from a hundred different boats. The Canal Parade draws thousands of onlookers – estimates put them at 350,000, and no one's clocking who's gay and who ain't.

As time goes on, everyone puts in overtime cultivating the following day's hangover – although they've probably drunk their way through the first one, as the partying technically starts on Friday. Or Thursday, depending on who you ask. Either way, the closing party takes place during late Sunday afternoon on Rembrandtplein, with a huge number of Dutch artists, DJs and those with enough energy left to sign off the celebration.

Like Queen's Day, when the city's population doubles and crams into the centre for the event, Pride is terribly Amsterdam. It's relaxed, tolerant, positive, outrageous and definitely worth celebrating.

't Arendsnest

Herengracht 90 (421 2057/www.
arendsnest.nl). Tram 1, 2, 5, 13,
14, 17. **Open** 4pm-midnight Mon-
Thur, Sun; 4pm-2am Fri, Sat. **Bar**.
Map p83 B2 ❻

A temple to the humble hop, the
'Eagle's Nest', in a lovely old canal
house, sells mainly Dutch beer. Many
of the customers are real ale types, but
even amateurs will have a ball sampling the wares: 23 drafts and over 120
bottled, from house ale Herengracht 10
to the aptly named Texelse
Skuumkoppe. Also available are 100+
Dutch jenevers and liquors and several Dutch whiskies.

Brandon

W Keizersgracht 157 (no phone). Tram
1, 2, 5, 13, 14, 17. **Open** 11am-1am
Mon-Thur, Sun; 11am-3am Fri, Sat.
No credit cards. **Bar**. **Map** p83 A3 ❾

When the previous owners hung up
their pinnies in the 1980s after 40 years
behind the bar, they sealed up their
café, retired upstairs and eventually
passed away. Twenty years later, the
new owners reopened this ghost bar
just as they found it: furniture, photos,
billiard room and all. A decidedly old-
fashioned ambience lingers, enhanced
by tasteful jazz music tinkling for
added effect in the background.

Envy

W Prinsengracht 381 (344 6407/
www.envy.nl). Tram 13, 14, 17. **Open**
6pm-1am Mon-Thur; noon-3pm, 6pm-
3am Fri, Sat; noon-3pm, 6pm-1am Sun.
€€€. **Global**. **Map** p83 A4 ❿

A poshed-up designer deli and restaurant serving an arsenal of delicacies
both from the streamlined cool cabinets
that line the walls and from the fancy
kitchen up front. Perfect for when you
want to try a little of everything.

Grey Area

Oude Leliestraat 2 (420 4301/www.
greyarea.nl). Tram 1, 2, 5, 13, 14, 17,
20. **Open** noon-8pm daily. No credit
cards. **Coffeeshop**. **Map** p83 B3 ⓫

Run by two blokes living the modern
American dream: get the f*@k out of
America. They did so by opening this
stellar coffeeshop, which offers some of
the best weed and hash on the planet
(try the Bubble Gum or Grey Mist
Crystals). Also on offer are large glass
bongs, a vaporiser and free refills of
organic coffee. The owners are highly
affable and often more baked than the
patrons: sometimes they stay in bed
and miss the noon opening time.

Kobalt

Singel 2a (320 1559/www.cafekobalt.
nl). Tram 1, 2, 5, 9, 13, 17, 24, 25.
Open 8am-1am Mon-Thur, Sun; 8am-
3am Fri, Sat. **Bar**. **Map** p83 B1 ⓬

This rather sophisticated bar near
Centraal Station is a great way of beating train delay blues. There's free Wi-
Fi, round-the-clock food from breakfast
to tapas to dinner, and any drink you
could name, from ristretto to champagne. DJs spin Friday nights, while
Sunday afternoons are dedicated to
slinky live jazz shows.

De Pels

Huidenstraat 25 (622 9037). Tram 1,
2, 5. **Open** 10am-1am Mon-Thur, Sun;
10am-3am Fri, Sat. No credit cards.
Bar. **Map** p83 B5 ⓭

The Nine Streets are littered with char-
acterful bars, and this one is a lovely
old-style, tobacco-stained example
with an intellectual bent. In fact, De
Pels can rightly claim a prime spot in
Amsterdam's literary and political
legacy: writers, journalists and social
activists regularly meet at this erstwhile Provo hangout to chew the fat,
although it's a nice spot to chill even if
you aren't feeling in a cerebral mood.

Twee Zwaantjes

Prinsengracht 114 (625 2729/www.
detweezwaantjes.nl). Tram 1, 2, 5, 13,
14, 17. **Open** 3pm-1am Mon-Thur,
Sun; 3pm-3am Fri, Sat. No credit cards.
Bar. **Map** p83 A3 ⓮

Oom-pah-pah, oom-pah-pah – that's
how it goes at this salt-of-the-earth bar
when the locals are out in force and the
air is filled with song. It's relatively

De Bazel's cosmic build

The spanking new City Archives in the **De Bazel building** on Vijzelstraat (www.gemeentearchief.amsterdam.nl), located between Keizersgracht and Herengracht, has a history shrouded in esoteric mists. Completed in 1926, it was originally the HQ for global trade association Nederlandsche Handel-Maatschappij.

It looks a muscular, highly logical monument to modernism, yet its architect, KPC De Bazel, was a strict follower of the religion-cum-philosophy-cum-science Theosophy, invented by chain-smoking Russian Madame Blavatsky. Followers were guided by the writings of millennia-old Tibetan masters and made to study Eastern literature, natural laws and the straight line.

After the architect embraced the new religion, he set up a bureau to put mysticism into practice, and this building is its greatest work. The pink and yellow façade represents masculinity and femininity; the grid is the *kundalini* or 'serpent power' most prevalent within Egyptian and Indian symbolism, and representing the 'total environment' or cosmic whole.

It's all at its most gloriously evident in the Schatkamer where every surface is decorated with a spiralling square pattern. It was painstakingly restored from original photographs, and is open to the public for exhibitions and guided tours.

quiet during the week, but weekends are real singalong, swingalong affairs, with revellers booming out tear-jerking tunes on such subjects as love, sweat and the Westerkerk.

Vyne

Prinsengracht 411 (344 6408/www. vyne.nl). Tram 1, 2, 5, 7, 10, 13, 14, 17. **Open** 6pm-midnight Mon-Thur; 5pm-1am Fri, Sat. **Bar. Map** p83 B4 ⑮
A tasteful – in every sense of the word – addition to the city's drinking scene. The gorgeous slimline interior is dominated by an amazing wall of wine and emphasis is on pairing drink with food, such as Weissburgunder with sausage, or smoked eel and Sancerre.

Shopping

Brilmuseum/Brillenwinkel

Gasthuismolensteeg 7 (421 2414/www. brilmuseumamsterdam.nl). Tram 1, 2, 5. **Open** 11.30am-5.30pm Wed-Fri; 11.30am-5pm Sat. No credit cards. **Map** p83 B4 ⑯
Officially, this 'shop' is an opticians' museum, but don't let that put you off. The fascinating exhibits are of glasses throughout the ages, and if you like what you see then most of the pairs on display are also for sale.

Frozen Fountain

Prinsengracht 645 (622 9375/www. frozenfountain.nl). Tram 1, 2, 5. **Open** 1-6pm Mon; 10am-6pm Tue-Fri; 10am-5pm Sat. **Map** p83 B5 ⑰
The 'Froz' is a paradise for lovers of contemporary furniture and design. It stays abreast of innovative Dutch designers like Piet Hein Eek, the maestro of furniture made from recycled wood; it also sells stuff by the non-Dutch likes of Marc Newsom, plus modern classics and photography.

De Kaaskamer

Runstraat 7 (623 3483). Tram 1, 2, 5. **Open** noon-6pm Mon; 9am-6pm Tue-Fri; 9am-5pm Sat; noon-5pm Sun. No credit cards. **Map** p83 B5 ⑱
De Kaaskamer offers over 200 varieties of domestic and imported cheeses, plus

AMSTERDAM BY AREA

Pâtisserie Pompadour

pâtés, olives, pastas and wines. Have fun quizzing shop staff on the different cheese varieties and random related trivia: they seriously know their stuff.

Kramer/Pontifex

Reestraat 18-20 (626 5274/www. pontifex.fiberworld.nl). Tram 13, 14, 17. **Open** 10am-6pm Mon-Fri; 10am-6pm Sat. **Map** p83 B4 ⑲
Broken Barbies and battered bears are restored to health by Mr Kramer, a doctor for old-fashioned dolls and teddies who has been here for 25 years. In the same shop, Pontifex is a candle seller.

Nic Nic

Gasthuismolensteeg 5 (622 8523/www. nicnicdesign.com). Tram 1, 2, 5, 13, 17. **Open** noon-6pm Mon-Fri; 11am-5pm Sat. **Map** p83 B4 ⑳
We consider this the best shop of its kind in Amsterdam, selling 1950s and '60s furniture, lamps, ashtrays and kitchenware, mostly in mint condition.

Pâtisserie Pompadour

Huidenstraat 12 (623 9554/www. patisseriepompadour.com). Tram 1, 2, 5, 7. **Open** 10am-6pm Mon-Fri; 9am-5pm Sat. **Map** p83 B5 ㉑

This fabulous bonbonnerie and tea-room – with a delightful 18th-century interior imported all the way from Antwerp – is likely to bring out the sweet-toothed little old lady in diners of all ages. Designer chocolates, pastries and cakes are all on hand for more discerning indulgers.

Ree-member

Reestraat 26 (no phone). Tram 1, 2, 5. **Open** 1-6pm Mon; 11am-6pm Tue-Sat; 1-6pm Sun. **Map** p83 A3/B3 ㉒
Ree-member stocks a terrific collection of vintage clothes and 1960s standards. The shoes are the best in town and boast prices to match, but if you're strapped for cash, then you'll be pleased to learn that the owners also sell less-than-perfect numbers over on Noordermarkt by the kilo.

Wella Warenhuis

NEW *Keizersgracht 300, (623 3766/ www.wellawarenhaus.nl). Tram 13, 14.* **Open** 1-6.30pm Mon-Wed, Fri-Sun; 1-8pm Thur. **Map** p83 B5 ㉓
A vast canalside office became this warehouse full of playful products from young Dutch designers, who take turns to man the cash register.

Arts & leisure

Galerie Binnen

NEW *Keizersgracht 82 (625 9603/www. galeriebinnen.nl). Tram 1, 2, 5, 13, 17.* **Open** noon-6pm Wed-Sat; or by appt. No credit cards. **Map** p83 A2 **24**

These industrial and interior design specialists have plenty of room in which to display work by lesser-known talents (Sottsass, Kukkapuro, Studio Atika) and unusual collections of things like toilet brushes, Benno Primsela vases or wacky linoleum.

Nightlife

Maloe Melo

Lijnbaansgracht 163 (420 4592/www. maloemelo.com). Tram 7, 10, 13, 14, 17. 9pm-3am Mon-Thur, Sun; 9pm-4am Fri, Sat. **Map** p83 A5 **25**

Well, I woke up this morning, feeling Maloe Melowed. Yes, you guessed it, this small, pleasantly pokey little juke joint is Amsterdam's native house of the blues. Quality rockabilly and roots acts play here on a regular basis, so shed your gloom and enjoy the boogie.

Southern Canal Belt

The Southern Canal Belt boasts two main squares: Rembrandtplein and Leidseplein. Rembrandtplein is unashamedly tacky and home to tasteless establishments from traditional striptease parlours to seedy modern peepshow joints and nondescript cafés. There are a few exceptions to the prevailing tawdriness – places like the grand café De Kroon (no.17), the art deco Schiller (no.26) and HL de Jong's eclectic masterpiece, the Pathé Tuschinski on Reguliersbreestraat. Also nearby is the floating flower market at the southern tip of Singel (the Bloemenmarkt). From the square, walk street along shopping and eating street Utrechtsestraat, or explore the scenic Reguliersgracht

and Amstelveld. Whichever you choose, you'll cross Herengracht as you wander.

As the first canal to be dug in the glory days, Herengracht attracted the richest of merchants and remains home to the most overblown houses on any of Amsterdam's canals. But it's on the stretch built between Leidsestraat and Vijzelstraat, known as the **Golden Bend**, that things really get out of hand. Around the corner on Vijzelstraat is the highly imposing **Gebouw de Bazel building**, since 2007 the new home of the city archives (see box p89). Nearby on Keizersgracht is the photography museum **Foam**.

Leidseplein, reached via the always chaotic pedestrian- and tram-packed Leidsestraat or the gallery-heavy strip of Nieuwe Spiegelstraat, is the tourist centre of Amsterdam. It's packed with merrymakers drinking at pavement cafés and is visually dominated by the **Stadsschouwburg** and many cinemas, theatres and restaurants. Max Euweplein offers a route to the greener pastures of Vondelpark.

Sights & museums

Foam (Photography Museum Amsterdam)

Keizersgracht 609 (551 6500/www. foam.nl). Tram 16, 24, 25. **Open** 10am-6pm Mon-Wed, Sat, Sun; 10am-9pm Thur, Fri. **Admission** €7; €5 students, seniors; free under-12s, MK. **Map** p93 C2 **26**

This excellent photography museum, located in a renovated canal house, holds exhibitions of works by shutter-button maestros like August Sander, Weegee and Richard Avedon. Shows cover everything from young talent to big names, and rough street photography to polished super-glamorous portraits of Kate Moss.

Huis Marselle p85

Museum Willet-Holthuysen

Herengracht 605 (523 1870/www. museumwilletholthuysen.nl). Tram 4, 9, 14. **Open** 10am-5pm Mon-Fri; 11am-5pm Sat, Sun. **Admission** €5; €3.75 seniors; €2.50 6s-18s; free under-6s, MK. **Map** p93 D1 ㉗

Upon the death in 1889 of Abraham Willet-Holthuysen, remembered as 'the Oscar Wilde of Amsterdam', his wife Sandrina Louisa, a hermaphrodite, left this 17th-century house and its contents to the city on the condition that it was preserved and opened as a museum. The family had followed the fashion of the time and decorated it in neo-Louis XVI style: it's densely furnished, with the over-embellishment extending to the collection of rare objets d'art, glassware, silver, china and paintings – including one of a rather shocked-looking Abraham (taken on his honeymoon perhaps?).

Tassenmuseum Hendrikje

NEW *Herengracht 573 (524 6452/ www.tassenmuseum.nl).* **Open** 10am-5pm daily (except 1 Jan, 30 Apr, 25 Dec). **Admission** €6.50; €5 groups of 10 or more, students, seniors; € 2.50 13-18s; free under-13s. **Map** p90 D1 ㉘

Bag habits are hard to break – so how about a bag break? This museum of bags and purses is the Western world's largest collection of its kind at a bag-gaga total of 3,500 items: anything from coin purses made of human hair to a Lieber rhinestone collectible named 'Socks' for Hillary Clinton's cat.

Eating & drinking

ARC

Reguliersdwarsstraat 44 (689 7070/ www.bararc.com). Tram 1, 2, 4, 5, 9, 16, 24, 25. **Open** 4pm-1am Mon-Thur, Sun; 4pm-3am Fri, Sat. **Bar**. **Map** p93 C1 ㉙

Still looking sleek and space age, gay bar ARC is well and truly established these days and continues to attract a stylish, moneyed, polysexual crowd. The cocktails and finger food are tasty, but service can be rather slow.

Bojo

Lange Leidsedwarsstraat 51 (622 7434/www.bojo.nl). Tram 1, 2, 5. **Open** 4.30pm-3am daily. €€. **Indonesian**. **Map** p93 B2 ㉚

Bojo is a fine Indo-eaterie, and one of very few places that stays open into the small hours. The price is right and the portions are large enough to glue your

insides together before or after an evening of excess. Its sister operation at no.49 compensates for its earlier closing time by serving alcohol.

Ctaste

NEW *Amsteldijk 55 (06-22335366/ www.ctaste.nl). Metro Weesperplein* **Open** 5.30-11pm Wed-Sun. €€€. **International. Map** p93 E2 ③①
The interior is dark – very dark. After being welcomed with a snack and a drink and asked to choose between meat, fish or vegetarian, you'll be led into pitch darkness by a blind person who will guide you through the meal. Keep claustrophobia at bay, and you'll learn how strongly taste is linked to vision; only on the way out can you ask what you've actually had.

Eat at Jo's

Marnixstraat 409 (638 3336). Tram 1, 2, 5, 6, 7, 10. **Open** noon-9pm Wed-Sun. €€. No credit cards. **Global. Map** p93 B2 ③②
Each day brings a new menu to this cheap and eminently cheerful international kitchen, where fish, meat and vegetarian dishes are all lovingly prepared. Star spotters take note: whichever act is booked to play at the Melkweg may well eat here beforehand.

Gala

Reguliersdwarsstraat 38 (623 6303/ www.restaurantgala.com). Tram 16, 24, 25. **Open** 6-10pm Tue-Fri; 6pm-midnight Sat, Sun. €€. **Catalan. Map** p93 C1 ③③
A peaceful and already popular new tapas hotspot that is in direct contrast to the more bustling Mexican noise fest Rose's Cantina, to which it is attached. Food at Gala is affordable and well prepared.

Hap Hmm

1e Helmerstraat 33 (618 1884/www. hap-hmm.nl). Tram 1, 6, 7, 10. **Open** 4.30-8pm Mon-Fri. €. No credit cards. **Dutch. Map** p93 A3 ③④
Hungry but hard up? You need some of the Dutch grandma cooking served in this canteen with a living-room feel,
which packs famished punters with meat and potatoes for around €6.

Kamer 401

Marnixstraat 401 (620 0614/www. kamer401.nl). Tram 1, 2, 5, 6, 7. **Open** 6pm-1am Wed, Thur; 6pm-3am Fri, Sat. No credit cards. **Bar. Map** p93 A2 ③⑤
Art students and the terminally hip gather at this red-lacquered temple to pleasure, where there is no food or frippery, just booze, DJ-spun music and a party vibe. Nearby establishment Lux (Marnixstraat 403, 422 1412) offers a similar formula.

Onder de Ooievaar

Utrechtsestraat 119 (624 6836/www. onderdeooievaar.nl). Tram 4. **Open** 10am-1am Mon-Thur; 10am-3am Fri, Sat; 10.30am-1am Sun. **Bar. Map** p93 D2 ③⑥
Here you have a highly uncomplicated venue for an evening's carousing among a mixed bunch of trendies, locals and the odd visitor. Highlights include 't IJ beer on tap, the downstairs pool table and the rather lovely Prinsengracht-side terrace.

La Rive

InterContinental, Prof Tulpplein 1 (520 3264/www.restaurantlarive.com). Tram 6, 7, 10/Metro Weesperplein. **Open** noon-2pm, 6.30-10.30pm Tue-Fri; 6.30-10.30pm Sat. Closed 1st 2 wks of Aug. €€€€. **French. Map** p93 E2 ③⑦
While Hôtel de l'Europe has Excelsior, it's La Rive at the InterContinental that overshadows the rest of the high-end competition, and it does so by serving chef Edwin Kats's superb French cuisine without excessive formality. Perfect when money is no object.

De Rokerij

Lange Leidsedwarsstraat 41 (622 9442 /www.rokerij.net). Tram 1, 2, 5, 6, 7, 10. **Open** 10am-1am daily. No credit cards. **Coffeeshop. Map** p93 B2 ③⑧
A marvellous discovery on an otherwise hideous touristy street by Leidseplein, De Rokerij is a real Aladdin's cave: lit by wall-mounted candles and beautiful metal lanterns,

De Kaaskamer p89

it's decorated with colourful Indian art and a variety of seating (ranging from mats thrown on to the floor to more formal decorative 'thrones').

Tempo Doeloe

Utrechtsestraat 75 (625 6718/www. tempodoeloerestaurant.nl). Tram 4, 6, 7, 10. **Open** 6-11.30pm daily. **€€€€**. **Indonesian**. **Map** p93 D2 ❸

This cosy and really rather classy Indonesian restaurant is widely thought of as one of the city's best and spiciest purveyors of rice table – and not without reason. Ring ahead, as reservations are required.

Van Dobben

Korte Reguliersdwarsstraat 5-9 (624 4200/www.vandobben.com). Tram 4, 9, 16, 24, 25. **Open** 9.30am-1am Mon-Thur; 9.30am-2am Fri, Sat; 11.30am-8pm Sun. **€**. No credit cards. **Dutch**. **Map** p93 C1 ❹

A kroket is the national version of a croquette: a mélange of meat and potato with a crusty, deep-fried skin best served on a bun with lots of hot mustard – and this 1945-vintage late-nighter is the uncontested champion.

Shopping

Bloemenmarkt (Flower Market)

Singel, between Muntplein & Koningsplein (no phone). Tram 1, 2, 4, 5, 9, 14, 16, 24, 25. **Open** 9am-6pm Mon-Sat; 11am-5.30pm Sun. No credit cards. **Map** p93 B1/C1 ❹

This fascinating collage of colour is the world's only floating flower market, with 15 florists and garden shops (although many also hawk rather cheesy souvenirs these days), all permanently ensconced on barges along the southern side of Singel. A good investment as the plants and flowers usually last well.

Concerto

Utrechtsestraat 52-60 (623 5228/ www.concerto.nu). Tram 4. **Open** 10am-6pm Mon-Wed, Fri, Sat; 10am-9pm Thur; noon-6pm Sun. **Map** p93 D2 ❹

Head here for classic Bach recordings, obscure Beatles items or that beloved old Diana Ross album that got nicked from your party. There are also second-hand 45s and new releases at very reasonable prices.

AMSTERDAM BY AREA

Lambiek

*Kerkstraat 132 (626 7543/www.
lambiek.nl). Tram 1, 2, 5.* **Open**
11am-6pm Mon-Fri; 11am-5pm Sat;
1-5pm Sun. **Map** p93 B2 **43**

Lambiek, founded in 1968, claims to be
the world's oldest comic shop and has
thousands of books from around the
world; its on-site cartoonists' gallery
hosts exhibitions every two months.

Shoe Baloo

*Koningsplein 7 (626 7993/www.
shoebaloo.nl). Tram 2, 3, 5, 12.*
Open noon-6pm Mon; 10am-6pm Tue,
Wed, Fri, Sat; 10am-9pm Thur; 1-6pm
Sun. **Map** p93 B1 **44**

A space age men's and women's shoe
shop with a glowing Barbarella-pod
interior. Über cool, but well worth taking the time to cruise for Miu Miu,
Costume Nationale and Patrick Cox.

Nightlife

Club Roque

NEW *Amstel 178 (421 0900/www.club
roque.nl). Tram 4, 9.* **Open** 9pm-4am
Wed, Thur; 9pm-5am Fri, Sat; 6pm-
midnight Sun. **Map** p93 D1 **45**

Until recently, this place was home to
YOUII, a smallish but hopping lesbian
club; now it's been poshed up, and seeks
to attract an open, mixed and relaxed
crowd. Reasonably priced cocktails, old-
school house and the latest dance tracks
do the rest.

Jimmy Woo's

*Korte Leidsedwarsstraat 18 (626 3150/
www.jimmywoo.com). Tram 1, 2, 5, 6,
7, 10.* **Open** 11pm-3am Thur, Sun;
11pm-4am Fri, Sat. **Map** p93 B2 **46**

Amsterdam has never seen anything
quite so luxuriously cosmopolitan as
club Jimmy Woo's. Now you too can
marvel at the lounge area filled with a
mixture of modern and antique furniture, and then confirm for yourself the
merits of its bootylicious light design
and sound system. If you have problems getting inside thanks to crowds,
cool off across the street at its sister
bar, the swanky Suzy Wong (Korte
Leidsedwarsstraat 45, 626 6769).

Melkweg

*Lijnbaansgracht 234A (531 8181/
www.melkweg.nl). Tram 1, 2, 5, 6,
7, 10.* **Open** 8.30pm-4am daily.
Membership €3/mth; €15/yr.
No credit cards. **Map** p93 A2 **47**

A former dairy (the name translates as
'Milky Way'), Melkweg has become
world renowned as an always innovative home to live music of all styles.
The complex also hosts a theatre, cinema, art gallery and café, and holds
weekend club nights to boot, so it's no
surprise it's a key cultural beacon in
the centre of the city. Membership is
compulsory for anyone wanting in.

Nachttheater Sugar Factory

*Lijnbaansgracht 238 (626 5006/www.
sugarfactory.nl). Tram 1, 2, 5, 7,
10.* **Open** 9pm-4am Thur, Sun;
9pm-5am Fri, Sat. No credit cards.
Map p93 A2/B2 **48**

This 'night theatre' club has found its
niche as a place where performance
meets clubbing, catering to both beat
freaks and more traditional music fans
at the same time. Weekly Vreemd
('Weird') sees various eclectic DJ acts;
WickedJazzSounds livens up Sunday
evenings; and the cutting-edge bash
Electronation brings top acts from the
worlds of 1980s synthesiser electro and
current day minimal techno.

Paradiso

*Weteringschans 6-8 (626 4521/www.
paradiso.nl). Tram 1, 2, 5, 6, 7, 10.*
Open varies. **Membership** €3/mth;
€18/yr. No credit cards. **Map** p93 B3 **49**

A cornerstone of the live music and
clubbing scene and a name synonymous with quality shows across the
city, this former church is in such
demand that it often hosts several
events in one day. The main hall has a
rare sense of grandeur, with multiple
balconies and stained-glass windows
peering down upon performers and
DJs. The smaller hall upstairs is a fantastic place to catch new talent.
Membership is compulsory. Concerts
by bigger-named stars such as Justin
Timberlake sell out weeks in advance.

The master of masters

Geert Jansen Gallery

It wouldn't be an implausible claim to say that Geert Jan Jansen, born in 1944, is the Netherlands' most prolific artist of all time. At the height of his career, a typical day would go like this: 'Before breakfast, a couple of Chagall drawings; during the morning, a couple of hefty Appels; and during the afternoon, a couple of Picassos. Only then would I feel satisfied.'

Jansen worked skilfully in a vast variety of media, from oils to etchings, and forged thousands of works by Beuys, Cocteau, Gauguin, Hockney, Kandinsky, Klimt, Magritte, Matisse, Miró and Warhol. Experts attested to their authenticity; even Appel verified several of Jansen's copies as his own, and it's said that Andy himself once gleefully watched Jansen signing a Warhol. This was real talent at work.

But in 1994, his chateau residence in Orléans was raided after a tip-off from a Munich gallery owner, who noticed a spelling mistake in the authentication certificate of a recently purchased Chagall. Jansen was arrested, and his collection of 1,600 paintings was impounded. Dubbed the 'Forger of the Century' by French and German police, he spent the next six months in jail, making a Picasso for the warden and writing his pithy memoirs, *Magenta: Adventures of a Master Forger*.

Today, as a free man, he's now the art dealers' neighbour: he has opened a gallery in Spiegelstraat, the city's high-end art and antiques street. The dropout from Amsterdam art history school shows little regret – 'At least I wasn't selling carcinogenic French fries' – but he has mellowed. He has repositioned himself as a 'master of masters', and now puts his own name to 'his' works.

Galerie Geert Jan Jansen

Nieuwe Spiegelstraat 61 (0343 552023/www.geertjanjansen.nl). **Open** 11am-6pm Tue-Sun.

Studio 80

*Rembrandtplein 17 (521 8333/www.
studio-80.nl). Tram 4, 9, 14.* **Open**
10pm-4am Wed-Thur, Sun; 11pm-5am
Fri, Sat. **Map** p93 C1 ⑩
In the midst of Rembrandt Square's
neon glitz and ice-cream eating crowds
lurks this former radio studio, a black
pearl waiting to be discovered. Dirty
disco, deep electronic acid and gritty
hip hop are shown off at very reasonable prices. The city's progressive techno and minimal crowds find their home
here and bring their record bag- and
synthesiser-wielding friends from
across Europe.

Arts & leisure

De Appel

*Nieuwe Spiegelstraat 10 (625 5651/
www.deappel.nl). Tram 16, 24, 25.* No
credit cards. **Map** p93 C2 ㉑
An Amsterdam institution that
showed its mettle by being one of the
first galleries in the country to embrace
video art. It still has a nose for all
things contemporary, and has the
courage to give international and
rookie guest curators real freedom to
follow their muse.

De Balie

*Kleine Gartmanplantsoen 10 (553
5151/www.debalie.nl). Tram 1, 2, 5, 6,
7, 10.* No credit cards. **Map** p93 B3 ㉒
Theatre, new media, photography, cinema and literary events sit alongside
lectures, debates and discussions about
social and political issues at this influential centre for the local intelligentsia.
Throw in a café and you've got healthy
food for both mind and body.

Boom Chicago

*Leidseplein Theater, Leidseplein 12
(423 0101/www.boomchicago.nl). Tram
1, 2, 5, 6, 7, 10.* **Map** p93 B2 ㉓
This American improv troupe is one of
Amsterdam's biggest success stories.
With several different shows running
seven nights a week (except Sundays
in winter), all in English, the group
offers a mix of audience-prompted
improvisation and sketches.

Koninklijk Theater Carré

*Amstel 115-125 (0900 252 5255
premium rate/www.theatercarre.nl).
Metro Weesperplein.* **Map** p93 E1 ㉔
It's the dream of many to perform in
this glamorous space, formerly home
to a circus and recently refurbished in
very grand style. The Carré hosts some
of the best Dutch cabaret artists and
touring operas, as well as the odd big
music name. If mainstream musical
theatre is more your thing, this is the
place to come to see and hear Dutch
versions of popular blockbusters like
Grease and *Cats*.

Mediamatic

*Vijzelstraat 66-80 (638 9901/www.
mediamatic.net).* **Open** varies. No
credit cards. **Map** p90 C2 ㉕
This bleeding-edge organisation is
dedicated to the outer reaches of technology and multimedia. It made the
move to its new location at the time of
going to press.

Pathé Tuschinski

*Reguliersbreestraat 26-34 (0900
1458/www.pathe.nl). Tram 4, 9, 16,
24, 25.* **Map** p93 C1 ㉖
This extraordinary exuberant cinema
is named after Abraham Tuschinski,
the city's most illustrious cinematic
entrepreneur, who built it in 1921
as a 'world theatre palace'. The
Tuschinski's interior and exterior are
a striking and appelling clash of roco-
co, art deco and Jugendstil.

Stadsschouwburg

*Leidseplein 26 (624 2311/www.
ssba.nl). Tram 1, 2, 5, 6, 7, 10.*
Map p93 B3 ㉗
The Stadsschouwburg (or Municipal
Theatre) is a seriously impressive 19th-
century building. Constructed in a traditional horseshoe shape, it seats 950 and
is known primarily for its progressive
theatre and opera productions – occasional contemporary music performances are also held. It's currently being
renovated, and will eventually link up
with the Melkweg.
Event highlights 'Angels in America'
(6-22 Feb 2009).

Café de Sluyswacht p104

Jodenbuurt, the Plantage & the Oost

Located south-east of the Red Light District, Amsterdam's Jewish neighbourhood is a mix of old and new architectural styles. Enter the skull-adorned gateway between Sint Antoniesbreestraat 130 and 132 to find the Zuiderkerk (South Church), scaling the tower of which allows more energetic tourists to survey the whole scene.

Crossing the bridge at the end of Sint Antoniesbreestraat leads you to the **Rembrandthuis**. Immediately before this, however, are steps to the **Waterlooplein** flea market, dominated by the Stadhuis-Muziektheater (the City Hall-Music Theatre). Also close at hand are the **Joods Historisch Museum** (Jewish Historical Museum) and **Hermitage aan de Amstel**.

The largely residential Plantage area lies south-east of Mr Visserplein and is reached via Muiderstraat. The attractive Plantage Middenlaan winds past the **Hortus Botanicus**, passes near the **Verzetsmuseum** (Museum of Dutch Resistance), and along the edge of zoo Artis towards the Tropenmuseum.

Jews began to settle here over 200 years ago, and the area was soon redeveloped on 19th-century diamond money. The Plantage is still wealthy, with graceful buildings and tree-lined streets, although its charm has sadly somewhat faded. The area has seen extensive redevelopment, which can be witnessed along Entrepotdok, where post-hippie houseboats and views of Artis provide a charming contrast to the apartment buildings.

Further south of Mauritskade is Amsterdam Oost (East), where the Arena hotel complex is located on the edge of Oosterpark. Disaster tourists, take note: near the corner of Oosterpark and Linneaustraat is the spot where film-maker Theo van Gogh was brutally murdered by an Islamic extremist in 2004 after making a film deemed to be offensive to Muslims. A sculpture in Oosterpark, *The Scream*, was unveiled in 2007 in his memory.

Sights & museums

Ajax Museum
ArenA Boulevard 29, Amsterdam Zuidoost (311 1336/www.amsterdam arena.nl). Metro Strandvliet or Metro/ NS rail Bijlmer. **Open** 9.30am-4.30pm Mon-Sat. **Admission** *museum* €3.50; including tour from €9.

Great for football fans of all ages, this museum covers the rich history of the club, offering photographs, memorabilia, trophies and videos documenting their greatest players and triumphs.

Artis
Plantage Kerklaan 38-40 (523 3400/www.artis.nl). Tram 9, 10, 14. **Open** *Summer* 9am-6pm Mon-Sat; 9am-sunset Sun. *Winter* 9am-5pm daily. **Admission** €17.70; €16.50 seniors; €14.50 3-9s; free under-3s. No credit cards. **Map** p101 C2 ❷

The first zoo in mainland Europe (and the third oldest in the world) provides a great day out for children and adults. Along with the usual animals, Artis has an indoor 'rainforest' for

nocturnal creatures and a 120-year-old aquarium that includes a simulated Amsterdam canal (the main difference is that the clear water improves your chances of spotting the eels). Yet further extras include savannah land, a geological museum, a zoological museum and, for kids, a petting zoo and playgrounds. A new butterfly greenhouse has also recently opened to set hearts of all ages aflutter.

Hermitage aan de Amstel
Gebouw Neerlandia, Nieuwe Herengracht 14 (530 8755/www. hermitage.nl). Tram 4, 9/Metro Waterlooplein. **Open** 10am-5pm daily. **Admission** €7; €5.60 seniors; free under-16s, MK. No credit cards. **Map** p101 A3 ❸

Partly opened in 2004 and due for completion in spring 2009, this 19th-century building is an outpost of the State Hermitage Museum in St Petersburg, the riches of which owe much to the collecting obsession of Peter the Great (1672-1725). Peter himself first came to Amsterdam to learn shipbuilding and how to build a city on a bog – the latter knowledge was applied to his pet project, St Petersburg – and while here he also bought the entire anatomical collection of Dr Frederik Ruysch, perhaps the greatest ever anatomist and preserver of body bits and bobs. With luck, some of Peter's own souvenirs – including Rembrandts – will return for a visit, but so far the collection is focused on Greek jewellery, the last Tsar and Tsarina, Nicolas and Alexandra, Persian treasures and a variety of modern art from the late 19th and early 20th centuries.

Hollandse Schouwburg
Plantage Middenlaan 24 (531 0340/www.hollandscheschouwburg.nl). Tram 9, 14. **Open** 11am-4pm daily. **Admission** free. **Map** p101 C2 ❹

In 1942, this grand theatre became a main point of assembly for between 60,000 and 80,000 of the city's Jews before they were taken to the transit camp at Westerbork. It's now a monu-

Jodenbuurt, the Plantage & the Oost

Legend:
- Sights & museums
- Eating & drinking
- Shopping
- Nightlife
- Arts & leisure

300 m
300 yds

Oosterpark

Tropenmuseum

ARTIS

Aquarium

Planetarium

THE PLANTAGE

Wertheim-park

Hortus Botanicus

Portuguese Synagogue

Joods Historisch Museum

Mozes en Aäronkerk

Rembrandthuis

Stadhuis

Muziektheater

JODENBUURT

THE OLD CENTRE

IJ-TUNNEL

Nederlands Scheepvaart Museum

Oosterdok

ment with a small but very impressive exhibition and a memorial hall displaying 6,700 surnames by way of tribute to the 104,000 Dutch Jews who were exterminated. The façade has been left intact, with most of the inner structure removed to make way for a memorial.

Hortus Botanicus

Plantage Middenlaan 2A (625 9021/ www.dehortus.nl). Tram 9, 14/Metro Waterlooplein. **Open** *Jan, Dec* 9am-4pm Mon-Fri; 10am-4pm Sat, Sun. *Feb-June, Sept-Nov* 9am-5pm Mon-Fri; 10am-5pm Sat, Sun. *Jul, Aug* 9am-7pm Mon-Fri; 10am-7pm Sat, Sun. **Admission** €7; €3.50 5-14s; free under-5s. No credit cards. **Map** p101 B3 ⑤

The Hortus has been here since 1682, although it was originally set up more than 50 years earlier when East India Company ships brought back tropical plants and seeds intended to supply doctors with medicinal herbs. Some of those same specimens (including the oldest potted plant in the world, a 300-year-old cycad) are still on display in the stunning palm greenhouse – which itself dates from 1912 – while three other greenhouses maintain desert, tropical and subtropical climates.

Joods Historisch Museum (Jewish Historical Museum)

Nieuwe Amstelstraat 1 (531 0310/ www.jhm.nl). Tram 9, 14/Metro Waterlooplein. **Open** 11am-5pm Mon-Wed, Fri-Sun; 11am-9pm Thur. Closed Jewish New Year & Yom Kippur. **Admission** €7.50; €4.50 students, seniors, €3 13-17s; free under-13s, MK. **Map** p101 B3 ⑥

Housed since 1987 in four erstwhile synagogues in the old Jewish quarter, the Jewish Historical Museum is full of religious items, photographs and paintings detailing the rich history of Jews and Judaism in the Netherlands. A recent revamping has created more warmth and a sense of the personal in its permanent displays, which concentrate on religious practice and Dutch Jewish culture. Among the exhibits is the painted autobiography of Jewish artist Charlotte Salomon, tragically killed at Auschwitz aged 26, which only shows once a year.

Portuguese Synagogue

Mr Visserplein 3 (624 5351/guided tours 531 0380/www.esnoga.com). Tram 9, 14/Metro Waterlooplein. **Open** *Jan-Mar, Nov, Dec* 10am-4pm Mon-Thur, Sun; 10am-2pm Fri.

Artis p100

Apr-Oct 10am-4pm Mon-Fri, Sun. Closed Yom Kippur. **Admission** €6.50; €5 students, seniors; €4 10-17s; free under-10s. No credit cards. **Map** p101 B3 **7**

Architect Elias Bouwman's mammoth synagogue, one of the largest in the world and reputedly inspired by the Temple of Solomon, was inaugurated in 1675. It's built on wooden piles and is surrounded by smaller annexes (offices, archives, the rabbinate and one of the world's oldest libraries). Renovation in the late 1950s restored the synagogue well and the low-key tours are very interesting.

Rembrandthuis

Jodenbreestraat 4 (520 0400 /www.rembrandthuis.nl). Tram 9, 14/Metro Waterlooplein. **Open** 10am-5pm daily. **Admission** €8 (incl. audio guide); €5.50 students; €1.50 6-16s; free under-6s, MK. **Map** p101 A2/3 **8**

You can't help but admire the skill and effort with which craftsmen have tried to recreate this house, bought by Rembrandt in 1639 for ƒ13,000 (around €6,000), a massive sum at the time, and occupied by the artist until bankruptcy forced him to move out in 1656. The presentation is, however, dry and unengaging on the whole. Nagging at you all the time is the knowledge that this isn't really Rembrandt's house, but rather a mock-up of it – which lends an unreal air that is only relieved when guest artists are allowed to use the studio. There's a remarkable collection of Rembrandt's etchings, which show him at his most experimental, but if it's his paintings you're after then make for the Rijksmuseum (p125).

Tropenmuseum

Linnaeusstraat 2 (568 8200/ www.tropenmuseum.nl). Tram 3, 7, 9, 10, 14/bus 22. **Open** 10am-5pm daily. **Admission** €7.50; €6 students, seniors; €4 6s-17s; free under-6s, MK. **Map** p101 E2 **9**

Visitors to this handsome building get a vivid glimpse of daily life in the tropical and subtropical parts of the world (a strange evolution for a museum originally erected in the 1920s to glorify Dutch colonialism), including Southeast Asia, Oceania, West Asia, North Africa, Latin America and a series called Man and Environment. Exhibits – from religious items and jewellery to washing powder and vehicles – are divided by region.

Verzetsmuseum (Museum of Dutch Resistance)

Plantage Kerklaan 61 (620 2535/ www.verzetsmuseum.org). Tram 9, 14/Metro Waterlooplein. **Open** 11am-5pm Mon, Sat, Sun; 10am-5pm Tue-Fri. **Admission** €6.50; €3.50 7-15s; free under-7s, MK. No credit cards. **Map** p101 C2 **10**

The Verzetsmuseum tells the moving story of the Dutch Resistance through a wealth of artefacts: false ID papers, clandestine printing presses and illegal newspapers, spy gadgets and an authentic secret door behind which Jews hid. The exhibits all help to explain the ways people in the Netherlands faced up to and dealt with the Nazi occupation, its disparate exhibits linked by personal testimonies from those who lived through the war. Regular temporary shows explore wartime themes and modern-day forms of oppression, and there's a small research room too.

Eating & drinking

Amstelhaven

Mauritskade 1 (665 2672/www. amstelhaven.nl). Tram 3/Metro Weesperplein. **Open** *Summer* 4pm-1am Mon-Thur, Sun; 4pm-3am Fri, Sat. *Winter* 4pm-1am Thur, Sun; 4pm-3am Fri, Sat. **Bar. Map** p101 D3 **11**

Occupying a prime spot on an arterial canal of the Amstel, this bar's cavernous insides are filled with yuppies chowing down on posh Dutch food and grooving to weekend DJs. But that's not the point. Amstelhaven's raison d'être is summer days spent sprawled on the vast deck's sofas and beanbags, watching boats bob as staff serve the resident salty dogs in situ.

Brouwerij 't IJ

Funenkade 7 (320 1786/www. brouwerijhetij.nl). Tram 6, 10. **Open** 3-8pm daily. **Bar**. **Map** p101 E1 ⑫

The famous tasting house at the base of the Gooyer windmill, where wares from award-winning local brewery 't IJ can be sampled. Inside is bare (still retaining the look of the municipal baths it once was) and seating minimal, so if water permits, plonk down on the pavement outside. Its standard range of tipples is always available for sampling behind the bar, from pale Plzen to the darker, head-poppingly strong brew known as Columbus.

Café de Sluyswacht

Jodenbreestraat 1 (625 7611/http:// sluyswacht.nl). Tram 9, 14/Metro Nieuwmarkt. **Open** 11.30am-1am Mon-Thur; 11.30am-3am Fri, Sat; 11.30am-7pm Sun. **Bar**. **Map** p101 A2 ⑬

Listing crazily, this wooden-framed bar has been pleasing drinkers for decades, though the building itself has been around since 1695, when it began life as a lock-keeper's cottage. Inside it's snuggly and warm, while outside has great views of Oude Schans.

Dauphine

Prins Bernardplein 175 (462 1646/ www.caferestaurantdauphine.nl). Tram 12/bus 15. **Open** 10am-1am Mon-Thur, Sat, Sun; 10am-2am Fri. **€€€€**. **French**. **Map** p101 E2 ⑭

This newcomer is located in a former Renault showroom and oozes old-school modernism in terms of both design and dining. Indulge in a menu packed with French bistro classics – from seriously swanky burgers to lobster – for breakfast, lunch or dinner.

Hesp

Weesperzijde 130-131(665 1202/www. cafehesp.nl). Tram 12. **Open** 10am-1am Mon-Thur; 10am-2am Fri, Sat; 11am-1am Sun. **Café**. **Map** p101 D3 ⑮

Hesp has occupied a lovely site on the river near Amstel station for 110 years, offering the joys of an old-fashioned boozer but moving with the times. The wine list is longer than most bars', snacks classy and classic, and entertainment ranges from big bands to Latin to lindyhop. In summer, the huge waterside terrace is lit by life-sized electric palm trees.

De Hogesluis

Sarphatistraat 23 (624 1521/www. hogesluis.nl). Tram 3, 7, 10/Metro Weesperplein. **Open** 11am-1am Mon-Sat; noon-midnight Sun. **Bar**. **Map** p101 C3 ⑯

From the Taittinger poster and the glowing fittings to the midnight-blue leather seats, this place oozes understated class, though it's not in the least bit snooty and welcomes visitors of all ages and inclinations. Half of the large space overlooking the river is given over to a (pricey) restaurant, but it's best used as the perfect spot for a sly sundowner in the summer months.

De Kas

Kamerlingh Onneslaan 3 (462 4562/ www.restaurantdekas.nl). Tram 9/ bus 59, 69. **Open** noon-2pm, 6.30-10pm Mon-Fri; 6.30-10pm Sat. **€€€€**. **Global**.

In Frankendael Park, way out east, is a renovated 1926 greenhouse. It's now a posh and peaceful restaurant that inspires much fevered talk among local foodies. Its international menu changes on a daily basis, and relies on fresh ingredients.

Shopping

Dappermarkt

Dapperstraat (no phone/www. dappermarkt.nl). Tram 3, 7, 9, 10, 14. **Open** 9am-5pm Mon-Sat. No credit cards. **Map** p101 E2 ⑱

Dappermarkt is a locals' market, which means that prices don't rise to match the number of visitors in attendance. It sells all the usual market fodder, plus plenty of cheap clothes.

Waterlooplein

Waterlooplein. Tram 9, 14, 20/Metro Waterlooplein. **Open** 9am-5.30pm Mon-Fri; 8.30am-5.30pm Sat. No credit cards. **Map** p101 A3 ⑲

Brouwerij 't IJ p104

Exit signs

Death Museum

Amsterdam might just have a new hangover cure. First, you score raw herring from a street fishmonger. Then chase it down with a trip to Amsterdam's Death Museum, or Nederlands Uitvaart Museum Tot Zover (Dutch Funerary Museum So Far). Opened in 2007 in Nieuw Oosterbegraafplaats cemetery in Watergraafsmeer, the museum even has a trendy café, complete with black-clad mourners.

'So Far' goes beyond objects and into text. Its arty displays are split into four themes. 'Rituals' is filled with coffins and notes from recently deceased; for instance, Merijn explains how to behave around his body. 'Make yourself at home. Make some coffee. Check the fridge. Don't touch my quiff, or it will be hard to get its shape back for the funeral.'

In the 'Body' section, visitors are introduced to the cremulator, a machine of literally bone-crushing power. Although corpses are cremated at 1200°C, that's not quite hot enough, and that's where the cremulator comes in, ensuring the urn doesn't rattle.

You can let that image settle while admiring a collection of spectacle frames made out of the titanium harvested from the machine.

'Mourning and Remembering' introduces the visitors to the more gentle world of hair paintings. The hair of the dearly departed has always been a popular keepsake, and in this sub-category of portraiture, the face of the deceased has his or her real hair draped around it.

The exhibition closes with a collection of objects linked to the theme of 'Memento mori', recalling the 16th- and 17th-century vanitas paintings that showed skulls, bones and hourglasses to remind the viewer of the inescapable fate. It concludes with a computer terminal with two words endlessly scrolling: Game Over.

Perhaps it's time for another stiff drink.

Nederlands Uitvaart Museum Tot Zover

Kruislaan 124 (694 0482/www. totzover.nl). **Open** 11am-5pm Tue-Sun. **Admission** €5.50.

Amsterdam's top bazaar is basically a huge flea market with the added attraction of loads of brand new clothes stalls (though gear can be a bit pricey and, at many stalls, a bit naff). Bargains can be found, but they may be hidden under cheap 'n' nasty toasters and down-at-heel (literally) shoes.

Nightlife

Club 3VOOR12

Studio Desmet, Plantage Middenlaan 4A (035 671 2222/www.3voor12.nl). Tram 9, 14. **Open** Airs between 10pm-1am Thur. **Admission** free. **Map** p101 B2 ⑳
This old film theatre bursts into life on Thursday nights to coincide with a live national radio and TV show. Each broadcast throws up a diverse lineup – one week it's three little-known local acts, the next it's international superstars in town for their sold-out gig. Entry is free, but there's limited capacity, so you must reserve a place at http://3voor12.vpro.nl/gastenlijst. The catch is not necessarily knowing who you're signing up for, which – needless to say – can work both for or against you.

Hotel Arena

's Gravesandestraat 51 (850 2420/ www.hotelarena.nl). Tram 3, 6, 9, 10, 14. **Open** 10pm-4am Fri-Sun. No credit cards. **Map** p101 D3 ㉑
Once an orphanage, then a youth hostel, now finding its feet as a trendy hotel, bar and restaurant. Big city folk already used to trekking long distances will no doubt laugh in the face of its (relative lack of) accessibility, but Amsterdammers tend to forego the small detour eastwards, making it hard for the Arena to truly kick clubbing butt. That said, monthlies like Salsa Lounge, with its funky Latin bias, provide notable exceptions.

Arts & leisure

Ajax

Amsterdam ArenA, Arena Boulevard 29, Amsterdam Zuidoost (311 1444/ www.ajax.nl). Metro Strandvliet/Arena or Bijlmer. **Map** p101 D3 ㉒
The country's most famous football club is renowned worldwide for flair on the field and its excellent youth training programme. Battles with main rivals Feyenoord and PSV are fought fiercely each season in the gladiatorial

Dauphine p104

Brewing up a storm

The art of brewing runs through Amsterdam's history like alcohol itself through the bloodstream, keeping the city's nightlife pumping and vital from as far back as the early 1300s, when hops were first brought to the country from abroad.

As the centuries passed and the population swelled, the city water became undrinkable. The only way to revitalise the supply again was to convert it into ale – hence the 17th and 18th centuries' Brouwersgracht ('brewer's canal'). Next up was **Heineken** (p135), invented locally in 1884 and brewed in the city until the 1980s, after which its departure reduced the number of local brewers to a handful. The best known of these is **'t IJ** (p104); free brewery tours take place every Friday at 4pm, and the in-house brews include Zatte, Struis and Columbus.

The **Bekeerde Suster** (p57) is lined with shimmering copper vats and once again allows real aficionados to take tours, while amateurs can sample the house *witbier* and blonde. Elsewhere, brewery-with-a-conscience **De Prael** (www.deprael.nl) is run by mentally disabled staff and produces beers named after various local singers.

All the local breweries also brew versions of seasonal bock beers, which have a kick like the deer they're named after. Try them at the **Bock Bier Festival**, held at the Beurs van Berlage during the last weekend of October.

ArenA – and sometimes out of it. Pre-season in July, some of the world's biggest teams are invited to come and take part in the hugely popular Amsterdam Tournament.

ARCAM

Prins Hendrikkade 600 (620 4878/ www.arcam.nl). Tram 9, 14/Metro Waterlooplein/bus 42, 43. **Open** 1-5pm Tue-Sat. **Admission** free. No credit cards. **Map** p101 B1 ㉓
The gallery here at the Architecture Centrum Amsterdam is obsessed with the promotion of Dutch contemporary architecture – from the early 20th-century creations of the world-famous Amsterdam School to more modern designs – and as a result organises a forums, lectures, its own series of architecture books and exhibitions in its fresh new 'silver snail' location.

Studio K

NEW *Timorplein 62 (692 0422/ticket office 06-1702 7407/restaurant 06-1702 7821/www.studio-k.nu). Tram 3, 7, 10, 14.* **Open** 11am-1am Mon-Thur, Sun; 11am-3am Fri, Sat. **Map** p101 E1 ㉔
Opened in late 2007, this former school turned cultural centre is, like mother ship Kriterion, entirely run by students. The place has a distinctive festival feeling as it puts on film, theatre, debates, exhibitions, comedy, club nights and food and drink. A new star in a revitalising Amsterdam East.

Tropentheater

Kleine Zaal Linnaeusstraat 2; Grote Zaal Mauritskade 63 (568 8500/ www.tropentheater.nl). Tram 3, 7, 9, 10, 14/bus 22. **Map** p101 E3 ㉕
The Tropentheater, next door to the Tropenmuseum, organises performances in music, dance, theatre and film that are related to various non-Western cultures. The programme is very varied: from classical Indian dance to salsa concerts and from Turkish films to African music. Tropentheater prides itself in offering shows that are at once engaging and culturally very enlightening.

The Waterfront & North

Amsterdam's historic wealth owes a lot to the waterfront: it was here that goods were unloaded, weighed and prepared for storage in the warehouses still found locally. At the time, the harbour and its arterial canals formed a whole with the city itself. A drop in commerce slowly unbalanced this unity and the building of Centraal Station in the late 19th century served as a final psychological cleavage. This neo-Gothic monument to modernity blocked both the city's view of the harbour and its own past.

Today, the area is about moving forward (see itinerary p44). One recent cultural success story was the massive reinvention of Post CS (Oosterdokskade 5), the former post office building just east of Centraal Station (CS). While the surrounding area is being made into a home for the city's music conservatory, the country's largest library and a whole mess of shops and hip hotels, Post CS has been tasked with serving as temporary home until mid 2008 for the Stedelijk Museum of Modern Art, **Mediamatic**, trendy club-restaurant 11 and other creative enterprises.

Directly south of Post CS, the Schreierstoren or 'Weeping Tower' is by far the most interesting relic of Amsterdam's medieval city wall. Built in 1487, it was from this point, on 4 April 1609, that Henry Hudson departed in search of shorter trade

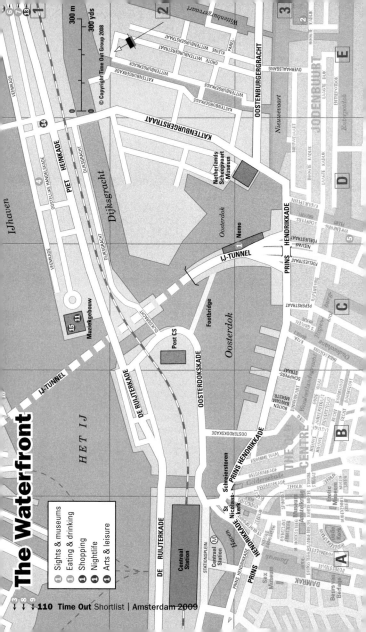

The Waterfront

- ● Sights & museums
- ● Eating & drinking
- ● Shopping
- ● Nightlife
- ● Arts & leisure

IJhaven

HET IJ

I J - T U N N E L

VEEMKADE

OOSTELIJKE HANDELSKADE

PIET HEINKADE

DIJKSGRACHT

Dijksgracht

VEEMKADE

DIJKSGRACHT

Muziekgebouw

DE RUIJTERKADE

Post CS

OOSTERDOKSKADE

Footbridge

Oosterdok

Oosterdok

Netherlands Scheepvaart Museum

Nemo

IJ-TUNNEL

PRINS HENDRIKKADE

PRINS HENDRIKKADE

OOSTENBURGERGRACHT

KATTENBURGERSTRAAT

KATTENBURGERKADE

KATTENBURGERGRACHT

WITTENBURGERKADE

GROTE WITTENBURGERSTRAAT

KLEINE WITTENBURGERSTRAAT

PARIL

Wittenburgervaart

Nieuwevaart

OOSTENBURGERVAART

JODENBUURT

OVERHAALSGANG

LAAGTE KADIJK

ENTREPOTDOK

HOOGTE KADIJK

KADIJKSPLEIN

Entrepotdok

DE RUIJTERKADE

DE RUIJTERKADE

Centraal Station

STATIONSPLEIN Ⓜ
Centraal Station

St Nicolaas-kerk

Schreierstoren

PRINS HENDRIKKADE

PRINS HENDRIKKADE

Hoven

VROME VLAAN

GELDERSEKADE

GELDERSEKADE

GELDERSEKADE

ZEEDIJK

Erotic Museum

Oude Kerk

Beurs van Berlage

SEX Museum

DAMRAK

Damrak

THE CENTRE

© Copyright Time Out Group 2008

300 m

300 yds

Boats and beaches

From artificial beaches to
revamped ferries and revitalised
shipyards, the far-flung areas of
the Waterfront offer some great
alternative opportunities for
eating, drinking and partying.

Blijburg

*Bert Haanstrakade 2004 (416
0330/www.blijburg.nl). Tram
26/bus 326.* **Open** *Summer*
noon-10pm daily. *Winter* 2-10pm
Thur-Sat; 10am-10pm Sun.
€€€. No credit cards. **Global**.
Being 25 kilometres (15 miles)
from the sea, Amsterdam was
hardly anyone's choice for a beach
holiday until sand was tipped on
to the artificial islands of IJburg,
where 45,000 people will
eventually live. Restaurant/bar
Blijburg – which has a regular
programme of barbecues, bands
and DJs – is on hand to cater
to your eating/drinking whims.

Hotel De Goudfazant

*Aambeeldstraat 10H (636
5170/www.hoteldegoudfazant.nl).
Ferry from Centraal Station.* **Open**
6pm-1am Tue-Sun. **€€€. Global**.
Deep in the north and yet deeper
within a former warehouse, this
is the post-industrial dining
experience at its atmospheric
best. Excellent, affordable food:
fine French cuisine and seafood.

Ot en Sien

*Buiksloterweg 27 (636 8233/
www.otensien.nl). Ferry from
Centraal Station.* **Open** noon-1am
Mon-Thur, Sun; noon-3am Fri, Sat.
No credit cards. **Bar**.
Just a ferry hop from Centraal
Station, this little bar feels like
it's in the heart of the countryside.
No pretensions, just friendly service

Pont 13

and a fantastic range of Dutch and
Belgian beers, including a mighty
La Trappe Quadrupel.

Pont 13

*W Stravangerweg 891 (770
2722/www.pont13.nl). Bus 22.*
Open 6-10pm daily. **€€€. Global**.
This renovated old ferry in the western havens – in a neighbourhood
of students living in revamped shipping containers – is all-round
intriguing. Simple, hearty fare
prepared with genuine flair.

NDSM

*TT Neveritaweg 15 (330
5480/www.ndsm.nl). Ferry from
Centraal Station/bus 35, 38, 94.*
NDSM was a shipbuilding yard at
the beginning of the last century.
Today, it's a cultural complex
more or less completed, satisfying
the constantly mutating needs
of Amsterdam's vibrant artistic
community. Small-scale workshops
and performances are held almost
daily in the studios here.

The rejuvenation of the Noord

There was a time when Amsterdam North was right off the map. Even in centuries past, the land on the other side of that big, watery body called the IJ was known as little more than the spot where the remains of freshly executed criminals were hung for public display. There was little of interest to pull short-term visitors northwards – except perhaps cycling routes towards such scenic fishing villages as Volendam and Marken, or the trip on the free ferry from the back of Centraal Station. But with the building of the Noord-Zuidlijn metro link that will unite this once isolated area with the rest of Amsterdam, and the accompanying redevelopment plans, things are set to change.

Already the cultural 'breeding ground' of **Kinetic Noord**, located in the former shipping yard NDSM (p111), is by far the largest in the country, with artists' studios, a skate hall and a slew of singular spaces. It sports a wonderful post-apocalyptic vibe that's ideal for parties, concerts and wacky theatre festivals like **Over het IJ** (p37) and **Robodock** (p33). It's got a surrounding district of student container dwellings, a 'clean energy' exhibition, a great restaurant and café (www.noorderlichtcafe.nl), and boasts regular visits from the alternative party boat **Stubnitz** (www.stubnitz.com), an inspired floating zone that books bands, DJs and artists.

And now this new ground zero for Dutch subculture is also home to the Benelux headquarters of MTV networks, which moved into a wildly revamped former woodwork factory in 2007. It's the hope of the powers-that-be to reinvigorate Amsterdam as a 'creative capital'. They also hope that much inspiration and money will be made by all – but as far as that goes, only time will tell.

routes to the Far East, and in failing discovered New Amsterdam, which later became known as Manhattan. Another eye-opener along the way is the Renzo Piano-designed **Nemo**, a science museum whose green building dominates the horizon. It dwarfs the silver shell-shaped ARCAM architecture gallery and the nautically inclined and grand Nederlands Scheepvaartmuseum, currently closed until 2009.

Sights & museums

science center NEMO

Oosterdok 2 (531 3233/www.e-nemo.nl). Bus 22, 42, 43. **Open** 10am-5pm Tue-Sun (daily Dutch school holidays). **Admission** €11.50; €6.50 students; free under-3s. **Map** p110 D3 ❶
Nemo opened in 1997 and has gone from strength to strength as a kid-friendly science museum. It eschews exhibits in favour of hands-on trickery, gadgetry and tomfoolery (in English and Dutch): you can play DNA detective games, blow mega soap bubbles or explode things in a 'wonderlab'. On top of that, Renzo Piano's mammoth structure (resembling the reflection of the tunnel below) never fails to raise a gasp from people setting eyes on it for the first time. The outdoor café, DEK5, at the top is a lovely place to while away an afternoon reading and relaxing.
Event highlights 'Wake up: Children's Lecture' (16 Nov 2008, 14 Dec 2008).

Werfmuseum 't Kromhout

Hoogte Kadijk 147 (627 6777/www.machinekamer.nl/museum). Bus 22, 26. **Open** 10am-3pm Tue. **Admission** €4.50; €2.75 under-15s. **Map** p110 E3 ❷
A nostalgic museum, full of old, silent ship engines and the proper tools for their construction. The shipyard is proud of the fact that it's the oldest remaining original yard still in use, but its 18th-century heritage is no longer

very apparent, nor is the yard itself especially active nowadays.

Eating & drinking

Bickers aan de Werf

Bickerswerf 2 (320 2951/www.bickersaandewerf.nl). Tram 3/bus 18, 22. **Open** noon-1am Wed-Fri; 1pm-1am Sat, Sun. **Bar**. **Map** p110 A1 ❸
The western islands feel like some secluded retreat from the city's bustle, and this modern glass cube is great for a break after aimless exploring. Food ranges from a slice of sponge cake to caviar; coffee becomes an indulgence with a side order of truffles from Jordino. The drinks menu is also outstanding: Japanese iKi beer alongside plenty of specialist whiskies and wines.

Fifteen

Pakhuis Amsterdam, Jollemanhof 9 (0900 343 8336 premium rate/www.fifteen.nl). Tram 25, 26. **Open** noon-3pm, 6pm-1am Mon-Sat; late lunch from 3pm Sun. **€€€€**. **Global**. No credit cards. **Map** p110 D1 ❹
While Jamie Oliver has only found one gap in his hectic schedule to visit the Amsterdam outpost of his food-based empire, this culinary franchise of sorts – complete with a TV show that documented the transformation of challenged street kids into a well-oiled kitchen brigade – is inspired by his love for dishes honest and fresh, offering a pre-set four-course tasting menu, which changes weekly (although it's quite cheeky having a premium rate number as the only telephone contact).

Kilimanjaro

Rapenburgerplein 6 (622 3485). Bus 22, 43. **Open** 5-10pm Tue-Sun. **€€€**. **African**. **Map** p110 D3 ❺
This relaxed and friendly pan-African eating place offers a reliable assortment of traditional recipes from as far afield as Senegal, the Ivory Coast, Tanzania and Ethiopia. Once you've eaten your way from the east all the way through to the west coast of Africa, you'll probably need some swift refreshment in the cooling form of

either fruity cocktails or the seriously potent regional beers.

Koffiehuis KHL

Oostelijke Handelskade 44 (779 1575/ www.khl.nl). Tram 10, 26. **Open** 11am-10pm Tue-Fri; noon-10pm Sat, Sun. No credit cards. **Bar**. **Map** p110 E1 ⑥

This beautiful, light-flooded interior harks back to the days in the early 20th century when it was a canteen serving staff of the Royal Holland Lloyd shipping line. Now it's a café-cum-meeting space serving the local community, with plenty to attract new visitors. There is art on the walls and regular live music for lifting spirits.

Odessa

Veemkade 259 (419 3010/www. de-odessa.nl). Tram 10, 26/bus 26. **Open** 6pm-1am Mon-Fri; 6pm-3am Sat, Sun. **€€€**. **Global**. **Map** p110 E1 ⑦

More dedicated trendsters regularly make the trek to the unlikely environs of an old Ukrainian fishing boat for Odessa's fusion food and tastefully revamped interior – the vibe is 1970s James Bond filtered through a modern lounge sensibility. On warmer nights, dine on the lit deck. DJs raise the tempo by spinning party tunes from 10pm on weekend evenings.

Onassis

Westerdoksdijk 40 (330 0456/www. onassisamsterdam.nl). Tram 3. **Open** 10am-midnight Mon-Thur; 10am-2am Fri, Sat. **Bar**. **Map** p110 A1 ⑧

Sleek lines, burnished mahogany, banquettes and voluptuous lounge decks: all of this luxury creates the mood of a yacht fit for a Greek shipping magnate. You'll also need the wealth of one to properly enjoy this place, with lunchtime sandwiches averaging €13. The bar (it also serves as a restaurant and club) is known for oyster slurping with mixed cocktails, plus in summer a team of in-house masseurs are on hand to ease away all your executive stresses.

Open!

NEW *Westerdoksplein 20 (620 1010/ www.open.nl). Bus 18, 21, 22, 48.* **Open** 10am-1am Mon-Thur, Sun; 10am-3am Fri, Sat. **Map** p110 A1 ⑨

Set in a box of steel and glass atop an unused railway bridge, this is one of the more attractive new restaurants in town. Its open kitchen pumps out simple classics for lunch and dinner, all at reasonable prices: try the steak tartare or steak béarnaise. For further regeneration, take a walk along the adjoining residential housing project that will lead to Prinseneiland.

Wilhelmina-Dok

Noordwal 1 (632 3701/www. wilhelmina-dok.nl). Ferry from Centraal Station. **Open** 11am-midnight daily. **€€€**. **Mediterranean**.

Through the large windows of this cubic building you get some terrific views of the eastern docklands. Come to devour soup and sandwiches by day and a daily menu of Mediterranean dishes by night.

Nightlife

Bimhuis

Piet Heinkade 3 (788 2188/www. bimhuis.nl). Tram 25, 26. **Open** *Phone reservations* noon-7pm Mon-Fri. *Box office* 7-11pm show nights; most shows start 9pm. **Map** p110 C1 ⑪

The name Bimhuis is familiar to jazz fans the world over, and musicians queue up for a chance to grace its stage. Even its transplant to a bizarre glass box jutting oddly out of the Muziekgebouw complex (p116) hasn't tarnished its reputation. Instead, the eye-catching building and familiar interior layout have provided the Bimhuis with a healthy future.

Café Pakhuis Wilhelmina

Veemkade 576 (419 3368/www.cafe pakhuiswilhelmina.nl). Tram 26; bus 42. **Open** hours vary Wed-Sun. No credit cards. **Map** p110 E1 ⑫

Wilhelmina is still often overlooked by casual clubbers. Is it the club's IJ location? The absence of bouncers? Or the

Book into the future

Opened on the auspicious date 7/7/07, the **Openbare Bibliotheek Amsterdam** is one of Europe's largest public libraries, and gives this tiny town a big city landmark. Designed by Jo Coenen, the building treats its arriving visitors to a soaring view up to the seventh floor café-restaurant, which, in turn, has a spectacular view of the city.

With its walnut floors and white shelves and walls, the interior is eminently unshowy, the idea being that colour will come from the books, and from the people using the free internet terminals and Wi-Fi – or perhaps having a nap in one of the polyester study 'pods'. The place was much praised when it opened, though critics have been asking impertinent questions such as 'Where exactly are the books?'.

As it happens, the library is only the first finished project in an all-out construction frenzy on the south side of Oosterdok island, beside Centraal Station. For a while, the only building still standing was Post CS, a 1969

Functionalist classic that was a post office, then temporary home to the **Stedelijk Museum of Modern Art** (see p126) and to creative companies, galleries, a restaurant and a nightclub. It's now being clad in slate, to reopen in 2009 as a commercial space.

Just as ambitious, due to open in late 2008, is the **Music Conservatory by De Architekten**, built in line with Japanese engawa principles: the hallways are set on the outside to maximise soundproofing for the students, but are transparent enough to be inviting to passers-by. And this building will be joined in 2009 by 'De Blub', a blob-shaped bar and restaurant designed by London's Future Systems. If it gets too much, you can always visit pagoda-shaped floating restaurant **Sea Palace**, which will stay docked in kitsch contrast opposite.

Centrale Bibliotheek Amsterdam
Oosterdokskade 143 (523 0900/www.oba.nl).

bottles of beer for only €2? Regardless, don't miss it if your heart lies with today's leftfield music scene. Professor Nomad does weekly improv and theme nights, Ichi One drops dubstep and filthy drum 'n' bass, and every first Thursday of the month brings the always enjoyable Hardrockkaraoke.

Panama

Oostelijke Handelskade 4 (311 8686/www.panama.nl). Tram 10, 26. **Open** 9pm-3am Thur, Sun; 10pm-4am Fri, Sat. **Map** p110 E1 ⑬

An increasing force in the Amsterdam nightlife, restaurant/theatre/nightclub Panama overlooks the IJ in one of the city's most booming areas. Regular Addicted and Houseplay evenings bring the best in national DJs, while well-known international artists such as Danny Howells and Sander Kleinenberg also find their way here. On Sunday, enjoy live music, mostly jazz and latin.

Arts & leisure

Galerie Paul Andriesse

Withoedenveem 8 (623 6237/www. galeries.nl/andriesse). Tram 26. **Open** 11am-6pm Tue-Fri; 2-6pm Sat; 2-5pm 1st Sun of mth. No credit cards. **Map** p110 D1 ⑭

Relocated in 2006, the Galerie Paul Andriesse may no longer be all that innovative, but there's still a very selective savvy at work that embraces both older and wiser artists (Marlene Dumas, Thomas Struth, Jan van de Pavert, Lidwien van de Ven, Luisa Lambri) and up-and-coming names such as Charlotte Dumas, Natasja Kensmil, Gianni Caravaggo and Antonietta Peeters.

Muziekgebouw

Piet Heinkade 1 (788 2010/tickets 788 2000/www.muziekgebouw.nl). Tram 25, 26. **Map** p110 C1 ⑮

Designed by the noted Danish architects 3xNielsen, this is one of the most innovative and interesting musical complexes in the whole of Europe, befitting its previous incarnation the IJsbreker's long-lasting ethos to promote modern variants of classical, jazz and world music. Never afraid to take risks, its weekly schedule typically bustles with delights, from cutting-edge multimedia works to celebrations of composers from the last 150 years.

NDSM p111

Kitsch Kitchen p121

The Jordaan

The Jordaan emerged when the city was extended in the 17th century, originally designated for the working classes and smelly industrial enterprises (although it also provided a haven for victims of religious persecution, such as Jews and Huguenots). But despite its working-class associations, properties are now highly desirable. While the residents are mainly fiercely community-spirited, the nouveaux riches have moved in to yuppify the 'hood.

The Jordaan has no major sights; it's more of a place to stumble across things. The area north of the shopping-dense Rozengracht, the Jordaan's approximate mid-point, is more interesting and picturesque, with the area to the south being more commercial. You will also stumble upon some of Amsterdam's more unusual and interesting galleries (see box p120).

Between scenic coffee breaks or decadent daytime beers, check out some of the specialist shops tucked away on these adorable side streets. Apart from the shops, many of the best outdoor markets are found nearby: Monday morning's bargain **Noordermarkt** and Saturday's organic foodie paradise **Boerenmarkt** are held around the **Noorderkerk**, the city's first Calvinist church, built in 1623. Adjacent to the Noordermarkt is the very reasonable Westermarkt, while another general market fills Lindengracht on Saturdays.

Between Brouwersgracht and the blisteringly scenic Westelijk Eilanden, more quirky shopping opportunities can be found on Haarlemmerstraat and its westerly

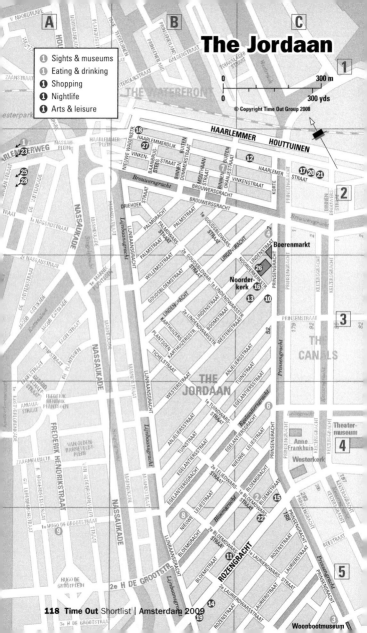

The Jordaan

Legend:
1. Sights & museums
2. Eating & drinking
3. Shopping
4. Nightlife
5. Arts & leisure

0   300 m
0   300 yds

© Copyright Time Out Group 2008

extension Haarlemmerdijk, where you'll see Haarlemmerpoort city gate, built in 1840. Behind it is wonderful Westerpark, which in turn connects to the happening arts complex Westergasfabriek.

Eating & drinking

Amsterdam

Watertorenplein 6 (682 2666/www. cradam.nl). Tram 10. **Open** 10.30am-midnight Mon-Thur, Sun; 10.30am-1am Fri, Sat. **€€€. Dutch. Map** p118 A2 ❶
This spacious monument to industry just west of the Jordaan pumped water from the coast's dunes for around a century. Now it pumps out honest Dutch and French dishes – from kroketten to caviar – under floodlighting rescued from the old Ajax stadium.

Café Chris

Bloemstraat 42 (624 5942/www. cafechris.nl). Tram 10, 13, 17. **Open** 3pm-1am Mon-Thur; 3pm-2am Fri, Sat; 3-9pm Sun. No credit cards. **Bar. Map** p118 C4 ❷
Not much has changed since 1624 at the oldest bar in town, where builders from the Westerkerk would come to receive their pay. Workers still come to unwind in unpretentious surroundings teeming with charming bric-a-brac.

Foodware

NEW *Looiersgracht 12 (620 8898/ www.foodware.nl). Tram 13, 14, 17.* **Open** noon-9pm Mon-Sat. **€€.** No credit cards. **Map** p118 C5 ❸
This takeaway (with a few chairs) does superlative soups, sandwiches, salads and meals; ask for a fork and make for a canalside bench. Order an Italian bollen and you'll come back for sure.

Proust

Noordermarkt 4 (623 9145/www. goodfoodgroup.nl). Tram 1, 2, 5, 10, 12, 13, 17. **Open** 9am-1am Mon; noon-1am Tue-Fri, Sun; 10am-3am Sat. **Bar. Map** p118 C2 ❹
Still trendy after all these years, and great for market pitstops or bar crawl kick-starts. Inside it's sleek and pared

down in style – like the punters. If full, try heading over to Finch next door; on warm days both bars' terraces merge into one convivial whole.

Semhar

Marnixstraat 259-261 (638 1634/ www.semhar.nl). Tram 10. **Open** 4-10pm Tue-Sun. **€€. African. Map** p118 B5 ❺
A great spot to tuck into the injera (tasty sourdough pancake) and veg-friendly food of Ethiopia (best washed down with a calabash of cold beer).

't Smalle

Egelantiersgracht 12 (623 9617). Tram 13, 17. **Open** 10am-1am Mon-Thur, Sun; 10am-2am Fri, Sat. No credit cards. **Bar. Map** p118 C3 ❻
This charming bar boasts some of the most scenic terraces on one of the prettiest canals in the city, so it's hardly surprising that waterside seats are snared early in the day. Its gleaming brass and candles hark back to the 18th century, when it was the Hoppe distillery.

Small World Catering

Binnen Oranjestraat 14 (420 2774/ www.smallworldcatering.nl). Bus 18, 22. **Open** 10.30am-8pm Tue-Sat; noon-8pm Sun. No credit cards. **Café. Map** p118 B2 ❼
The base for this catering company is a tiny homey deli. Besides superb coffee and fresh juice, enjoy salads, lasagnes and gourmet sandwiches.

De Vliegende Schotel

Nieuwe Leliestraat 162-168 (625 2041/ www.vliegendeschotel.com). Tram 13, 14, 17. **Open** 4-11.30pm daily. **€€. Vegetarian. Map** p118 B5 ❽
Venerable Flying Saucer serves up a splendid array of innovative meat-free dishes in a hearty buffet format. If it's booked up, try nearby De Bolhoed (Prinsengracht 60-62, 626 1803) for lovely vegan dishes.

Yam-Yam

Frederik Hendrikstraat 88-90 (681 5097/www.yamyam.nl). Tram 3. **Open** 6-10pm Tue-Sun. **€€. Italian. Map** p118 A4 ❾

Groovy little gallery trail

You could easily fill a holiday trawling the 40-odd Jordaan galleries. Since they occupy places that were once homes or shops, none are big, and most specialise – in photography, for example, or modern Dutch art.

At **Rockarchive** (110 Prinsengracht, 423 0489, www.rockarchive.com), owned by photographer Jill Furmanovsky, there's always a selection of iconic pictures from cameras of the calibre of Gered Mankowitz, Sheila Rock and the owner herself, and rare silver gelatine prints can be bought.

There are more high-quality photos at **Gallery Vassie** (1e Tuindwarsstraat 16, 489 4042), run by an ex-V&A curator. Artists from Lee Miller to Antoni & Alison have been shown here, as well as treasures from Walfred Moisio.

If you're feeling flush, head to the **Arthouse Marc Chagall** located at Bloemgracht 134 (330 7577, www.chagallkunst.com). Open in the afternoons (noon-6pm Mon-Fri), it houses a collection of lithographs, graphic works and woodcuts by the Russian master, many signed. At the opposite end of the spectrum is **KochxBos Gallery** (1e Anjeliersdwarsstraat 3, 681 4567, www.kochxbos.nl), which specialises in art from the dark side – such as queasy surrealist Ray Caesar.

Other peddlers of out-there art include the **Stedelijk Museum Bureau Amsterdam** (Rozenstraat 59, 422 0471, www.smba.nl), **Torch** (Lauriergracht 94, 626 0284, www.torchgallery.com), **Galerie Diana Stigter** (Hazenstraat 17, 624 2361, www.dianastigter.nl) and the **Galerie Fons Welters** (Bloemstraat 140, 423 3046, www.fonswelters.nl).

Open Ateliers Jordaan (www.openateliersjordaan.nl) offers a chance to poke your nose into more than 70 artists' studios.

Unparalleled and inexpensive pastas and wood-oven pizzas in a hip, casual atmosphere: no wonder Yam-Yam is a firm favourite with both hungry postclubbers and locals alike.

Shopping

Boerenmarkt

Westerstraat/Noorderkerkstraat (no phone). Tram 3, 10. **Open** 9am-3pm Sat. No credit cards. **Map** p118 C3 ➓
Every Saturday, the Noordermarkt turns into an organic farmers' market. Groups of singers or medieval musicians sometimes make a visit feel more like a day trip than a grocery shop.

Broer & Zus

Rozengracht 104 (422 9002/www. broerenzus.nl). Tram 13, 14, 17. **Open** noon-6pm Mon; 10.30am-6pm Tue-Fri; 10am-6pm Sat. **Map** p118 B5 ⓫
For the baby or toddler who has it all, Broer & Zus offers handmade toys and adorable T-shirts with goofy slogans. It's recently added a section for kids up to ten years old.

Crumpler

W Haarlemmerdijk 31 (620 2454/ www.crumpler.nl). Tram 1, 2, 4, 5, 13, 14, 16, 17, 24, 25. **Open** 1-5pm Mon; 11am-6pm Tue-Fri; 11am-5pm Sat; 1-5pm Sun. **Map** p118 C2 ⓬
Bags for the boys – OK, so the girls love 'em too, but oh how the fellas fall for the trendy laptop containers from Crumpler.

Delicious Food

Westerstraat 24 (320 3070). Tram 3. **Open** 10am-6.30pm Mon, Wed-Fri; 9am-6pm Sat. **Map** p118 C3 ⓭
Organic produce has reached a pinnacle of urban 'rustic' chic at what can only be described as a bulk food boutique. An enticing spread of the finest pastas, nuts, spices, oils and vinegars.

De Kasstoor

Rozengracht 202-210 (521 8112/ www.dekasstoor.nl). Tram 10, 13, 14, 17. **Open** 10am-6pm Tue-Sat. **Map** p118 B5 ⓮

De Kasstoor is not your average Dutch interior design shop; it also has hand-picked collectors' pieces from Le Corbusier, Eames and Citterio, and an extensive upholstery and fabrics library.

Kitsch Kitchen

Rozengracht 8 (428 4969/www. kitschkitchen.nl). Tram 13, 14, 17. **Open** 10am-6pm Mon-Sat. **Map** p118 C4/5 ⓯
Mexican Mercado with a twist. Even the hardiest denouncers of tat will love their colourful culinary and household objects, wacky wallpapers included.

Noordermarkt

Noordermarkt (no phone). Tram 3, 10. **Open** 7.30am-1pm Mon. No credit cards. **Map** p118 C3 ⓰
North of Westermarkt, Noordermarkt is frequented by the serious shopper. The stacks of (mainly second-hand) clothes, shoes, jewellery and hats need to be sorted with a grim determination, but there are real bargains to be had. Arrive early to nab the best stuff.

Reprezent

Haarlemmerstraat 80 (528 5540/ www.reprezent.nl). Tram 3/bus 18, 22. **Open** 10.30am-6.30pm Mon-Wed, Fri; 10.30am-8pm Thur; 10.30am-6pm Sat. **Map** p118 C2 ⓱
Custom skateboards, snowboarding threads from Volcom, Grenade and Special Blend and various ass-kicking accessories. The staff also organise in-house surf and snowboard tours.

Schaak en Go het Paard

Haarlemmerdijk 173 (624 1171/ www.schaakengo.nl). Tram 3/bus 18, 22. **Open** 1-5.30pm Mon; 10am-5.30pm Tue, Wed, Fri, Sat; 10am-8pm Thur. **Map** p118 B2 ⓲
This is the place to come for a truly glorious selection of handmade chess sets, from African to ultra-modern.

SPRMRKT

Rozengracht 191-193 (330 5601/ www.sprmrkt.nl). Tram 13, 14, 17. **Open** noon-6pm Mon, Sun; 10am-6pm Tue, Wed, Fri, Sat; 10am-8pm Thur. **Map** p118 B5 ⓳

A whopping 450sq m of exceptionally cool duds. The prize is the shop-with-in-the-shop, SPR+, featuring picks from Margiela, Acne Jeans, Peachoo + Krejberg and more. Also has a tasty selection of 1960s and '70s furniture plus coffee-table design books.

Unlimited Delicious

Haarlemmerstraat 122 (622 4829/ www.unlimiteddelicious.nl). Tram 3/ bus 18, 22. **Open** 9am-6pm Mon-Sat. **Map** p118 C2 ⑳

Known for such twisted treats as a caramel-balsamic-chocolate pie with a brownie bottom, Unlimited Delicious also offers courses in bonbon making.

Vlaamsch Broodhuis

W Haarlemmerstraat 108 (528 6430/www.vlaamschbroodhuys.nl). Tram 3/bus 18, 22. **Open** 11am-6.30pm Mon; 8.30am-6.30pm Tue-Fri; 9am-5pm Sat. No credit cards. **Map** p118 C2 ㉑

The name may be a bit of a mouthful, but it's worth a visit to wrap your gums around the tasty sourdough breads, fine French pastries and fresh salads from restaurant/greenhouse De Kas (p104), among other treats.

Wegewijs

Rozengracht 32 (624 4093/www. wegewijs.nl). Tram 13, 14, 17. **Open** 8.30am-6pm Mon-Fri; 9am-5pm Sat. No credit cards. **Map** p118 C5 ㉒

The Wegewijs family started this shop over a century ago. They stock 50 foreign cheeses and 100 varieties of caseus, including graskaas, a grassy-tasting cheese that's only available in summer.

Nightlife

Flex Bar

NEW *Pazzanistraat 1 (486 2123/ www.flexbar.nl). Tram 3, 10/bus 18, 21, 22.* **Open** 10pm-5am Fri, Sat; 10pm-4am Sun. **Map** p118 A2 ㉓

Electronic sounds provided by local DJs such as Rogerseventytwo & The Walk, Fightclub and Beat Dimensions Crew. Flexbar consists of two spaces, often with different programmes.

WestergasTerras

NEW *Klönneplein 4-6 (684 8496/ www.westergasterras.nl). Tram 10 /bus 21.* **Open** 11am-1am Wed, Thur; 11am-3am Fri; 10am-3am Sat; 10am-1am Sun. No credit cards. **Map** p118 A2 ㉔

A perfect place to get that sunny Sunday feeling, thanks to a warm and funky vibe and great tapas; it's located in the heart of Westergasfabriek. For a more rocking evening feeling, go to near-neighbour Pacific Parc (Polonceaukade 23, 488 7778, www.pacificparc.nl).

Arts & leisure

Noorderkerk

Noordermarkt 44 (626 6436/www. noorderkerkconcerten.nl). Tram 3, 10. No credit cards. **Map** p118 C3 ㉕

Sure, the wooden benches in this early 17th-century church are a little on the hard side, but all is soon forgiven thanks to its programme of recitals, which attracts accomplished musicians. Reservations recommended.

The Movies

Haarlemmerdijk 161 (638 6016/ www.themovies.nl). Tram 3. **Map** p118 B2 ㉗

The oldest cinema still being used in Amsterdam has been circulating celluloid since 1912, and still exudes a genteel atmosphere. The adjoining Wild Kitchen serves decent set dinners that cost between €27 and €35; prices include a ticket for a film.

Westergasfabriek

Haarlemmerweg 8-10 (586 0710/ www.westergasfabriek.com). Tram 10, 12/bus 21s. **Map** p118 A2 ㉘

With a plethora of industrial areas being cleverly reinvented as performance, event and exhibition spaces, this former gas works is quickly evolving into one of Amsterdam's premier cultural and creative hubs. It's also the new home base for Cosmic (606 5050, www.cosmictheater.nl), an inspired theatre troupe. Sporadic club nights.

Concertgebouw p130

The Museum Quarter, Vondelpark & the South

The heart of the late 19th-century Museum Quarter is Museumplein, the city's largest square, bordered roughly by the **Rijksmuseum**, the **Stedelijk Museum of Modern Art**, the **Van Gogh Museum** and the **Concertgebouw**. However, the heart will be beating fainter in the coming few years, with the Rijksmuseum partially closing and the Stedelijk relocating to the Post CS building. Museumplein itself is not really an authentic Amsterdam square, but recent additions include grass, a wading pool, a skate ramp, a café and a wacky amendment to the Van Gogh Museum.

As you'd expect in such cultural surroundings, property doesn't come cheap, and the affluence is apparent. Housing covers more than its fair share of overly elegant 19th-century mansions, while Van Baerlestraat and PC Hooftstraat are as close as Amsterdam gets to Rodeo Drive, their boutiques offering solace to ladies who might otherwise lunch.

Vondelpark is the city's largest and most central park, and the last few years have seen much renovation as the park has sunk two to three metres (seven to ten feet) since it was first built – some

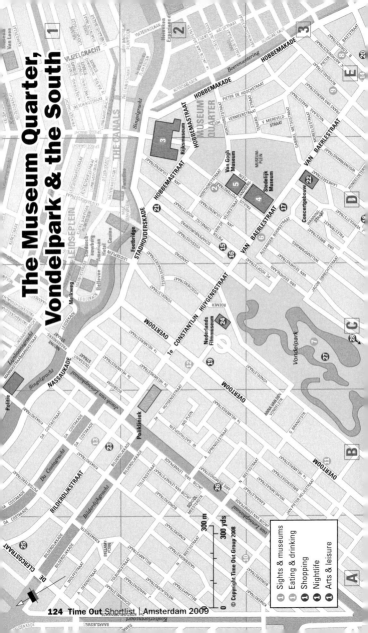

The Museum Quarter, Vondelpark & the South

Map Legend

- **Sights & museums**
- **Eating & drinking**
- **Shopping**
- **Nightlife**
- **Arts & leisure**

© Copyright Time Out Group 2008

300 m
300 yds

of the larger trees are, in fact, 'floating' on huge blocks of styrofoam or are slyly reinforced with underground poles. There are several ponds and lakes in the park – no boating, though – plus a number of play areas and cafés; most pleasant are 't Blauwe Theehuis and Café Vertigo at the Nederlands Filmmuseum. Vondelpark gets fantastically busy on sunny days and Sundays, when bongos abound, dope is toked and football games take up any space that happens to be left over. Films, plays and public concerts are also put on, with a festival of free open-air performances in summer.

Stretching out in the rough shape of a ring beneath Vondelpark is a fairly indeterminate region known as Nieuw Zuid (New South), which is itself bordered to the north by Vondelpark, to the east by the Amstel and to the west by the 1928 Olympisch Stadion (www.olympisch-stadion.net).

Sights & museums

CoBrA Museum of Modern Art

Sandbergplein 1, Amstelveen (547 5050/www.cobra-museum.nl). Tram 5/Metro 51/bus 170, 171, 172. **Open** 11am-5pm Tue-Sun. **Admission** €9.50; €6.50 seniors; €5 6s-18s, students; free under-6s, MK.

The CoBrA group (it's an acronym of Copenhagen, Brussels and Amsterdam) attempted to radically reinvent the language of paint in 1948, preaching an ethos of participation and believing everyone should make art, regardless of their ability or education. Artists such as Karel Appel, Eugene Brands and Corneille were once regarded as little more than eccentric trouble-makers; they've now been absorbed into the canon. This museum, way out in the south in the people's suburb of Amstelveen, provides a sympathetic

environment in which to trace the development of one of the most influential Dutch artistic movements of the 20th century.

Event highlights 'New Leipzig School' (4 Oct 2008-11 Jan 2009). 'CoBrA 60' (18 Oct 2008-25 Jan 2009).

House of Bols

Paulus Potterstraat 14 (570 8575/ www.houseofbols.nl). Tram 2, 5. **Open** noon-6pm Mon, Wed-Sun. **Admission** €10 (over-18s only, includes free cocktail). **Map** p124 D2 ❷

The Bols were one of the first producers of fine jenever – the original gin – and began it all in 1575. Besides a 'World of Bartending', their centre also has a 'Hall of Taste' where you can taste with your eyes, hands and nose. A bit naff perhaps, but lots of fun if you are in the right mood. Hell, you even get a free cocktail in the 'Mirror Bar' after the tour. It's only too bad that it doesn't serve absinthe – that might combine nicely with a visit to the Van Gogh Museum directly across the street.

Rijksmuseum

Jan Luijkenstraat 1 (674 7000/www. rijksmuseum.nl). Tram 2, 5, 6, 7, 10, 12. **Open** 9am-6pm Mon-Thur, Sat, Sun; 9am-8.30pm Fri. **Admission** €10; free under-19s, MK. **Map** p124 D2/E2 ❸

Designed by PJH Cuypers and opened in 1885, the Rijksmuseum holds the country's largest collection of art and artefacts, including an impressive 40 Rembrandts and four Vermeers. However, most of the museum's million exhibits will be out of the public eye until after the summer of 2013 while the Rijksmuseum gets a €227 million facelift. The closure is in fact somewhat of a blessing in disguise: instead of overdosing on the vastness of the place, visitors will be able to see the 400 most masterful masterpieces in the Philips Wing. Some parts of the collection will also be in exhibitions organised by other museums throughout the Netherlands. In short: there will still be plenty of Golden Age art to look at, but check in with the museum's excellent website before you turn up.

Event highlights 'Heavenly Sculptures from the East and West' (to Feb 2009).

Stedelijk Museum of Modern Art

Paulus Potterstraat 13 (573 2911/ www.stedelijk.nl). Tram 2, 3, 5, 12. **Open** 10am-6pm daily (Post CS). **Admission** €9; €4.50 7-16s; free under-7s, MK. **Map** p124 D3 ❹

After enjoying a temporary home in the Post CS building near Centraal Station, the beloved Stedelijk will finally return to its old haunt on Paulus Potterstraat, scheduled to reopen at the end of 2009. Meanwhile, Stedelijk in de Staat (Stedelijk in the City) will hold various exhibitions around town throughout the year. Check the website to get the latest information. Wherever it finds itself, the museum has an amazing and diverse collection to draw from. Pre-war highlights include works by Cézanne, Picasso, Matisse and Chagall, plus a collection of paintings and drawings by Malevich. Post-1945 artists represented include De Kooning, Newman, Ryman, Judd, Stella, Lichtenstein, Warhol, Nauman, Middleton, Dibbets, Kiefer, Polke, Merz and Kounellis.

Van Gogh Museum

Paulus Potterstraat 7 (570 5200/ www.vangoghmuseum.nl). Tram 2, 3, 5, 12. **Open** 10am-6pm Mon-Thur, Sat, Sun; 10am-10pm Fri. **Admission** €10; €2.50 13-17s; free under-13s, MK. Temporary exhibition prices vary. **Map** p124 D2 ❺

After a major and impressive refurbishment, the enlarged Rietveld building remains home base to the 200 paintings and 500 drawings by Van Gogh forming the museum's permanent collection, while the new wing by Japanese architect Kisho Kurokawa is usually home to temporary exhibitions that focus on Van Gogh's contemporaries and his influence on other artists. These shows are assembled from both the museum's own extensive archives and private collections. Do yourself a favour and try going around midday (from 11am) or late afternoon (around 4.30pm): the queues during most other hours can get frustratingly long, and the gallery unbearably busy. It's also well worth noting that Friday evenings at the museum often feature lectures, concerts and films.

Event highlights '125 Favourites' (3 Oct 2008-18 Jan 2009). 'Welcoming the Rijksmuseum: Indian Miniatures' (17 Oct 2008-4 Jan 2009).

Eating & drinking

Bagels & Beans

Van Baerlestraat 40 (675 7050/www. bagelsbeans.nl). Tram 3, 5, 12. **Open** 8am-6pm Mon-Fri; 9.30am-6pm Sat, Sun. **Café**. **Map** p124 D3 ❻

An Amsterdam success story, this branch of B&B also boasts a wonderfully peaceful back patio. Perfect for an economical breakfast, lunch or snack;

Vondelpark p123

Twist and shut

Rijksmuseum

Everything is closed – or so it seems. The Royal Palace on the Dam will be closed for renovations until at least 2009; ditto with the Dutch Shipping Museum. And the Stedelijk Museum of Modern Art (see p126) lost its temporary home in Post CS in July 2008 – but at least its renovation on Museumplein is now on a tight schedule, with the design of a new wing by Benthem Crouwel Architekten. A giant synthetic 'bath tub' – as the locals are already calling it – will form its new entrance when it opens at the end of 2009.

But the real story is the Rijksmuseum (see p125). It closed in 2003, with the plan to reopen in 2008 after completion of its facelift by Spanish architect Cruz y Ortiz; now it emerges that the museum will not reopen until 2013, earliest. In February 2008, the only remaining contractor (BAM) presented its estimate

to complete the project: €222 million, €88 million more than the national government had budgeted for. Minister of Culture and Education Ronald Plasterk announced that he would not be 'held hostage', and decided to split the project into smaller portions so that more companies could participate. BAM denied taking advantage of its singular position, and instead blamed the stressed building market, the time frame and the historical nature of the building.

In the interim, the Rijksmuseum will continue with its satellite programmes such as the Schiphol Airport location and lending out parts of its collection to other museums. As it happens, the 'best of' exhibition in the Philips Wing, with its 400 paintings and objects, is more than enough for the average human being to absorb. Sometimes it's good to have focus.

Get your skates on

Friday Night Skate

It's 9pm on a Friday night. Most of the locals are slumped in front of the telly or drinking in a bar – but not the people currently assembling in the Vondelpark. Unless it's raining, every Friday a group of skate fanatics meets to snake the 20-kilometre (12.4-mile), three-hour-long **Friday Night Skate** through central Amsterdam (www.fridaynightskate.com).

It all started in 1997, when three friends decided to do something special to kick off the weekend. Ten years later, that same group varies from a small handful of die-hards in winter to hundreds in summer, but whatever the cause they all have one thing in common: a love of skating around the city. Forget tracing circles around boring parks – it's high bridges, car parks, tunnels and noisy roads this lot are after.

Things never get stale. Each week there is a new route but the start and finish is always in Vondelpark, directly opposite the Filmmuseum (p132). There are teams of 'blockers', who block the roads so cars and cyclists can't get in the way, plus 'flying nurses' who'll come to your assistance if ever you have an unscheduled meeting with the hard tarmac. Some skaters even carry sound systems on their backs, providing tunes to help people move with purpose. It's free, it's fun and it's a great way to make new friends.

sun-dried tomatoes are a speciality, always employed with particular skill.

't Blauwe Theehuis

Vondelpark 5 (662 0254/www.blauwe theehuis.nl). Tram 1, 2, 6. **Open** 9am-11pm Mon-Thur, Sun; 9am-1am Fri, Sat. **Bar. Map** p124 C3 **7**
One of the few local landmarks that you can nestle down inside with a beer, HJAB Baanders' extraordinary 1930s teahouse – a sort of UFO-hat hybrid – is a choice spot for fair-weather drinking. In summer there are DJs and barbecues, though it's a romantic spot for dinner and drinks all year round.

Eetcafé I Kriti

Balthasar Floriszstraat 3 (664 1445/ www.ikriti.nl). Tram 3, 5, 12, 16. **Open** 5pm-1am daily. €€€. **Greek. Map** p124 E3 **8**
Eat and party Greek style in this evocation of Crete. On a lucky night, the owner and chef Yannis steps out of the kitchen to sing and play guitar for guests, sometimes boosted by plate-lobbing antics.

Le Garage

Ruysdaelstraat 54-56 (679 7176/www. restaurantlegarage.nl). Tram 16, 24. **Open** noon-2pm, 6-11pm Mon-Fri; 6-11pm Sat, Sun. €€€€. **French. Map** p124 E3 **9**
Don your glad rags to blend in at this extremely fashionable brasserie, which is great for emptying your wallet while watching a cross-section of the Dutch glitterati do exactly the same thing. The authentic French regional cuisine – and 'worldly' versions thereof – is pretty damn good, as you'd expect.

Kashmir Lounge

Jan Pieter Heijestraat 85-87 (683 2268). Tram 1, 6, 7, 11, 17. **Open** 10am-2am Mon-Thur; 10am-3am Fri, Sat; 11am-1am Sun. No credit cards. **Coffeeshop. Map** p124 A3 **10**
Lit with little beyond candlelight, Kashmir may seem too dark at first, but once your eyes adjust it's an opulent cavern of Indian tapestries, ornate tiles, hand-carved walls and

comfy cushions swathed in zebra and cheetah prints. With a multitude of obscure corners and partially enclosed tables, you can feel like a VIP at no extra charge.

De Peper

Overtoom 301 (412 2954/www. depeper.org). Tram 1, 6. **Open** 6pm-1am Tue, Thur, Fri, Sun. €. No credit cards. **Vegetarian. Map** p124 B3 **11**
This purveyor of the cheapest and best vegan food in town is a collectively organised, non-profit project combining culture with an awesome kitchen.

Peperwortel

Overtoom 140 (685 1053/www.peper wortel.nl). Tram 1, 3, 10, 12. **Open** 4-9pm Mon-Fri; 3-9pm Sat, Sun. €€. No credit cards. **Global. Map** p124 C2 **12**
You could survive for weeks on takeaways from Pepper Root (which, if you follow the name's Jewish Amsterdam roots, translates to Horse Radish), with its range of dishes embracing everything from Dutch to Mexican, Indian and Spanish cuisines.

Riaz

Bilderdijkstraat 193 (683 6453/www. riaz.nl). Tram 1, 3, 7, 12, 17. **Open** 11.30am-9pm Mon-Fri; 2-9pm Sun. €€. No credit cards. **South American. Map** p124 B1 **13**
A Surinamese joint where you might be lucky enough to see Ruud Gullit; it's where he scores his rotis when he happens to be in town.

Wildschut

Roelof Hartplein 1-3 (676 8220/www. goodfoodgroup.nl). Tram 3, 5, 12, 24. **Open** 9.30am-noon Mon-Fri; 10am-1am Sat, Sun. **Bar. Map** p124 E3 **14**
A stunning example of Amsterdam School architecture, this elegant semi-circular building puts the 'grand' into grand café and positively drips with elegant nouveau detail. The drink and food menu mirrors the upmarket surroundings, as does the regular clientele, which includes flush locals, loud yuppies and usually a crowd of art-weary tourists.

Shopping

Azzurro Due

Pieter Corneliesz Hooftstraat 138 (671 9708). Tram 2, 5. **Open** 1-6pm Mon; 10am-6pm Tue, Wed, Fri; 10am-9pm Thur; 10am-6pm Sat; noon-5pm Sun. **Map** p124 D2 ⓯

If you've got to splurge on cutting-edge fashion, this is as good a spot as any. Saucy picks from Marni, Miu Miu, Chloé and Stella McCartney attract the usual hordes of mediacrities.

For Our Friends Store (Blue Blood Store)

NEW *PC Hooftstraat 142 (676 6220/ www.bluebloodbrand.com). Tram 2, 5.* **Open** noon-6pm Mon, Sun; 10am-6pm Tue-Wed, Fri; 10am-9pm Thur. **Map** p124 D2 ⓰

The concept store for local jeans icon Blue Blood stocks not just its own denims, but also the works of Dutch designers like Francisco van Benthum and Daryl van Wouw, and must-have scooters, vintage watches, high-tech gadgets and art. A second location, Blue Blood Boutique (Cornelis Schuytstraat 18, 673 3847), puts more emphasis on vintage couture.

Intertaal

Van Baerlestraat 76 (575 6760/www. intertaal.nl). Tram 3, 5, 12, 16. **Open** 10am-6pm Tue-Fri; 10am-5pm Sat. **Map** p124 D3 ⓱

Dealing in language books, CDs and teaching aids, Intertaal will be of use to all learners of a new foreign language, whether they're grappling with basic Dutch or improving their English.

Lairesse Apotheek

Lairessestraat 40 (662 1022/www. delairesseapotheek.nl). Tram 3, 5, 12, 16. **Open** 8.30am-6pm Mon-Fri; 10am-5pm Sat. **Map** p124 D3 ⓲

One of the largest suppliers of alternative medicines in the country, from chemist Marjan Terpstra. The shop is out of the way if you're just popping in for haemorrhoid cream, but the interior is inspiring enough to be on any design junkie's must-see list.

Pied-à-Terre

Overtoom 135-137 (627 4455/www. piedaterre.nl). Tram 1, 2, 5. **Open** 1-6pm Mon; 1am-6pm Wed, Fri; 10am-9pm Thur; 10am-5pm Sat. No credit cards. **Map** p124 C2 ⓳

Travel books, guides and maps for active holidays. Adventurous walkers can seek advice from the helpful staff for out-of-town trips.

Waterwinkel

Roelof Hartstraat 10 (675 5932/www. springwater.nl). Tram 3, 24. **Open** 10am-6pm Mon-Fri; 10am-5pm Sat. **Map** p124 E3 ⓴

The variety of native and imported water in this unusual store will charm many, but may induce an emergency in the more weak-bladdered.

Nightlife

The Mansion

Hobbemastraat 2 (616 6664/www.the-mansion.nl). Tram 2, 5. **Open** 6.30pm-1am Wed, Thur, Sun (restaurant only Sun); 6.30pm-3am Fri, Sat. **Map** p124 D2 ㉑

This restaurant/bar/club is less Hugh Hefner and more gentleman's club with chicks allowed. The staff are decked out in designer outfits, and the decor is plush chinoiserie. Expect DJs, dancing and a hole in your wallet.

Arts & leisure

Amsterdam RAI Theater

Europaplein 8-22 (549 1212/www.rai theater.nl). Tram 4, 15/Metro Amstel. This huge convention and exhibition centre by day turns into an enormous theatre by night and on weekends. Musicals, operas, comedy nights, ballets, spectacular shows – all can be enjoyed in a venue created to make each visit an inspiring experience.

Concertgebouw

Concertgebouwplein 2-6 (reservations 671 8345/24hr information in Dutch & English 573 0511/www. concertgebouw.nl). Tram 2, 3, 5, 12, 16, 24. **Map** p124 D3 ㉒

Delicious Amsterdam

These days, mention Dutch food and most serious gastronomes will barely be able to repress a snigger. And yet once upon a time, according to über-food critic Johannes van Dam, the national dishes were serious stuff indeed.

'Dutch cuisine was as rich as Belgian or French until the end of the 19th century,' he says. That was when *huishoudscholen* – 'household schools', whose noble intention was teaching impoverished Amsterdammers to make more easy, affordable meals – stripped the cuisine of its many riches, leaving nothing in their wake except meat, vegetables and potatoes.

Recent years, however, have seen a fiercely renewed interest in traditional food across the city. Johannes praises **Greetje** (Peperstraat 23, 779 7450) for reinventing old favourites like eel soup, blood sausage and liquorice ice-cream, and singles out **De Roode Leeuw** (Damrak 93-94, 555 0666) and **Moeders Pot** (Vinkenstraat 119, 623 7643) as the best places to taste real home-style Dutch cooking.

Geographical phenomena have also shaped the national fare: tasty North Sea shrimps flavour *kroketten* – try it for yourself at **Holtkamp** (Vijzelgracht 15, 624 8767), whose luxury lines also include calves' sweetbreads with mushrooms. The other standard snack is raw herring, of which van Dam cautions: 'If you don't watch out, you will undoubtedly be served onion with your fresh fish. Good herring is ruined by onion.' Don't say we didn't warn you.

Most people, however, tend to say 'cheese' if they need to name a staple. The most famous is gouda, but van Dam says that fans should avoid factory-made versions. Look instead for *boeren* (farmers') gouda. This can be bought at specialist cheese retailers (such as **De Kaaskamer**, Runstraat 7, 623 3483), and at most markets. Yet more tasty variations include spicy leidsekaas with cumin seeds and Friesland's nagelkaas with cloves, both unusual and delicious.

While Dutch cuisine hasn't fully recovered from past misguided intentions, it is doing well enough for the arch critic himself to have recently written a book in English about local cuisine. Its name? *Delicious Amsterdam*, of course.

With its beautiful architecture and clear acoustics, the Concertgebouw is a favourite venue of many of the world's top musicians, and is home to its very own world-famous Royal Concertgebouw Orchestra. As you'd expect, the sound in the Grote Zaal (Great Hall) is excellent. The Kleine Zaal (Recital Hall) is perhaps less comfortable, but is the perfect size for both chamber groups and soloists.

Gasthuis Werkplaats & Theater

Marius van Bouwdijk Bastiaansestraat 54 (616 8942/www.theatergasthuis.nl). Tram 1, 3, 7, 17, 12. No credit cards. **Map** p124 B2 ㉓

The Gasthuis emerged from a group of squatters who became critical darlings in just a few years. Even when their home, a former hospital, was threatened with demolition, their artsy activities contributed a great deal towards the building's ultimate salvation. The rolling programme is, as you might expect, mainly youthful and experimental. Some productions are in English; be sure to check the website beforehand to guarantee a comprehensible evening's entertainment.

Nederlands Filmmuseum (NFM)

Vondelpark 3 (589 1400/www. filmmuseum.nl). Tram 1, 2, 3, 5, 6, 12. No credit cards. **Map** p124 C2 ㉔

This stylish building overlooking the Vondelpark is both a cinema and a museum. The most important centre of cinematography in the Netherlands, it collects films to add to its vast catalogue and restores copies that have been ravaged by the passage of time. It also regularly screens silent films, authentically accompanied by an old-fashioned pianola, and specialises in major retrospectives and edgier contemporary fare. In the summer, be sure to take in an outdoor screening on the terrace of the in-house Café Vertigo. And enjoy it while you can. It's moving to a new location near Centraal Station in 2010.

Serieuze Zaken Studioos

Bilderdijkstraat 66 (427 5770/www. galerieserieuzezaken.com). Tram 10, 12. **Open** 1-6pm Wed-Sat. No credit cards. **Map** p124 A1 ㉕

Rob Malasch was already known as a quirky theatre type and journalist before opening this gallery. Shows here might feature anything from Brit Art to work by modern Chinese painters.

Smart Project Space

Arie Biemondstraat 101-11 (427 5951/ www.smartprojectspace.net). Tram 1, 17. No credit cards. **Map** p124 B2 ㉖

Relocated in a former pathology lab and reopening in 2007, Smart will no doubt remain loyal to 'hardcore art' in its huge new exhibition space, which also has three cinemas, a media centre, a lecture hall, and a decent in-house café and restaurant for hungry Bohos.

Vondelpark Openluchttheater

Vondelpark (673 1499/www.openlucht theater.nl). Tram 1, 2, 3, 5, 7, 10, 12. No credit cards. **Map** p124 C3 ㉗

Theatrical events have been held in Vondelpark since 1865, and the tradition continues each summer with a variety of shows. Wednesdays offer a lunchtime concert and a mid-afternoon children's show; Thursday nights find a concert on the bandstand; there's a theatre show Friday evenings and various events (many child-friendly) on both Saturday and Sunday afternoons. Gets especially packed in summer.

Vondeltuin

Vondelpark 7 (664 5091/www.vondel tuin.nl). Tram 1, 2. No credit cards. **Map** p124 C3 ㉘

Rollerblades, skates and accessories are rented to those looking to make the most of the surrounding area's potential for concrete cruising. If you're seeking less sedate thrills, make a beeline for ramp-happy SkateparkAmsterdam (www.skateparkamsterdam.nl) at the NDSM yard (p111), offering both lessons for beginners, competitions for the more experienced and plenty of all-in rail riding.

Albert Cuypmarkt p138

The Pijp

While it's hardly a historical treasure trove of sights, the Pijp's time is the present. Well over 150 different nationalities keep its global village vibe alive, and the recent economic boom has seen the opening of more upmarket eateries and bars than ever before. The gentrification process, it seems, is in full swing. This trend will be heightened over the next few years by the construction of the Metro's controversial new Noord-Zuidlijn, which will run pretty much directly beneath bustling Ferdinand Bolstraat.

The Pijp is the best known of the working-class quarters built in the late 19th century. Harsh economics saw the building of long, narrow streets, which led to its appropriate nickname, 'the Pipe'. Because rents were high, many tenants were forced to sublet rooms to students and artists, who then gave the area its bohemian character.

The Pijp today houses a mix of nationalities, providing locals with halal butchers, Surinamese, Spanish, Indian and Turkish delicatessens, and restaurants offering authentic Syrian, Moroccan, Thai, Pakistani, Chinese and Indian cuisine. Thanks to these low-priced exotic eats, the Pijp is quite simply the best place in town for quality snacking treats, the many ingredients for which are almost always bought fresh from the single largest daily market in all of the Netherlands: Albert Cuypmarkt, the hub around which the Pijp turns. The market attracts thousands of customers every day to the junctions of Sweelinckstraat, Ferdinand Bolstraat and 1e Van der

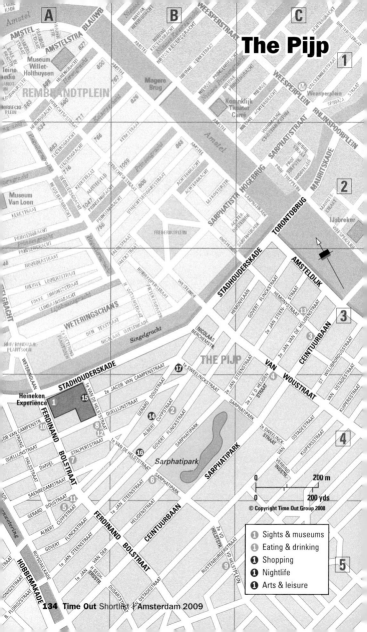

The Pijp

A | **B** | **C**

1 | **2** | **3** | **4** | **5**

AMSTEL

Museum Willet-Holthuysen

REMBRANDTPLEIN

Magere Brug

Koninklijk Theater Carré

Museum Van Loon

Amstel

SARPHATISTR. HOGEBRUG

TORONTOBRUG

AMSTELDIJK

STADHOUDERSKADE

IJsbreker

WETERINGSCHANS

Singelgracht

NICOLAAS BERCHEMSTR.

THE PIJP

VAN WOUSTRAAT

CEINTUURBAAN

Heineken Experience

FERDINAND BOLSTRAAT

Sarphatipark

SARPHATIPARK

STADHOUDERSKADE

FERDINAND BOLSTRAAT

CEINTUURBAAN

HOBBEMAKADE

0   200 m
0   200 yds

© Copyright Time Out Group 2008

❶ Sights & museums
❶ Eating & drinking
❶ Shopping
❶ Nightlife
❶ Arts & leisure

Helststraat, north into the lively Gerard Douplein, and also south towards Sarphatipark. Another particularly pretty street, and also one rich with cafés and bars, is the always lovely Frans Halsstraat.

Sights & museums

Heineken Experience

Stadhouderskade 78 (523 9666/www. heinekenexperience.com). Tram 6, 7, 10, 16, 24, 25. **Open** 10am-6pm (no entry after 5pm) Tue-Sun. **Admission** €10. **Map** p134 A4 ❶

After Heineken stopped brewing here in 1988, the company kept the building open for endearingly unflashy tours: for a charitable donation of €2 (less than €1 in today's money), you got an hour-long guided walk followed by as much Heineken as you could consume. Unfortunately, the company cottoned on to the fact that most people were there for the booze, and renovated the huge building as the Heineken Experience. While it's a lot flashier, it's a little less illuminating and a lot less fun. Plus points: the quasi-virtual reality ride through a brewery from the perspective of a Heineken bottle is easily the most ludicrous exhibit in all Amsterdam, and you still get three free beers as well as a surprise free gift at the end of the tour.

Eating & drinking

Bazar

Albert Cuypstraat 182 (675 0544/ www.bazaramsterdam.nl). Tram 16, 24. **Open** 11am-1am Mon-Thur; 11am-2am Fri; 9am-2am Sat; 9am-midnight Sun. **€€**. **North African**. **Map** p134 B4 ❷

If you fail to find Bazar, look up at the sky and search there for an angel. This former church, now downgraded to an Arabic-kitsch café, is one of the real glories of Albert Cuypmarkt. Sticking to the winning formula set by its Rotterdam mothership, it boasts a menu that travels the world but lingers lovingly in the environs of North

Africa. Whether it's for breakfast, lunch or dinner, Bazar is a real winner.

Bloemers

Hemonystraat 70 (400 4024). Tram 3, 4, 25. **Open** 10am-1am Mon-Thur, Sun; 10am-3am Fri, Sat. **Bar**. **Map** p134 C3 ❸

A justifiably popular neighbourhood bar on the eastern fringes of the Pijp, with a dark wood interior enlivened by old posters and chandeliers. The kitchen turns out well-priced and tasty international classics for lunch and dinner. Capacity doubles when the terrace, complete with swing seats, opens during the summer.

Buna Bet

Van Woustraat 74 (673 9449). Tram 25. **Open** 8am-5pm Mon-Sat. **Café**. **Map** p134 C4 ❹

There's no booze on offer here, but plenty of coffee with a conscience on Amsterdam's up-and-coming foodie street. Choose from a range of fairtrade coffees and cakes.

Burger Meester

NEW *Albert Cuypstraat 48 (670 9339/ www.burgermeester.eu). Tram 16, 24, 25.* **Open** noon-11pm daily. **€€**. **Burgers**. No credit cards. **Map** p134 A5 ❺

A new designer burger specialist. Order your beef, lamb, tuna or falafel burger with toppings that include wild mushrooms, wasabi, grilled peppers or pancetta – and it will arrive complete with a baked potato or an enticingly good salad.

Café Krull

Sarphatipark 2 (662 0214). Tram 3, 4, 24, 25. **Open** 9am-1am daily. **Bar**. **Map** p134 B4 ❻

Light from the enormous windows floods this delightful locals' café that's busy at all hours, with lap-toppers taking advantage of Wi-Fi, parents treating their lucky offspring to a hot chocolate, and – later on – evening imbibers of every stripe. The barman's music choice is exquisite (disco, Motown, easy listening, rockabilly), plus the outdoor picnic tables are every summer drinker's dream.

Gollem

Daniel Stalpertstraat 74 (676 7117/ www.cafegollem.nl). Tram 3, 12, 16, 24, 25. **Open** 4pm-1am Mon-Thur, Sun; 2pm-2am Fri, Sat. No credit cards. **Café. Map** p134 A4 ⑦
An outstanding place to get sozzled, this dark and very cosy Belgian beer specialist offers more than 150 bottled bevvies – including 42 abbey beers and 14 trappists – and 14 on tap. The helpful menu lists the strengths of the brews on offer.

Mamouche

Quellijnstraat 104 (673 6361/www. restaurantmamouche.nl). Tram 3, 12, 16, 24, 25. **Open** 6.30-10pm daily. €€€. **Moroccan. Map** p134 A4 ⑧
In the heart of the multicultural Pijp is this Moroccan restaurant with a real difference: it's posh, stylish (in a sexy, minimalist sort of way) and provides a groovy kind of background soundtrack music that can only be described as 'North African lounge'.

Renato's Trattoria

Karel du Jardinstraat (673 2300). Tram 12, 25. **Open** 6-11pm daily. €€. No credit cards. **Italian. Map** p134 B5 ⑨
Dropping in here is like briefly stepping into Italy itself, with hearty hospitality and raw kitchen action to match. Pizza – heavily loaded but with a delicious crispy crust – is the house speciality, popular with all ages but a real hit with kids.

De Taart van m'n Tante

Ferdinand Bolstraat 10 (776 4600/ www.detaart.com). Tram 16, 24. **Open** 10am-6pm daily. No credit cards. **Café. Map** p134 A4 ⑩
The café – affectionately known as My Aunt's Cake – started its existence as a purveyor of over-the-top cakes (which it still produces) before becoming the campest tearoom in what can be a very camp town. Set in a glowing pink space filled with charmingly mismatched furniture, it's particularly gay-friendly (try the Tom of Finland cake). It also features a delightful and welcoming B&B (www.cakeundermy pillow.com).

Warung Spang-Makandra

Gerard Doustraat 39 (670 5081/www. spangmakandra.nl). Tram 16. **Open** 11am-10pm Tue-Sat; 1-10pm Sun. €. **Global. Map** p134 A4 ⑪
An Indonesian-Surinamese restaurant serving tasty and addictive Javanese *rames*. The decor is very simple, but the relaxed vibe and beautifully presented dishes will make you want to linger for a while over your meal, rather than take it away.

Wijnbar Boelen & Boelen

1e Van der Helststraat 50 (671 2242/ www.wijnbar.nl). Tram 3, 4, 16, 24, 25. **Open** 6pm-midnight Tue-Sun. **Bar. Map** p134 A4 ⑫
Many of the regulars come here just to sample the Frenchified food, but as the name implies, the wine's the real star of the show at this compact yet airy bar, located on the edge of the Pijp's main nightlife strip. The emphasis is really on old world tipples, but there are also well-edited selections from Australia, New Zealand and North and South America, and the friendly owners can offer suggestions for those of you who are less well versed in the ways of the grape.

Yo-Yo

2e Jan van der Heijdenstraat 79 (664 7173). Tram 3, 4. **Open** noon-7pm Mon-Sat. No credit cards. **Coffeeshop. Map** p134 C3 ⑬
Located on a leafy residential street near Sarphatipark and the Albert Cuypmarkt, this chill-out spot lacks the commercialism and crowds found in other more central shops. The herb here is all-organic, and the place is run by a very pleasant lady who bakes her own fresh apple pie every day – a truly awesome and delicious cure for the chronic munchies if ever there was one.

The Amsterdam School

Amsterdam's monuments are not products of imperial imaginations imposing their stone wills on an unwilling populace, but rather the homes of merchants and working men and women. And it was also for those same workers that the Amsterdam School built its gentler versions of Gaudí-style buildings, working with a socialist vision in the early 20th century.

While due credit can be given to the stonemasons who perforce had to practise non-geometrical brickwork when repairing houses slowly sinking into the mud, it was Hendrik Berlage who pioneered the main movement by not only stripping things down, rejecting all the neo-styles that had defined 19th-century Dutch architecture, but also by providing a much-needed opportunity to experiment with new forms by starting **Plan Zuid**, an urban development meant to provide housing for the working classes south of the Pijp.

Although the Amsterdam School was short-lived – the money ran out – examples remain liberally dotted around the city. Located along the waterfront, the eerie and epic **Scheepvaarthuis** (Prins Hendrikkade 108-114) is most usually considered to be the school's first work and has reopened as the Hotel Amrâth (see box p157). The school's real playground is at Plan Zuid, on the border of the Pijp and Rivierenbuurt. **Josef Israelkade**, between 2e Van der Helststraat and Van Woustraat, is a pleasant stretch along the Amstelkanaal; enter PL Takstraat and then circle Burg Tellegenstraat, popping your head into the **Cooperatiehof** courtyard. It's the school at its hallucinatory best, incongruous with its surroundings yet utterly inspired.

It's a different story elsewhere, though. Backtrack and cross the Amstelkanaal, and then walk down **Waalstraat**; here you'll find later examples of the school's work, where tightening purse strings led to greater restraint. It's also worth visiting the extraordinary **Spaarndammer** neighbourhood on the other side of town near the Westerpark.

One of the school's most frolicsome works, the Ship, is home to the **Museum Het Schip** (Spaarndammerplantsoen 140, 418 2885, www.hetschip.nl, 1-5pm Wed-Sun; pictured), which operates Amsterdam School boating and walking tours, and also boasts an exhibition space devoted to its architectural legacy.

AMSTERDAM BY AREA

Shopping

Albert Cuypmarkt

Albert Cuypstraat (no phone). Tram 4, 16, 24, 25. **Open** 9.30am-5pm Mon-Sat. No credit cards. **Map** p134 B4 ⓮
Amsterdam's largest general market sells everything from pillows to prawns at great prices. The clothes on sale tend to be run-of-the-mill cheapies.

Dirk van den Broek

Marie Heinekenplein 25 (673 9393/ www.lekkerdoen.nl). Tram 16, 24, 25. **Open** 8am-9pm Mon-Sat. **Map** p134 A4 ⓯
Suddenly fashionable – its red bags are now must-haves for Amsterdam's designer lemmings and have even been spotted on the arms of the fashion rat-pack overseas – Dirk remains cheaper than Albert Heijn, while its choice has improved, although it has to be said that it's not the most glamorous of the city's supermarkets.

Runneboom

1e Van der Helststraat 49 (673 5941). Tram 16, 24, 25. **Open** 7am-5pm Mon-Fri; 7am-4pm Sat. No credit cards. **Map** p134 B4 ⓰
This Pijp bakery is a staunch favourite with locals, who queue far into the street come rain or shine. A huge selection of French, Russian, Greek and Turkish loaves is offered, with rye bread the house speciality. Delicious cakes and pastries are also sold.

Nightlife

Badcuyp

1e Sweelinckstraat 10 (675 9669/ www.badcuyp.nl). Tram 3, 4, 12, 16, 24, 25. **Open** 11am-1am Tue-Thur, Sun; 11am-3am Fri, Sat. **Map** p134 B3 ⓱
Small and friendly, the focus at this popular nightspot is firmly placed on world and jazz music. Besides the intriguing range of international talents in the main hall, the cute café plays host to regular salsa, African, jazz and open jam evenings that are always a hoot.

Bazar p135

Kijk-Kubus p148

Day Trips

There's more to the Netherlands than just its capital city, of course, and for a relatively compact country it boasts an astonishing variety of landscapes, from beaches and dykes to thick woods and forests to real urban jungles. Amsterdam itself is part of one of the most densely populated areas in the world: no fewer than 40 per cent of the country's entire population inhabit the built-up sprawl known as the Randstad or 'Edge City'. It's made up of Delft, Haarlem, the Hague, Leiden and Utrecht, as well as bitter urban rivals Amsterdam and Rotterdam. Each of the destinations we describe below can easily be explored in day trips undertaken from the capital, although they also stand up to more leisurely and sustained exploration.

Delft

Imagine a miniaturised Amsterdam– canals reduced to dinky proportions, bridges narrowed, merchants' houses shrunk – and you have the essence of Delft. Though it's small and often scoffed at for its sleepiness, Delft is a student town with plenty going on. Its bars and cafés may appear to outsiders to be survivors of a bygone era – white-aproned waiters, high-ceilinged interiors and all – but it's the norm in Delft. Other cities offer hot chocolate finished with aerosol cream; cafés here use real cream and accompany it with a fancier brand of biscuit.

Everything you're likely to want to see is in the old centre. As soon as you cross over the road from the station towards the city centre, you encounter an introduction to Delft's past: a representation of Vermeer's famous *Milkmaid* in stone.

Delft was traditionally a centre for trade, producing and exporting butter, cloth, beer – at one point in the past, 200 breweries could be found alongside its canals – and, later, 'Royal Blue' pottery. Its subsequent loss in trade has been Rotterdam's gain, but the aesthetic benefits can be seen in the city's centuries-old gables, hump-backed bridges and shady canals. To appreciate how little has changed, walk to the end of Oude Delft, the oldest canal in town, cross the busy road to the harbour and compare the view to Vermeer's *View of Delft*, now on display in the Mauritshuis in the Hague (p144).

Sights & museums

De Delftse Pauw
Delftweg 133 (015 212 4920/www. delftsepauw.com). **Open** *Apr-Oct* 9am-4.30pm daily. *Nov-Mar* 9am-4.30pm Mon-Fri; 11am-1pm Sat, Sun. **Admission** free.
Delft is famous for its blue and white tiles and pottery, known as Delft Blue (internationally as Royal Blue). One of the few factories open to visitors.

Legermuseum
Korte Geer 1 (015 215 0500/www. legermuseum.nl). **Open** 10am-5pm Tue-Fri; noon-5pm Sat, Sun. **Admission** €7.50; €3 seniors, 5-17s; free under-5s, MK.
Gun nuts, take note: the 'Army Museum' houses the country's largest military collection.

Museum Lambert van Meerten
Oude Delft 199 (015 260 2199). **Open** 10am-5pm Tue-Sat; 1-5pm Sun. **Admission** €6; €5 seniors; free under-12s.
Offers an overview of the Delft Blue industry and includes a huge range of tiles, with everything from battling warships to randy rabbits.

Nieuwe Kerk
Markt 80 (015 212 3025/www.nieu wekerk-delft.nl). **Open** Apr-Oct 9am-5pm Mon-Sat. Nov-Mar 11am-4pm Mon-Fri; 10am-5pm Sat. **Admission** €3.20; €2.70 seniors; €1.60 under-12s. (*Tower* €2.70; €2.20 seniors; €1.10 under-12s.
The 'New Church' took almost 15 years to construct and was finished in 1396. It contains the mausoleums of lawyer-philosopher and founder of 'natural law' theory Hugo de Groot (also known as 'Grotius') and William of Orange (interned alongside his dog, which faithfully followed him into death by refusing food and water), in a black and white marble mausoleum by Hendrick de Keyser. De Keyser also designed the epic 1620 Stadhuis across the Markt.

Oude Kerk
Heilige Geestkerkhof 25 (015 212 3015/www.oudekerk-delft.nl). **Open** *Apr-Oct*; 9am-6pm Mon-Sat. *Nov-Mar* 11am-4pm Mon-Fri; 10am-5pm Sat. **Admission** €3.20; €2.70 seniors; €1.60 under-12s.
The town's other splendid house of worship, the Gothic 'Old Church' (c1200), is known as 'Leaning Jan' because its tower stands 2m (over 6ft) off-kilter. Art-lovers should note that it's the final resting place of Vermeer.

De Porceleyne Fles
Rotterdamseweg 196 (015 251 2030/ www.royaldelft.com). **Open** *Apr-Oct* 9am-5pm daily. *Nov-Mar* 9am-5pm Mon-Sat. **Admission** €4.50 guided tour.
Another look behind the scenes of a Delft Blue pottery factory.

Het Prinsenhof Municipal Museum
Sint Agathaplein 1 (015 260 2358/ www.prinsenhof-delft.nl). **Open** 10am-5pm Tue-Sat; 1-5pm Sun. **Admission** €6; €5 seniors, 12-16s; free under-12s.
This castle-like structure in the former convent of St Agatha, has exhibitions, plus displays on William of Orange, assassinated here in 1584. The bullet holes are still visible on the stairs.

Day Trips

Nieuwe Kerk p141

Reptielenzoo Serpo

Stationsplein 8 (015 212 2184/www.
serpo.nl). **Open** 10am-6pm Mon-Sat;
1-6pm Sun. **Admission** €7.50; €6.50
seniors; €5.50 4-11s; free under-4s.
Europe's largest collection of poiso-
nous snakes, and other scaly creatures.

Getting there

Delft is 60 kilometres (37 miles)
south-west of Amsterdam on the A4.
Trains from Amsterdam Centraal
Station take just under an hour (you
may need to change at the Hague).

Tourist information

Toeristische Informatie Punt (Tourist Information Point)

Hippolytusbuurt 4 (0900 515 1555
premium rate/www.delft.nl). **Open**
Apr-Sept 10am-4pm Mon; 9am-6pm
Tue-Fri; 10am-5pm Sat; 10am-4pm

Sun. *Oct-Mar* 11am-4pm Mon; 10am-
4pm Tue-Sat; 10am-3pm Sun.

Haarlem

Although Amsterdam is also located
in Noord-Holland, Haarlem, 15
minutes away by train, is the
provincial capital. A cycle ride from
the lovely beaches of Zandvoort-
and Bloemendaal-aan-Zee, Haarlem
is a smaller, gentler and older
version of Amsterdam. All traces of
the city's origins as a tenth-century
inland sea settlement disappeared
when the Haarlemmermeer was
drained in the 19th century. But it
hasn't lost its appeal: the centre,
with its lively square, canals and
charming almshouses, is beautiful.

Sights & museums

Frans Halsmuseum

Groot Heiligland 62 (023 511 5775/
www.franshalsmuseum.nl). **Open**

11am-5pm Tue-Sat; noon-5pm Sun. **Admission** €7.50; €3.75 19-24s; free under-18s, MK.

Housed in what was an elderly men's almshouse and orphanage (well worth a visit in themselves), this museum has a magnificent collection of 16th- and 17th-century portraits, still lifes, genre paintings and landscapes. The highlight is a group of eight portraits of militia companies and regents from the brush of Frans Hals. The museum also has vast collections of period furniture, Haarlem silver and an 18th-century apothecary with Delftware pottery.

De Hallen

Grotemarkt 16 (023 511 5775/www. dehallen.com). **Open** 11am-5pm Tue-Sat; noon-5pm Sun. **Admission** €5; €2.50 19-24s; free under-18s; MK.

A genuinely up-to-the-minute modern art museum housed in two interesting old buildings, the Verweyhal (a 19th-century gentleman's club) and the atmospheric Vleeshal or 'meat hall', a 17th-century butcher's market. Exhibitions focus on cutting-edge artists such as Tracey Emin, Sarah Lucas and the German Jonathan Meese.

St Bavo

Grotemarkt (023 553 2040/www. bavo.nl). **Open** 10am-4pm Mon-Sat. **Admission** €2; free under-12s.

This truly enormous church, dominating Grotemarkt, the main square, provides an excellent point to begin exploring Haarlem's long history. Built around 1313, it suffered fire damage in 1328 and rebuilding lasted another 150 years. It's surprisingly bright inside: cavernous white transepts stand as high as the nave and make a stunning sight. The floor is made up of 1,350 gravestones, including one featuring only the word 'Me' and another long enough to hold a famed local giant. In the interests of balance, there's also a dedication to a local midget who died of injuries from a game of dwarf-tossing. Ironic really, as it was a sport he'd invented himself. The centrepiece is the famous Müller organ (1738) – the most photographed organ in the world. An extraordinary gold and red instrument, it boasts an astonishing 5,068 pipes. In its time it has been played by Handel, as well as the ten-year-old Mozart, who squeezed out a few tunes in 1765 while he was on a tour of the Netherlands with his family.

Teylers Museum

Spaarne 16 (023 516 0960/www. teylersmuseum.nl). **Open** 10am-5pm Tue-Sat; noon-5pm Sun. **Admission** €7; €2 6-17s; free under-6s, MK.

Though somewhat in the shadow of the Frans Halsmuseum, the Teylers is a good example of an old-fashioned Age of Enlightenment museum of everything. Founded in 1784, it's the oldest museum in the Netherlands. Fossils and minerals sit beside antique scientific instruments, and there's a superb collection, spanning the 16th to the 19th centuries, of more than 10,000 drawings by Old Masters including Rembrandt, Michelangelo and Raphael. A new wing hosts temporary art and science exhibitions.

Getting there

By car, Delft is ten kilometres (six miles) west on the A5. Trains from Amsterdam Centraal Station take roughly 15 minutes.

Tourist information

VVV

Stationsplein 1 (0900 616 1600 premium rate/www.vvvzk.nl). **Open** *Oct-Mar* 9.30am-5pm Mon-Fri; 10am-3pm Sat. *Apr-Sept* 9am-5.30pm Mon-Fri; 10am-4pm Sat.

The Hague

Beginning life in the 13th century as a hunting ground for Dutch counts, its full name, 's Gravenhage, means 'the Count's Hedge'. But the Hague (*Den Haag* in Dutch) is not in fact officially a city. In days of yore, the powers that be did not want to offend its more ancient neighbours, Leiden and Utrecht, and so never granted the Hague a status beyond that of a mere town. Nevertheless, it is the nation's hub of power and a centre for international justice.

Sights & museums

Binnenhof

Binnenhof 8A (070 364 6144/www. binnenhofbezoek.nl). **Open** 10am-4pm Mon-Sat. **Admission** €6-8; €1 students, under-13s.
The Hague's history begins right here, where, in 1248, William II built a castle. Now parliament buildings occupy the site, and every September Queen Beatrix arrives in a golden coach for the state opening of parliament. Tours are organised daily around the Knights' Hall, where the ceremony takes place.

Escher in Het Paleis

Lange Voorhout 74 (070 427 7730/ www.escherinhetpaleis.nl). **Open** 11am-5pm Tue-Sun. **Admission** €7.50; €5 7-15s; free under-7s.
The Gemeentemuseum's new sister museum, Escher in het Paleis, is filled with further examples of the artist's mind-melting work.

Gemeentemuseum Den Haag

Stadhouderslaan 41 (070 338 1111/ www.gemeentemuseum.nl). **Open** 11am-5pm Tue-Sun. **Admission** €8.50; €6.50 seniors; free under-18s; MK.
The star of this gallery is Piet Mondrian's *Victory Boogie Woogie*, which sold for €36 million in 1998. The museum also holds the world's largest collection of Mondrians, plus several pieces by MC Escher – not to mention one of the ever best fashion collections. Event highlights 100% Make up (until 12 Oct 2008).

Madurodam

George Maduroplein 1 (070 416 2400/www.madurodam.nl). **Open** Jan-Mar, Sept-Dec 9am-6pm daily. *April-June* 9am-8pm daily. *July, Aug* 9am-11pm daily. **Admission** €13.75; €12.75 over-65s; €9.75 3-11s; free under-3s.

An insanely detailed miniature city that dishes up every Dutch cliché in the book: windmills turn, ships sail and trains speed around on the world's largest model railway. If you visit on a summer's evening, when the models are lit from within by 50,000 miniature lamps, be prepared for your ironic appreciation to evaporate completely and be replaced by unalloyed, child-like wonder.
Event highlights Sesamstraat in Madurodam (Until 26 Oct 2008).

Mauritshuis

Korte Vijverberg 8 (070 302 3456/ www.mauritshuis.nl). **Open** Jan-Mar, Sept-Dec 10am-5pm Tue-Sat; 11am-5pm Sun. April-Aug 10am-5pm Mon-Sat; 11am-5pm Sun. **Admission** €9.50 incl audio tour; €4.75 seniors; free under-18s, MK.
Once a home for local counts, like much of the Hague, the Mauritshuis is now open to the public and houses one of the most famous art collections in the world, boasting works by Rubens, Rembrandt and Vermeer.
Event highlights Jacob van Ruisdael in Bentheim (Feb-May 2009). Philips Wouwerman (Nov 2009-Feb 2010).

Panorama Mesdag

Zeestraat 65 (070 364 4544/www. mesdag.nl). **Open** 10am-5pm Mon-Sat; noon-5pm Sun. **Admission** €5; €4 over-65s; €2.50 3-13s; free under-3s.
This building houses the largest painting in the country, measuring 120m (400ft) in circumference, from which the museum takes its name. Painted by Hendrik Willem Mesdag (and with the assistance of the great Amsterdam painter George Hendrik Breitner, then still a student) it's a view of the landscape of Scheveningen, which visitors examine from an observation platform. The museum also displays works from the Hague (with mainly seascapes by Roelof and Mauve) and Barbizon (peasant life and landscape by the likes of Alma-Tadema) Schools.

Traditional attractions: windmills, tulips and clogs

These perennial Dutch clichés beguile most visitors, no matter how cool they may think they are. And rightly so. They're part of the Netherlands' DNA: you can stroll into a gallery anywhere in the world and see a Van Gogh, but there aren't many places where you can sip beer by a windmill.

Clogs make groovy wall-decorations and are even seen on feet: mostly workmen's (they're EU-recognised safety shoes), kids' and occasionally those of hicks from the sticks. The improbably fascinating **Klompenmakerij De Zaanse Schans** (Kraaienest 4, Zaandam, 075 617 7121, www.zaanseschans.nl) is a museum detailing the shoe's unique history and symbolism.

Tulips, meanwhile, are ubiquitous, and play a crucial role in the economy. The most famous place to buy them is Amsterdam's **floating flower market** (p95). It's less dazzling than it sounds, but still pretty. For real action, head to Aalsmeer's **flower auction** (Legmeerdijk 313, 0297 392185, www.vba-aalsmeer.nl), which shifts 19 million blooms daily.

Eight windmills remain to this day in Amsterdam; most famous is **De Gooyer** (Funenkade 5), abutting the award-winning brewery 't IJ. There are also photogenic examples on Haarlemmerweg: **De 1200 Roe** (No.701) was built in 1632, while **De Bloem** (No.465) is a mere whippersnapper dating from 1878. Both were in use until the 1950s. Grab a chance to see the improbably urban **De Otter** (Gillisvan Ledenberchstraat 78) in Westerpark while you can. Its future is being wrangled over by the highest court in the land, which is currently deciding whether it should be moved to a place where wind can actually get to it.

Getting there

By car, the Hague is 50 kilometres (31 miles) south-west of Amsterdam on the A4, then the A44. Trains from Amsterdam Centraal Station to Den Haag station take 50 minutes; you may need to change at Leiden.

Tourist information

VVV

Hofweg 1, outside Centraal Station (0900 340 3505 premium rate/www. denhaag.com). **Open** 10am-6pm Mon-Fri; 10am-5pm Sat; noon-5pm Sun.

Leiden

Canal-laced Leiden derives a good deal of its charm from the fact that it is home to the Netherlands' oldest university. It was founded here in 1575 and boasts such notable alumni as René Descartes, sixth president of the US John Quincy Adams and many a Dutch royal. The old town teems with students, bikes and bars, has the highest concentration of historic monuments of anywhere in the country, and is ideal for a charming weekend away from Amsterdam.

Sights & museums

Hortus Botanicus Leiden

Rapenburg 73 (071 527 7249/www. hortusleiden.nl). **Open** *Apr-Oct* 10am-6pm daily. *Nov-Feb* 10am-4pm Mon-Fri, Sun. *Mar* 10am-4pm daily. **Admission** €5; €3 seniors; €2.50 4-12s; free under 4s, MK.
Over 6,000 species of flora are represented here at one of the world's oldest botanical gardens, including descendants of the country's first tulips.

Molenmuseum de Valk

2e Binnenvestgracht 1 (071 516 5353/ http://home.wanadoo.nl/molenmuseum). **Open** 10am-5pm Tue-Sat; 1-5pm Sun. **Admission** €3; €1.80 seniors, 6-15s, concessions; free under-6s, MK.

If Dutch clichés are what you came here to see, head straight to the 'Falcon Windmill Museum', an erstwhile mill where you can see the old living quarters, machinery and a picturesque view over Leiden. (A better panorama, though, can be had from the top of the Burcht, a 12th-century fort on an ancient artificial mound in the centre.)

Naturalis

Darwinweg (071 568 7600/www. naturalis.nl). **Open** 10am-5pm Tue-Fri; noon-5pm Sat, Sun. **Admission** €9; €6 13-17s; €5 4-12s; free under-3s; MK.
There are a staggering ten million fossils, minerals and assorted stuffed animals at this natural history museum.

Rijksmuseum van Oudheden

Rapenburg 28 (071 516 3163/www. rmo.nl). **Open** 10am-5pm Tue-Fri; noon-5pm Sat, Sun. **Admission** €8.50; €5.50 4-17s; €7.50 seniors; free under-4s, MK.
Perhaps Leiden's most noteworthy museum, this houses the largest collection of archaeological artefacts in the Netherlands. Of particular interest are the unique display of Egyptian mummies, and an exhibition of bog finds.

Rijksmuseum voor Volkenkunde

Steenstraat 1 (071 516 8800/www. rmv.nl). **Open** 10am-5pm Tue-Sun. **Admission** €7.50; €4 reductions; MK.
The National Museum of Ethnology showcases cultures of Africa, Oceania, Asia, the Americas and the Arctic.

Stedelijk Museum de Lakenhal

Oude Singel 28-32 (071 516 5360/ www.lakenhal.nl). **Open** 10am-5pm Tue-Fri; noon-5pm Sat, Sun. **Admission** €4; €2.50 seniors; free under-18s, MK.
In the Golden Age of the late 16th and 17th centuries, Leiden grew fat on textiles. It also spawned three great painters: Rembrandt van Rijn, Jan van Goyen and Jan Steen. Although few works by these masters remain in Leiden today, the Lakenhal Municipal

Rotterdam

Museum does have a Rembrandt, plus works by other Old Masters and collections of pewter, tiles, silver and glass.

Getting there

By car, Leiden is 40 kilometres (24 miles) south-west of Amsterdam on the A4. Trains from Amsterdam Centraal Station take 35 minutes.

Tourist information

VVV

Stationsweg 2D (071 516 1211/www. vvvleiden.nl). Open *Jan-Mar, Sept-Dec* 11am-5.30pm Mon; 9.30am-5.30pm Tue-Fri; 10am-4.30pm Sat. *Apr-Aug* 11am-5.30pm Mon; 9.30am-5.30pm Tue-Fri; 10am-4.30pm Sat; 11am-3pm Sun.

Rotterdam

The antithesis of Amsterdam both visually and in vibe, this port city – its nickname is the Haventstad or 'harbour city' – brings a bit of urban grit to the Dutch landscape. Almost completely flattened during World War II, it has blossomed into a concrete-and-glass jungle,

and what it lacks in charm it makes up for with creativity and innovation. In fact, the city remains in an almost continuous state of regeneration:a fine example of this is Rotterdam Centraal Station, currently being rebuilt. It may mean your entry point into the city is a building site, but the changes promise to be breathtaking – and well worth the long wait – when the station finally opens in 2010.

Sights & museums

Euromast

Parkhaven 20 (010 436 4811/www. euromast.nl). Open *Apr-Sept* 9.30am-11pm daily. *Oct-Mar* 10am-11pm daily. Admission €8.30; €5.40 4-11s; free under-4s.

A bird's-eye view of the whole city and its docklands – and way beyond – can be had from the nearby Euromast, if you can handle the precipitous height of 185m (607ft). Some 100m up there's a café-restaurant and even two hotel suites. There are also three rather vertiginous thrills: Euroscoop is a rotating lift, and the foolhardy can abseil or take a deathslide from 100m.

Euromast p147

AMSTERDAM BY AREA

Kunsthal

Westzeedijk 341 (010 440 0301/ www.kunsthal.nl). **Open** 10am-5pm Tue-Sat; 11am-5pm Sun. **Admission** €8.50; €8 seniors; €5 students; €2 6-18s; free under-6s.
Designed by Rem Koolhaas's locally based OMA bureau, the Kunsthal offers more than 3,000 sq m of art, design and photography, and also features regular travelling exhibitions.

Museum Boijmans van Beuningen

Museumpark 18-20 (010 441 9400/ www.boijmans.rotterdam.nl). **Open** 11am-5pm Tue-Sun. **Admission** €9; €4.50 students; free under-18s; free on Wed, MK.
The city's principal art museum is home to a quite magnificent collection of both traditional and contemporary art, including works by such unsurpassed masters as Bruegel, Van Eyck and Rembrandt.

Netherlands Architecture Institute

Museumpark 25 (010 440 1200/ www.nai.nl). **Open** 10am-5pm Tue-Sat; 11am-5pm Sun. **Admission** €8; €5 seniors, students, 12-18s; €1 4-12s; free under-4s, MK.
Favourite city son and architectural wizard Rem Koolhaas designed Rotterdam's cultural heart, the Museumpark, where you'll find outdoor sculptures and five museums. This one, which opened in 1993, gives an overview of the history and development of architecture, with particular emphasis on the city of Rotterdam itself. It also hosts regular temporary exhibitions on architecture-related subjects and has an extensive archive that will be of interest to experts.

Getting there

By car, Rotterdam is 73 kilometres (45 miles) south of Amsterdam on firstly the A4, and then the A13. Direct trains from Centraal Station in Amsterdam take roughly one hour.

Historical Museum Rotterdam

Korte Hoogstraat 31 (010 217 6767/ www.hmr.rotterdam.nl). **Open** 11am-5pm Tue-Sun. **Admission** €3; €1.50 seniors; free under-16s.
Includes the Dubbelde Palmboom ('Double Palm Tree'), housed in an old granary in Delfshaven and exploring life in the Meuse delta from 8000 BC to the present, and Het Schielandshuis, a 17th-century mansion, another of few buildings spared in the bombing.

Kijk-Kubus

Overblaak 70 (010 414 2285/www. cubehouse.nl). **Open** 11am-5pm daily. **Admission** €2.50; €2 students, seniors; €1.50 4-12s; free under-4s.
Rotterdam's Oude Haven (Old Harbour) is now a work of imaginative modernism, the pinnacle of which is Piet Blom's witty yellow cubic houses. Built in the 1970s, Kijk-Kubus remains a modernist monument. Some are private houses; one cube is being converted into a hostel, due to open in 2008.

Tourist information

Use-it

Schaatsbaan 41-45 (010 240 9158/ www.use-it.nl). **Open** *Jan-Mar, Sept-Dec* 9am-5pm Tue-Sat. *May-Aug* 9am-6pm Tue-Sun.

A kind of 'young person's VVV', this place offers loads of tips for trips to the city, plus some free lockers to ditch your backpack.

VVV

Coolsingel 5 (0900 403 4065 premium rate/www.rotterdam.info). **Open** 9am-5.30pm Mon-Thur, Sat; 9am-11pm Fri; 10am-5pm Sun.

Utrecht

Utrecht is one of the oldest cities in the Netherlands. And during its Middle Ages salad days, it was the biggest. A religious and political centre for hundreds of years, at one point there were around 40 houses of worship in the city, all with towers and spires. From a distance, it must have looked like a holy pincushion. But there's more to Utrecht than just history: the university is one of the largest in the Netherlands – still expanding and employing architects like Rem Koolhaas (who designed the Educatorium) – and the centre bustles with trendy shops and cafés. Happily, too, the Hoog Catharijne, the country's biggest shopping mall, will soon be knocked down. But until then, you'll have to negotiate the labyrinthine layout, following the signs to 'Centrum' to exit Centraal Station.

Utrecht is in an area rich in castles, forests and arboretums. **Slot Zuylen** (Zuylen Castle, Tournooiveld 1, Oud Zuilen, 030 244 0255, www.slotzuylen.com) overlooks exquisite waterfalls and gardens. Check out the concerts and shows in **Kasteel**

Utrecht

Groeneveld's gorgeous gardens (Groeneveld Castle, Groeneveld 2, Baarn, 035 542 0446, www.kasteelgroeneveld.nl), to the north-east of Utrecht. Take a stroll in the **Arboretum von Gimborn** (Vossensteinsesteeg 8, 030 253 1826/www.bio.uu.nl/bottuinen) in Doorne, then pop over to **Kasteel Huis Doorn** (Doorn Castle, Langbroekerweg 10, 034 342 1020, www.huisdoorn.nl). This will answer a question that's probably been puzzling you for ages: what happened to the Kaiser after World War I? Wilhelm II lived here in exile for 20 years before eventually passing away in 1941.

Sights & museums

Centraal Museum

Nicolaaskerkhof 10 (030 236 2362/ www.centraalmuseum.nl). **Open** 11am-5pm Tue-Sun. **Admission** €8; €6 seniors, 13-17s; €2 under 12s, MK.

Domtoren

The St Catharine Convent Museum is located in a beautiful late-medieval building. Mainly dedicated to Dutch religious history, it also has a great collection of paintings by Old Masters, including Rembrandt.

Nationaal Museum van Speelklok tot Pierement

Steenweg 6 (030 231 2789/www. museumspeelklok.nl). **Open** 10am-5pm Tue-Sun. **Admission** €8; €7 seniors; €4.50 4-12s; free under-4s; MK. Though it sounds as if it's only for hurdy-gurdy fanciers and organ grinders, this museum, the world's biggest collection of automated musical instruments, is actually great fun, especially the regular guided tours that bring the street organs, cuckoo clocks and rabbits in hats to life for visitors of all ages.

Rietveld-Schröderhuis

Prins Hendriklaan 50 (030 236 2310/ www.rietveldschroderhuis.nl). Tour bus from Centraal Museum, leaving Thur-Sun hourly between 11.45am and 2.45pm. **Open** 11am-5pm Thur-Sun. **Admission** €16; €14 12-18s, over-65s; €8 under-12s.
Another Utrecht-born celebrity in the Centraal Museum's collection is De Stijl architect and designer Gerrit Rietveld, best known for his rectangular chairs and houses. The Rietveld-Schröderhuis, on the outskirts of the city centre, can be reached on the Centraal Museum's tour bus.

A varied collection, from Van Goghs to modern art and fashion. A wing is dedicated to Miffy creator Dick Bruna, who was born and lives in the town.

Domtoren

Domplein (030 236 0010/www. domtoren.nl). **Open** noon-6pm Mon; 10am-6pm Tue-Fri; 10am-5pm Sat, Sun. **Admission** €7.50; €4.50 concessions; free under-4s.
At over 112m (367ft), the cathedral tower is the highest in the country. The panorama is worth 465 steps: vistas stretch 40km (25 miles) to Amsterdam. The neighbouring space was once occupied by a huge church, destroyed by a tornado in 1674. Inside the Domkerk you'll see before and after sketches.

Museum Catharijneconvent

Lange Nieuwstraat 38 (030 231 3835/ www.catharijneconvent.nl). **Open** 10am-5pm Tue-Fri; 11am-5pm Sat, Sun. **Admission** €8.50; €7.50 seniors; €4.50 6-17s; free under-6s.

Getting there

Utrecht is 40 kilometres (25 miles) south-east of Amsterdam. Direct trains from Amsterdam Centraal Station take half an hour.

Tourist information

VVV

Domplein 9 (0900 128 8732 premium rate/www.utrechtyourway.nl). **Open** noon-6pm Mon; 10am-6pm Tue-Wed, Fri; 10am-8pm Thur; 10am-5pm Sat; noon-5pm Sun.

Essentials

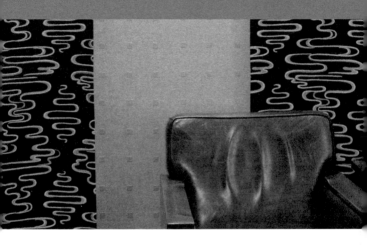

Grand Hotel
Krasnapolsky p155

Hotels

Tiny town that it is, Amsterdam
has always battled against a
shortage of hotels. But in the next
couple of years, there will finally
be a veritable explosion of new
accommodation – of mostly the
large and seriously high-class kind
– as the building frenzy finally
reaches completion stage. In
keeping with the city's push to
redevelop the area around the
waters of the IJ, this has been –
and will be for some time yet – the
main focus of the boom. A highly
handsome branch of the Swiss
Mövenpick chain recently opened
next door to the Muziekgebouw;
just a few short minutes' walk
away over on Oosterdokseiland,
near the station, digging has
already begun on what will be the
biggest (550 rooms) hotel in town,
at a cost of €150 million. Operated
by the UK's City Inn chain, it will
open in 2010.

Across the road, the Grand
Hotel Amrâth Amsterdam (see
box p158) opened in late 2007,
converting one of the city's
landmarks, the Scheepvaarthuis,
into an extremely smart hotel.

Lower down the budget scale
it's business as usual, with fewer
facilities, smaller rooms, compact
bathrooms (showers are standard;
baths a luxury, even at the top end)
and vertiginous stairwells making
things awkward for disabled
travellers. This is a reflection of a
lack of accommodation and land in
a country conjured out of the sea.

Nor is Amsterdam, hotel-wise
at least, the place to come for a
cheap weekend away – and prices
continue to creep up. For some
reason, boutique hotels haven't

really caught on here; we've listed the finest of the few there are below. But Stayokay Amsterdam Zeeburg hostel was revamped in 2007 to a point that it now combines reasonable prices with almost designer-hotel pretensions.

Perhaps the best way to experience a local version of the phenomenon is to stay in a B&B. Far from the dowdy, seaside images the term usually conjures up, B&Bs are often designed to their stylish owners' very high specifications, but be warned: bed-and-breakfasting is seldom a budget option.

Hotels cluster around particular areas of Amsterdam: the Museum District and the Canals have plenty, while the Pijp and Jordaan, alas, contain few. A general rule of thumb should be to avoid – with a couple of exceptions – hotels near the station or Red Light District.

Money matters

Credit card payment isn't always accepted in this quaint old city, particularly in smaller places, so check first. A rate may or may not include the city tax of five per cent, which could be added on to your final bill. Before booking, it's always worth checking for special deals on hotels' own websites, or on more commercial hotel websites – www.bookings.nl (also in English) is a good place to start.

The Old Centre

Amstel Botel

NDSM Werf Pier 3 (626 4247/ www.amstelbotel.nl). Ferry. €
Convenient for Centraal Station, this is good, clean accommodation with a few frills like in-house movies. The bar (9am-1am) has pinball, pool and a juke-box. Housed in a large boat, it's recently changed locations to the other side of the water at NDSM.

ESSENTIALS

Wanted.
Jumpers, coats and people with their knickers in a twist.

From the people who feel moved to bring us their old books and CDs, to the people fed up to the back teeth with our politicians' track record on climate change, Oxfam supporters have one thing in common. They're passionate. If you've got a little fire in your belly, we'd love to hear from you. Visit us at **oxfam.org.uk**

Be Humankind **Oxfam**

Barbizon Palace

Prins Hendrikkade 59-72 (556 4564/ www.nh-hotels.com). Tram 1, 2, 4, 5, 9, 13, 16, 17, 24, 25, 26. €€€

This flash branch of the reliable home-grown NH chain is opposite Centraal Station, and so ideal if you're hopping off the train with luggage. Public areas are decked out in sleek monochrome, making the rooms themselves (in bland hotel beige) a bit disappointing. That said, facilities include conference rooms in a 15th-century chapel and a Michelin-starred restaurant.

Flying Pig Downtown

Nieuwendijk 100 (420 6822/group bookings 421 0583/www.flyingpig. nl). Tram 1, 2, 3, 5, 13, 17. €

Not so much a hostel, more a way of life, and a stalwart of the Inter-railing scene. Young (it doesn't accept guests over 40 or under 18) backpackers flock here from around the world: they organise walking tours and in-line skating for free, and plus regular parties and cheap beer. There are also branches near to the Vondelpark and on the beach at Noordwijk-aan-Zee; the latter is open all year but comes into its own in the summer, when watersports, beach activities and barbecues are the order of the day.

Grand Hotel Krasnapolsky

Dam 9 (554 9111/www.nh-hotels.com). Tram 1, 2, 4, 5, 9, 13, 16, 17, 24, 25, 26. €€€€

Bang in the centre of Amsterdam, right opposite the Royal Palace, facilities here are really excellent: restaurants, bars, a ballroom, beauty salon and a winter garden for a relaxing weekend brunch. Options range from suites to compact rooms at the back. Less expensive rooms lack baths, but come with invigorating multi-head showers.

Greenhouse Effect

Warmoesstraat 55 (624 4974/ www.greenhouse-effect.nl). Tram 4, 9, 17, 24, 25. €

If you're planning to disappear in a cloud of cannabis smoke, this place above a coffee shop (p58) is where to

Amstel p153

rest your addled head. Some rooms feature shared facilities, several are kitted out in trippy styles and others are just plain, old-fashioned nice with good canal views. Breakfast is served until midday and the attached bar has an all-day happy hour and DJ nights.

Hotel des Arts

Rokin 154-156 (620 1558/www. hoteldesarts.nl). Tram 4, 9, 14, 16, 24, 25. €€

A snug hotel exuding a touch of faded glamour, rooms here tend to be decorated with clunky, polished period furniture and ornate chandeliers – although some of them are also a little dark. Most are very spacious, however, and are geared towards groups and families. Near the main shopping street, with most sights within easy walking distance.

Hotel de l'Europe

Nieuwe Doelenstraat 2-8 (531 1777/ www.leurope.nl). Tram 4, 9, 16, 24, 25. €€€€

Another landmark hotel with views across the Amstel, this is the place for indulgent splurges or honeymoon hide-aways: think marble bathrooms and Bulgari toiletries. The bridal suite has a four-poster bed and a two-person jacuzzi in the room; it's also one of the few hotels in Amsterdam to boast a swimming pool, and there's a highly rated restaurant, Excelsior.

Ibis Amsterdam Centre

Stationsplein 49 (638 9999/www. ibishotel.com). Tram 1, 2, 5, 9, 13, 17, 24, 25. 26. **€€**

If you're arriving late or leaving first thing, this place is ideal. Right next to Centraal Station, there's 24-hour take-away food (pizzas and smoothies) and very early (4am onwards) breakfast. There's nothing fancy – just the reliable Ibis formula of basic but comfortable rooms and reasonable facilities.

Nova

Nieuwezijds Voorburgwal 276 (623 0066/www.novahotel.nl). Tram 1, 2, 5. **€€**

The five charming townhouses that make up Nova are comfortable, plainly furnished (yet good-looking in an IKEA sort of way), and smell fresh as daisies since the place went totally no-smoking in February 2007. The hotel is also handily located for the Nieuwezijds nightlife as well as the main cultural sights.

Renaissance Amsterdam

Kattengat 1 (621 2223/www.marriott. com). Tram 1, 2, 4, 5, 9, 13, 16, 17, 24, 25, 26. **€€€**

An upmarket option for exploring the bohemian charms of the Harlemmerstraat and Jordaan, this 400-roomed place compensates for flowery decor with luxuries like in-house movies, interactive videos and DVDs, and even PlayStations, making it a good bet for flush families with recalcitrant kids. There's also a babysitting service. In 2008, the rooms and restaurant were renovated, an executive lobby was added and the hotel in general spruced up.

Residence Le Coin

Nieuwe Doelenstraat 5 (524 6800/ www.lecoin.nl). Tram 4, 9, 16, 24, 25. **€€**

On a quiet, café-lined street between the Old Centre and the central shopping district, this medium-sized hotel arranged across seven buildings has spacious, very stylish rooms in muted colours. Drenched in light thanks to big windows, furnishings are a classy mix of old and new, with designer chairs and lots of shiny wood. The attic rooms are particularly full of character, and many rooms come with kitchenettes, making this a good bet for families.

RHO Hotel

Nes 5-23 (620 7371/www.rhohotel.nl). Tram 1, 2, 4, 5, 9, 13, 16, 17, 24, 25, 26. **€€**

If your budget doesn't stretch as far as the swankier and more expensive hotels on and around Dam square, this one matches on location, if not on interior design or style. On a backstreet bustling with bars, restaurants and theatres, the art deco lobby harks back to the days when it was a gold merchant's, although the rooms themselves are surprisingly plain.

Sofitel the Grand Amsterdam

Oudezijds Voorburgwal 197 (555 3111/www.thegrand.nl). Tram 4, 9, 16, 25. **€€€€**

Centuries of history in a luxurious courtyard hotel. Rooms are spacious and airy thanks to big windows; bathrooms are embellished with Roger & Gallet smellies; and the suites range from junior to royal. Not exactly a bargain getaway destination, but there are nevertheless deals like the appropriately named Dream Package, which includes champagne, dinner and use of the spa. Indulgent Sunday brunch (€75) in the Council Chamber is open to non-guests also.

Swissotel

Damrak 96 (522 3000/www. amsterdam.swissotel.com). Tram 1, 2, 4, 5, 9, 13, 16, 17, 24, 25, 26. **€€€**

ESSENTIALS

Shipshape at the Amrâth

The lovely new **Grand Hotel Amrâth Amsterdam** nods handsomely to Dutch seafaring supremacy (Cornelis Houtman and Peter de Keyser sailed from this spot to the East Indies in 1595), and to the birth of an architectural movement.

Considered to be the first true example of Amsterdam School architecture, the Scheepvaarthuis ('Maritime House'), which houses the hotel, was built between 1913 and 1916 by Johan van der Mey. Also involved were two other leading lights of Dutch modernism: Piet Kramer and Michel de Klerk. The carvings that cover the façade – of fish, animals and the busts of Dutch explorers – were the first commission for Hildo Krop, later the official city sculptor.

Upon originally opening, the Scheepvaarthuis was home to several shipping offices, a function it fulfilled for the best part of the 20th century – the last of its old tenants, the KNSM, finally set sail from the building in 1981. After that, it fulfilled a rather more prosaic role as offices for public transport and the city's parking services.

Happily, a brand new chapter in the Scheepvaarthuis's history is unfolding, and the opening of the Amrâth has seen all those same gloriously fine details restored to glowing health. Now the building consists of 137 rooms and 26 suites – one of which is three storeys high, set in the imposing tower at the front. In addition to the usual embellishments, the Amrâth subscribes to that growing deluxe trend of a free minibar. It also joins the exclusive club of Amsterdam hotels boasting pools.

Grand Hotel Amrâth Amsterdam

Prins Hendrikkade 108-114 (552 0000/www.amrathamsterdam.nl). Tram 1, 2, 5, 9, 13, 17, 24. €€€

One of the best-looking of the big international chains, this place is geared towards the business market, but it's still a good destination for pleasure seekers. It's next to Dam square and near department store De Bijenkorf, and all rooms have big beds and on-demand films and music. Pricier rooms come with espresso machines and suites overlook Dam square.

Victoria

Damrak 1-5 (623 4255/www.parkplaza. com/amsterdamnl_victoria). Tram 1, 2, 4, 5, 9, 13, 16, 17, 24, 25. €€
A stalwart of the hotel scene, the public areas of this 300-roomed hotel opposite Centraal Station look very dapper indeed, decked out in browns, creams and reds. Rooms are a good size, and come with all the trappings. A big plus is the excellent health club and pool, which are open to non-guests, for a fee.

Winston Hotel

Warmoestraat 129 (623 1380/ www.winston.nl). Tram 4, 9, 14, 16, 24, 25. €
The legendary Winston has a youthful, party-loving atmosphere and rooms decorated in eccentric, eclectic style, ranging from monochrome to kinky S&M den decor. Cheaper dormbeds are available, but are much less fun. There's also a bar and club (p67).

Western Canal Belt

Ambassade Hotel

Herengracht 341 (555 0222/www. ambassade-hotel.nl). Tram 1, 2, 5. €€€
Staff in this literary hotel are discreet and attentive, and rooms – from single to suite to apartment – are decorated in Louis Quatorze style. There's also a library, the many shelves of which are loaded with signed tomes by illustrious previous guests, which residents are free to peruse at their leisure.

Amsterdam Wiechmann

Prinsengracht 328-332 (626 3321/www.hotelwiechmann.nl). Tram 1, 2, 5, 7, 17. €€

From a suit of armour in reception to teapots and toasters in the breakfast room, retro touches adorn this long-established Jordaan hotel. Decor errs to the chintzy, but it's cosy nevertheless, and costlier rooms look on to the canal.

Belga

Hartenstraat 8 (624 9080/www. hotelbelga.nl). Tram 1, 2, 5. €€
Both family friendly and affordable, which is rare in Amsterdam. In contrast to the stealth wealth of the surroundings, rooms are functional but clean, and the breakfast room is a kitsch, colourful delight. There is a resident cat, so avoid if allergic.

Dylan

Keizersgracht 384 (530 2010/www. dylanamsterdam.com). Tram 1, 2, 5. €€€€
Outrageous elegance is the key in the Dylan's raspberry, turmeric or coal rooms, detail-obsessed bar and restaurant boasting chef Dennis Kuipers's French-inspired menu. Everything, from the alignment of the cushions to the service , is well thought out.

Flying Pig p155

Winston p159

Estherea

Singel 303-309 (624 5146/www. estherea.nl). Tram 1, 2, 5. €€€

Spread over several elegant houses at the spectacular epicentre of the canals, this hotel has been run by the same family for decades. The emphasis is on understated luxury: rooms are swathed in Fortuny-style fabrics and have DVD players (on request) and marble bathrooms, ensuring that once you're in, you won't want to stray back out of your front door. For those hot summer days, management has recently added air-conditioning to the entire building.

't Hotel

Leliegracht 18 (422 2741/www.thotel. nl). Tram 1, 2, 5, 13, 17. €€

A stylish bolthole on a beautiful canal in the Jordaan, this prosaically named place is fitted throughout in 1920s-inspired style. Bauhaus prints adorn the walls, the colour scheme is muted and the armchairs are design classics. All rooms have great views on to the canal or the rear garden and all are spacious. Split-level room eight, tucked away up in the eaves of the building, is especially full of character.

Hotel Brouwer

Singel 83 (624 6358/www.hotel brouwer.nl). Tram 1, 2, 5. 16, 24. €

These eight neat, en suite rooms all look on to the Singel canal, but it's not the place for extras. If you want well-priced accommodation in a longstanding family hotel, though, you're in for a treat. Unusually for budget class, there's a lift, plus TVs in the doubles.

Hotel Pulitzer

Prinsengracht 315-331 (523 5235/ www.pulitzer.nl). Tram 13, 14, 17. €€€€

Sprawling across 25 canal houses, rooms are big and stylish in this glamorous hotel. There's a lovely garden and, in August, the classical music Grachtenfestival takes place in and around the grounds, making it an excellent choice for music fans.

Singel Hotel

Singel 13-17 (626 3108/www. singelhotel.nl). Tram 1, 2, 5. €

This medium-sized, 32-roomed place is ideally located for canal and Jordaan hikes, and for arrival and departure by train (it's a five-minute walk from

Centraal Station). Inside its solid 17th-century walls, rooms are plain and furnished in a modern, basic style; they are generally clean and tidy, and all ensuite. Front-facing rooms can be noisy.

Toren
Keizersgracht 164 (622 6352/www. *hoteltoren.nl). Tram 13, 14, 17.* **€€€**
This building has been a Golden Age mansion, a prime minister's home, a university and even a hiding place for persecuted Jews during World War II. Now it's a family-run hotel and comes with all the usual trappings: opulent fabrics, grand public rooms and attentive staff. Standards are a bit of a cramp, but deluxe rooms have jacuzzis, and the bridal suites even come with elegant double whirlpool baths.

Southern Canal Belt

American Hotel
Leidsekade 97 (556 3000/www. *amsterdamamerican.com). Tram 1, 2, 5.* **€€€€**
This dazzling art nouveau monument looks extra spruce now that a fountain has been added to its terrace, and its public areas – like the buttressed in-house Café Americain – are all eye-pleasing. Rooms (not including suites) are pretty cramped, although they do enjoy views of the canal or square below. The decor is smart-but-bland hotel standard.

Amsterdam Marriott Hotel
Stadhouderskade 12 (607 5555/www. *marriott.com). Tram 1, 2, 5.* **€€€€**
Set right next to the lovely Vondelpark, the Marriott was given an overhaul last year, so it's goodbye to the dowdy green and brown gentleman's club styling and hello to soothing yellows and modern furnishings. All 392 rooms now come equipped with high-thread-count linen and luxury duvets. Bathrooms have gone similarly upmarket, with cherry wood and granite surfaces and cascade showerheads. The restaurant, Quoy, is something of a well-kept secret.

Banks Mansion
Herengracht 519-525 (420 0055/www. *banksmansion.nl). Tram 16, 24, 25.* **€€€**
Once you check into this grand hotel in a former bank building, everything is for free – yep, drinks in the lounge, movies in your room, and even the minibar. This classy form of an all-inclusive holiday also involves a pillow menu, cascade showerheads, plasma TVs and DVD players. Needless to say it's hardly bargain basement stuff, but look out for deals on the website.

Bridge Hotel
Amstel 107-111 (623 7068/www. *thebridgehotel.nl). Tram 4, 6, 7, 9, 10, 14.* **€€**
Gloriously isolated on the eastern bank of the Amstel, this private hotel in a former stonemason's workshop is just a few minutes from the bright lights of Rembrandtplein, and well situated for the Plantage and Jodenbuurt. Rooms are simple and bright; river views cost more. There are apartments and a studio for stays longer than three days.

Dikker & Thijs Fenice Hotel
Prinsengracht 444 (620 1212/www. *dtfh.nl). Tram 1, 2, 5, 6, 7, 10.* **€€€**
This well-established place is owned by a publisher, so authors often drop in. Set in an 18th-century warehouse near Leidseplein, rooms are plain but smart, while the glamorous penthouse has glass walls for unsurpassed views over the rooftops. At breakfast, guests are bathed in jewel-coloured light from the stained-glass windows.

Hotel 717
Prinsengracht 717 (427 0717/www. *717hotel.nl). Tram 1, 2, 5.* **€€€€**
The epitome of understated glamour, this small, flower-filled place emphasises searching the globe for the best accoutrements: linens from the USA, bespoke blankets from Wales, spring mattresses from London. There is afternoon tea daily and a garden. Guests are the type who shed euros on antiques in the Spiegelkwartier.

The best guides to enjoying London life

(but don't just take our word for it)

'Armed with a tube map and this guide there is no excuse to find yourself in a duff bar again'

Evening Standard

'I'm always asked how I keep up to date with shopping and services in a city as big as London. This guide is the answer'

Red Magazine

'You will never again be stuck for interesting things to do and places to visit in the capital'

Independent on Sunday

Rated 'Best Restaurant Guide'

Sunday Times

TIME OUT GUIDES
WRITTEN BY
LOCAL EXPERTS
timeout.com/shop

Hotel Agora

Singel 462 (627 2200/www. hotelagora.nl). Tram 1, 2, 5. €€
Ideal for botanists stocking up on bulbs, this homely little place is in an 18th-century house on a canal near the floating flower market. What Agora lacks in extras, it more than makes up for with nice touches like conservatory breakfasts and a garden. Rooms are plain but neat and comfortable and all enjoy lovely canal or garden views.

Hotel Leydsche Hof

Leidsegracht 14 (623 2148/www.free webs.com/leydschehof). Tram 1, 2, 5. €
A hidden gem on a genteel canal just minutes from Leidseplein; the Piller family lovingly cares for the seven bright, simply decorated rooms in their charming 17th-century house. All are are done out in dark wood, and the high-ceilinged breakfast chamber boasts a striking marble fireplace.

Hotel de Munck

Achtergracht 3 (623 6283/www. hoteldemunck.com). Tram 4. €€
This higgledy-piggledy place in an old Dutch East India Company captain's house is perched on a secluded little canal near the river. Rooms here are plain and basic (and some are looking rather tired), though they are clean and neat. The breakfast room is a delight, though, with a 1950s jukebox and walls plastered with old album covers.

Hotel Prinsenhof

Prinsengracht 810 (623 1772/www. hotelprinsenhof.com). Tram 4. €
This dinky, ten-room hotel is near the nightlife and foodie Utrechtsestraat and has helpful staff. Rooms themselves (some have canal views) are simple, some share facilities, and they're all clean and tidy. Those physically less able should note that the stairs are very steep.

InterContinental Amstel Amsterdam

Professor Tulpplein 1 (622 6060/ www.intercontinental.com/ams-amstel). Tram 7, 10. €€€€
They don't come much posher than this: if movie stars or royalty are in town, they almost always lay their heads in one of the huge, soundproofed rooms or luxury suites here. Staff are liveried, the restaurant is Michelin-starred (now with chef Roger Rassen), and every service imaginable is present, pool included. If money is no object or it's a once-in-a-lifetime splurge, this is the place for you.

Kamer01

3e Weteringdwarsstraat 44 (625 6627/ www.kamer01.nl). Tram 7, 10, 16, 24, 25. €€€
A stylish, gay-friendly B&B. The Red Room comes with a huge shower (big enough for two – or more), while the Blue Room – with its circular bed and private roof terrace – is sleek and modern, though, with its angled attic ceilings, is not recommended for very tall guests. Both come with iMacs, flat-screen TVs and DVD players. There's a minimum two-night stay.

Marcel van Woerkom

Leidsestraat 87 (622 9834/www. marcelamsterdam.com). Tram 1, 2, 5. €€
Artist Marcel has been letting rooms in his stylish 'creative exchange' since 1970: chances are you'll run into artists or designers admiring the artworks. Despite it being classed as a B&B, you only get the bed, but there are plenty of breakfast choices nearby. Book well in advance.

Mercure Hotel Arthur Frommer

Noorderstraat 46 (622 0328/www. mercure.com). Tram 4, 16, 24, 26. €€€
On a residential street within walking distance of the sights and the local nightlife, this courtyard hotel is in one of the nicest locations in town by far, near Amstelveld and with restaurant-lined Utrechtsestraat also very close at hand. Rooms are spacious and smart, though not overburdened with fancy extras. There's also a bar that's popular with guests and non-guests.

ESSENTIALS

Nicolaas Witsen

Nicolaas Witsenstraat 4 (623 6143/ www.hotelnicolaaswitsen.nl). Tram 4. €€

One of the few hotels to fill the gap between museums and the Pijp, this place, though plain, functional (and a tad overpriced), is well placed for both serious culture vultures and fun-seekers. Ground-floor rooms can get noisy but plusses include free Wi-Fi and a lift. The excellent deli on the corner encourages in-room midnight feasting.

Seven Bridges

Reguliersgracht 31 (623 1329/www. sevenbridgeshotel.nl). Tram 16, 24, 25. €€

The ideal destination for hermits who want a luxury hidey-hole far from the madding crowd, this hotel is also convenient for the museums and trips into the city centre. There are no public spaces, just eight antique-packed rooms. Breakfast is served in bed on Villeroy and Boch crockery. One of Amsterdam's best-kept secrets.

Jodenbuurt, the Plantage & the Oost

Arena

's Gravesandestraat 51 (850 2400/ www.hotelarena.nl). Tram 3, 6, 9, 10, 14. €€

A hotel, restaurant and club in an old orphanage, a ten-minute tram ride from town, it's the one-stop-shop of food, booze and boogie. Standard and larger rooms are a bit boring, but pricier, extra large ones and suites are kitted out by leading local designers.

Eden Lancaster

Plantage Middelaan 48 (535 6888/ www.edenhotelgroup.com). Tram 9, 14. €€

If you're planning on taking the kids to the excellent Artis zoo , then this hotel is just across the road, and its triple and quad rooms are very much aimed at families. Even though it's a little out of the way of the more central sights, the main railway station is a short tram ride or 20-minute walk away, and there are several good cafés in the immediate vicinity.

Hotel Adolesce

Nieuwe Keizersgracht 26 (626 3959/ www.adolesce.nl). Trams 4, 6, 7, 9, 10/Metro Weesperplein. €

You won't get any breakfast at this unfussy place near the Skinny Bridge, but guests can help themselves to drinks, fruit and chocolate in the lounge. Rooms are plain – the attic room is nicest – but it's close to both the Hermitage Museum and Waterlooplein flea market.

Stayokay Amsterdam Zeeburg

Timorplein 21 (551 3190/www. stayokay.com). Trams 7, 10, 14. €

This new branch of the reliable hostel chain in a grand old school building is aimed at families and discerning hostellers. Rooms sleep two to eight; there are no dorms. Designed in warm reds with mosaic floors and sleek furniture, hostelling never looked so good.

The Waterfront & North

Ideaal II

Opposite Levantkade 51 (419 7255/ www.houseboats.nl). Tram 10, 26. €€

An inspired and indulgent option, this converted cargo boat near the up-and-coming cultural quarter sleeps up to five, and comes with two bathrooms, jacuzzi, stainless steel kitchen and decks dedicated to sunbathing and swimming. At night, you'll sleep on (what else?) a waterbed. Overnight stays are possible, but longer ones make more economic sense. Check the website for excellent last-minute deals.

Mövenpick Hotel Amsterdam City Centre

Piet Heinkade 11 (519 1200/www. moevenpick-hotels.com). Tram 25, 26. €€€

A glamorous multi-storey branch of the Swiss chain recently opened on the

Check in to the Lloyd

The idea was simple: to create as much space and freedom as possible. The reinvention of a youth prison into a hotel and 'cultural embassy' – complete with 120 rooms, running the range from one to five stars – took eight long years, the Lloyd Hotel finally opening amid the up-and-coming eastern docklands area in 2004.

But this is no mere designer hotel. MVRDV, the insanely inspired architects who gave the world the unrealised Pig City (a strange skyscraper for pig breeding), have turned a once claustrophobic hell-hole into a bastion of light while respectfully retaining such original elements as stained-glass windows, tiled walls, exposed timbers and jail doors reinvented as linen storage units. Meanwhile, some of the more high-profile names in the Dutch design world – Atelier van Lieshout, Bureau Lakenvelder,

Richard Hutten, Marcel Wanders and Hella Jongerius, for example – took responsibility for the interiors of the rooms themselves.

Many rooms are best described via their bathrooms: some are shared, some fold away, some have strange translucent walls and some only exist as an open shower in the middle of the room. Besides the requisite bar and two restaurants (one 'fast', the other 'slow'), there's almost always something special going on for guests to join in with, be it an artist's party or happenings like 2006's Full Llove Inn, the latter a room in an Opel Kadett atop a four-and-a-half-metre-high pole. In short, expect the unexpected – in the nicest possible way, of course.

Lloyd Hotel
Oostelijke Handelskade 34 (561 3604/www.lloydhotel.com). Tram 10, 26. €€€€€

banks of the IJ. Rooms are decorated in muted modern greys and woods. The more expensive ones include access to the 'executive lounge' and have great views over the water and the city.

The Jordaan

Frederic Rentabike
Brouwersgracht 78 (624 5509/www. frederic.nl). Bus 18, 22. No credit cards. €€
This bike shop also does a nice sideline in renting out six houseboats all around town, from sleek vessels to more homely numbers. Houseboat no.3, on the Prinsengracht, is big, stylish, central and has internet access.

Truelove Antiek & Guesthouse
Prinsenstraat 4 (320 2500/06 248 056 72 mobile after 6pm/www.truelove.be). Tram 1, 2, 5. €€
Above an antiques shop (now the hotel reception), this dinky place is decorated with the odd decoratvie piece from downstairs. The attic room is best, but all come with CD player, TV and kettle. There's also an apartment located on Langestraat.

The Museum Quarter, Vondelpark & the South

Between Art and Kitsch
Ruysdaelkade 75 (679 0485/www. between-art-and-kitsch.com). Tram 16, 24. €
Technically speaking it's between the museums and the Pijp, actually. This B&B has just two rooms: one is decorated in mock art deco with authentic period knick-knacks, the other in faux Baroque, and yes, rooms do live up to the name's promise. On a nice canal, it's great for culture vultures keen to get out there and explore.

Bilderberg Jan Luyken
Jan Luykenstraat 58 (573 0730/www. bilderberg.nl). Tram 2, 5, 10, 12. €€

One of the city's most stylish secrets, this place – complete with spa and a wine bar – is just a skip from the upmarket shops along PC Hooftstraat. Rooms feature designer touches and wall-mounted CD players, and are something of a bargain for a place with these looks and facilities. Check for special packages: the Amsterdam Beauty Arrangement, for example, gets you a cocktail, B&B, and a spa session for under €110 per person.

College Hotel
Roelof Hartstraat 1 (571 1511/www. thecollegehotel.com). Tram 3, 5, 12. €€€
Part of the city's hotel and catering college and thus staffed by students. Boutique styling and some glam touches ensure that prices are far from pocket-money. Some rooms, though lovely, are small; pay top dollar to get oodles of space, though most of the suites have now converted into two or three separate spaces, ideal for families. There's a bar and an ambitious modern Dutch restaurant. Perhaps because of the hotel's educational function, service can be unpredictable.

Hotel V
Victorieplein 42 (662 3233/www. hotelv.nl). Tram 4, 12, 25. €€
Hotel V is a bit of a hike from the sights and the centre, but tram no.4 stops right outside to whisk you into town within ten minutes, and the less mainstream lures of the Pijp are a 15-minute walk away. This boutique B&B-style hotel is ideal for business travellers sick of sterility: it's near the RAI and business areas of Zuid. There's sleek decor in all rooms, but you won't find much in the way of extras. That said, the lounge, with its pebbly fireplace and furry pouffes, looks lovely.

Hotel Vondel
Vondelstraat 28-30 (612 0120/www. hotelvondel.nl). Tram 1, 2, 5, 7, 10. €€€
Another well-hidden gem near the museums and Amsterdam's more upmarket shopping district, this chic

little place is covered with art and boasts a lovely decked garden. Rooms, from small to extra large via a junior and family suite, are designer driven, with Burberry-check blankets, chandeliers and nice swanky bathrooms. Unusually for such a trendy hotel, families are encouraged.

Xaviera Hollander Bed & Breakfast

Stadionweg 17 (673 3934/www. xavierahollander.com). Tram 5, 24. €€
Prudes avert your eyes, since you won't want to stay in the home of the original Happy Hooker. Rooms, upstairs in Xaviera's own banker-belt villa or in a hut at the bottom of her garden, are nice, but guests come here mainly for a truly outrageous anecdote – or several – from the lady herself.

The Pijp

Hotel Okura Amsterdam

Ferdinand Bolstraat 333 (678 7111/ www.okura.nl). Tram 12, 25. €€€€
This multi-storey, multi-tasking, very smart business-class stopover has everything captains of industry need:

a top-floor, top of the range French restaurant, Le Ciel Bleu; a full-size pool and health club; and sushi bars. Rooms are done up in suitably masculine style and range from small standards to the huge (and hugely expensive) presidential suite on the 21st floor.

Hotel Savoy

Ferdinand Bolstraat 194 (644 7445/ www.savoyhotel.nl). Tram 3, 12, 16, 24, 25. €€€
One of a limited number of accommodation options in the area, this hotel in an imposing red-brick Amsterdam School building came under new ownership in 2006. It has been restyled as a swanky concept hotel, which should suit the Pijp right down to the ground.

Van Ostade Bicycle Hotel

Van Ostadestraat 123 (679 3452/ www.bicyclehotel.com). Tram 12, 16, 24, 25. €
This staging post for pedal-pushers was one of the first places to stay in the Pijp. Staff can suggest trips and rent out bikes. Rooms are comfy and there are loads of excellent places nearby to refuel for the day ahead or wind down after a long, hard ride around town.

Banks Mansion p161

Getting Around

Arriving & leaving

By air

Schiphol Airport

0900 0141 premium rate/
www.schiphol.nl
Amsterdam's airport is 18
kilometres (11 miles) south-west
of the city. There's only one
terminal building, and within that
four departure and arrival halls.

Connexxion Airport Hotel Shuttle

Connexxion counter, Section A7,
Arrivals, Schiphol Airport (038 339
4741/www.airporthotelshuttle.nl).
This bus from Schiphol to
Amsterdam departs every 30
minutes between 6am and 9pm.
Anyone who buys a ticket (€12
single) can use it, not just hotel
guests. Drop-off points are the
100-odd allied hotels; see the
website for schedules, destination
hotels and their booking service.

Airport trains

Trains leave approximately every
ten minutes between 5am and
midnight (after which they are
hourly), at 11, 18, 31, 41 and 48
minutes past the hour, and on
the hour. The journey to Centraal
Station takes about 20 minutes.
Buy your ticket (€3.60 single, €6.10
return) before you board, or you're
highly likely to incur a €35 fine.

By taxi

A fixed fare from the airport to the
south and west of the city is about
€25, and to the city centre is about
€35. Bear in mind that there are
always plenty of licensed taxis
beside the main exit.

By bus

Long-distance international
Eurolines coaches (560 8788/
www.eurolines.nl) stop at Amstel
station, Julianaplein 5, in the south-
east of the city, connected to
Centraal Station by Metro.

By train

A range of national trains operated
by NS (www.ns.nl), as well as
international services, stop at
Centraal Station in the city centre.

In town

Getting around Amsterdam is very
easy: there are efficient, cheap and
integrated trams, metros and buses,
and in the centre most places can
be got to on foot. Locals tend to
get around by bike, and there are
also boats and water taxis. Public
transport provision for those with
disabilities, however, is dire.

    The best way to travel is by tram,
with a network of routes through
the centre (buses and the Metro are
more for outlying suburbs).

GVB

Stationsplein CS, Old Centre: New Side
(0900 8011 premium rate/www.gvb.nl/
english). Tram 1, 2, 4, 5, 9, 13, 16, 17,
24, 25, 26. **Open** *Phone enquiries* 8am-
10pm daily. *In person* 7am-9pm Mon-
Fri; 10am-6pm Sat, Sun.
The GVB runs Amsterdam's Metro,
bus and tram services, and can also
provide detailed information and
departure and arrival times on all
of them, as well as sell tickets.

Fares & tickets

A *strippenkaart* (strip ticket)
system operates across trams,
buses and metros: prices begin at
€1.60 for a strip of two units (one

journey in one zone) bought on the tram/bus, or purchased from machines for the Metro. Cheaper are 15-unit (€6.90) or 45-unit (€20.40) cards, bought from GVB offices, post offices, train stations, and many supermarkets and tobacconists. Kids under three travel free; older children (four to 18) and seniors (65+) pay reduced fares. *Strippenkaarten* must be stamped on boarding trams/buses or entering Metro stations. For convenience's sake, Amsterdam is divided up roughly into five separate zones: Noord (north), West, Centrum, Oost (east) and Zuid (south); most of central Amsterdam falls within the main Centrum zone.

Journeys work on the principle of one unit for the journey, plus one unit for each zone, so for a single zone, stamp two units; for two zones stamp three and so on.

If the tram is conductorless, stamp the *strippenkaart* in the yellow box near the doors: fold it so the unit you need to stamp is at the end. On conductored trams and buses, the *strippenkaart* is stamped for you. On the Metro, stamping machines are located near the entrance. More than one person can travel on one strip ticket, but the correct number of units must be stamped per person.

Stamped cards are valid for an hour and allow transfer to other buses/trams/metros, or across all three. *Strippenkaarten* are valid for a year from the date of first stamping. Unlimited 24-hour tickets costing €7 (or for 48 hours at €11.50, 72 hours at €14.50 and 96 hours at €17.50), and the Iamsterdam Pass valid for one day at €24 (including canalbus ticket), can also be purchased from either the GVB or Amsterdam Tourist Board. Don't even think about travelling without a ticket:

inspectors make regular checks, and passengers without tickets are hit with €35 on-the-spot fines.

Trams & buses

Trams run from 6am Mon-Fri, 6.30am Sat and 7.30am Sun. Night buses (numbered 351 to 363) take over later (12.30am-7.30am daily), and all go to Centraal Station. Night bus stops are indicated by a black square with the bus number printed on it. During off-peak hours and at quiet stops, stick out your arm to let the driver know you want to get on. Signs at tram and bus stops show the name of the stop and line number, and boards indicate the full route.

The yellow and decorated trams are synonymous with Amsterdam, but the newer, bluer and higher-windowed ones are becoming more common. Other road users must remember that a tram will only stop if absolutely necessary. Cyclists should listen for tram warning bells and cross tramlines at an angle that avoids the front wheel getting stuck. Motorists should avoid blocking tramlines: cars are allowed to venture on to them only if turning right.

Metro

The Metro uses the same ticket system as trams and buses (see above) and serves suburbs to the south and east. Three separate lines, 51, 52 and 53, terminate at Centraal Station (sometimes abbreviated to CS). Trains on the city Metro run from 6am Mon-Fri (6.30am Sat, 7.30am Sun) to around 12.15am on a daily basis.

Taxis

Most taxis are operated by the central office **TCA**. They're hard to hail on the street, but ranks are found around the city; most central are the ones at Centraal Station, by the bus station at the junction of Kinkerstraat and Marnixstraat, on Rembrandtplein and Leidseplein. Cabs can be ordered on 777 7777. Wheelchairs will only be carried in taxis if folded, but there is a service for wheelchair users (633 3943, 7am-5pm daily); be sure to book journeys at least a day in advance.

Getting a taxi in Amsterdam is relatively straightforward, but check that the meter starts at the minimum charge (€7.50, with first two kilometres included) and ask the rough cost of the journey before setting out. Even short journeys are expensive: on top of the minimum charge, it costs €2.20 per kilometre for the first 25 kilometres, €1.75 per kilometre for the next 25 kilometres, and €1.45 thereafter.

If you feel you've been ripped off (relatively rare), ask for a receipt and contact the TCA (650 6506, 9am-5pm Mon-Fri) or the police.

There are companies out to break the monopoly of TCA. One such is the popular **Tulip Taxi** (636 3000), which offers a minimum charge of €2.55, with €0.85 for the first 15 kilometres and €1.50 per kilometre thereafter, saving up to 50% on inner-city rides. Bear in mind that it's a very small fleet, so waiting times are often long.

Driving

If you absolutely must bring a car to the Netherlands, join a national motoring organisation beforehand. This should then issue you with booklets that explain what to do in the event of a breakdown in Europe. To drive a car within the Netherlands, you need a valid national driving licence, although **ANWB** (see below) and many car hire firms favour photocard licences (Brits need the paper

version as well for this to be legal; the photocard takes a couple of weeks to come through if you're applying from scratch). You'll need proof that the vehicle has passed a road safety test in its country of origin, as well as an international identification disk, a registration certificate, and – needless to say – relevant insurance documents.

Car hire

Local car hire (*autoverhuur*) firms generally expect at least a year's experience, and demand a valid national driving licence (with photo) and passport, and drivers to be over 21. All require a credit card deposit with hire.

Adam's Rent-a-Car
685 0111/www.adamsrentacar.nl

Dik's Autoverhuur
662 3366/www.diks.net

Hertz
612 2441/www.hertz.nl

Parking

Parking is a nightmare: the centre is metered from 9am until at least 7pm (midnight in many places), setting you back up to €4.80 an hour; ticketing is extremely common. Parking passes for daytime (9am-7pm, €27.60) or evening (7pm-midnight, €18.40), and weekly passes (9am-7pm, €165.60; 24 hours, €248.40) can be bought from **Stadstoezicht** (www.stadstoezicht.amsterdam.nl). Bear in mind that after controlled hours, parking at meters across the city is completely free.

Car parks

Car parks are indicated by a white 'P' on a blue square sign. **ANWB Parking Amsterdam Centraal** (Prins Hendrikkade 20A in the Old Centre: New Side, 638 5330) is open

24 hours daily and charges €4 per hour, or €50 per day. Many nearby hotels offer a 10% discount on parking here. Europarking (Marnixstraat 250, 0900 446 6880 premium rate) in Oud West is cheaper, charging €3 per hour, or €30 per day, but is only open 6.30am-1am Mon-Wed; 24 hours Thur-Sat; 7am-1am Sun. Both accept payment by credit card. When leaving your car, empty it of valuables: cars with foreign number plates are particularly vulnerable to break-ins.

Clamping & fines

On 13 February 2008, Amsterdam city council voted to end clamping, saying that they plan to fully abolish it by the end of 2008. If you manage to get clamped before the end date, a sticker on your windscreen tells you to phone 251 2222 (24-hour pay-and-go service). Someone will come to remove the clamp for the €103.60 fine (payable by credit card). During business hours, go to any of the clamping offices on www.stadstoezicht. amsterdam.nl and hand over your money; if you have to pay in cash after business hours, go to the pound at Daniel Goedkoopstraat 7-9, then back to the car to wait for someone to remove the clamp.

If you don't pay within 24 hours, you'll be towed: this costs €150 or more, plus a parking fine, plus a tariff per kilometre to reclaim it from the pound within 24 hours, plus €58 for every 12 hours after. Take your passport, licence number and cash or major credit card.

Petrol

There are 24-hour petrol stations (*tankstations*) at Gooiseweg 10, Sarphatistraat 225, Marnixstraat 250 and Spaarndammerdijk 218.

Water transport

Amsterdam is best seen from the water. Sure, there are canal cruises, but they don't offer the freedom to do your own exploring. You can try to bond with a local boat owner; otherwise your options are limited to the pedal-powered canal bike or pedalo. Upon rental, don't ignore the introductory rundown of the rules of the water (put at its most basic: stick to the right and be very wary of canal cruisers, who always assume that size makes right).

Pedaloes

Canal Bike
Weteringschans 24, Southern Canal Belt (626 5574/www.canal.nl). **Open** *Summer* 10am-6pm daily (in good weather until 9.30pm). *Winter* 10am-5.30pm daily at Rijksmuseum; also weekends at Westerkerk and Leidseplein.

Canal buses

Canal Bus
Weteringschans 26, Southern Canal Belt (623 9886/www.canal.nl). Tram 16, 24, 25. **Open** 10am-7pm daily.

Water taxis

Water Taxi Centrale
Stationsplein 8, Old Centre: New Side (535 6363/www.water-taxi.nl). Tram 1, 2, 4, 5, 9, 13, 16, 17, 24, 25, 26. **Open** 8am-midnight daily.

Cycling

There are bike lanes on most roads, marked by white lines and bike symbols. Never leave a bike unlocked, and use two locks. Most bikes have pedal-backwards (as opposed to handlebar-mounted) brakes, which take some getting used to.

ESSENTIALS

Resources A-Z

Accident & emergency

In the case of minor accidents, you can just turn up at the outpatient departments at the following city hospitals (*ziekenhuis*). All are open 24 hours a day, seven days a week, and stay open all year round.

Academisch Medisch Centrum
Meibergdreef 9, Zuid (566 9111/first aid 566 3333). Metro Holendrecht.

Boven IJ Ziekenhuis
Statenjachtstraat 1, Noord (634 6346/first aid 634 6200). Bus 34, 37, 92, 93, 94, 173.

Onze Lieve Vrouwe Gasthuis
's Gravesandeplein 16, Oost (599 9111/first aid 599 3016). Tram 3, 7/bus 37/Metro Weesperplein or Wibautstraat.

St Lucas Andreas Ziekenhuis
Jan Tooropstraat 164, West (510 8911/first aid 510 8161). Tram 13/bus 19, 47, 80, 82, 97.

VU Ziekenhuis
De Boelelaan 1117, Zuid (444 4444/first aid 444 3636). Tram 16, 24/Metro Amstelveenseweg/bus 62, 142, 166, 170, 171, 172, 176, 222.

Banks

There's little difference between the rates of exchange offered by banks and bureaux de change, but banks do tend to charge less commission. Dutch banks will buy and sell foreign currency and exchange travellers' cheques, but bear in mind that few of them will give cash advances against credit cards.

ATMs

Cash machines are only found at banks. If your cashcard carries the Maestro or Cirrus symbols, you should be able to withdraw cash from ATMs, though it's worth checking with your bank that it's possible, and what the charges are.

Customs

EU nationals over 17 years of age may import limitless goods into the Netherlands for their personal use. Other EU countries may still have limits on the quantity of goods they permit on entry. For citizens of non-EU countries, however, the old limits continue to apply as before. These are as follows:

- 200 cigarettes or 50 cigars or 250 grams tobacco;
- two litres of non-sparkling wine or one litre of spirits (over 22 per cent alcohol), or two litres of fortified wine (under 22 per cent alcohol);
- 60cc/ml of perfume;
- 500g coffee or 200g coffee extracts or coffee essence;
- 100g tea or 40g tea extracts or tea essence;
- other goods to the value of €175.

Dentists

To find a dentist (*tandarts*), call 0900 821 2230. Operators can put you in touch with your nearest dentist, and lines are open 24 hours for those with more urgent dental emergencies. Otherwise, you'll need to make yourself an appointment at one of the following.

AOC

Wilhelmina Gasthuisplein 167, Oud West (616 1234). Tram 1, 2, 3, 5, 6, 12. **Open** 9am-noon, 1-4pm Mon-Fri. Emergency dental treatment. They also have a recorded service in Dutch on 686 1109 that tells you where a walk-in clinic will be open at 11.30am and 9.30pm that day.

TBB

570 9595/0900 821 2230 premium rate.
A 24-hour service that can refer callers to a dentist.

Disabled

Winding, cobbled streets, poorly maintained pavements and steep canal house steps can present real problems, but the pragmatic Dutch can generally solve problems quickly. Most large museums, cinemas and theatres have decent disabled facilities (but little for the partially sighted and hard of hearing). The Metro is accessible to wheelchair users with normal arm function, but most trams are inaccessible to wheelchair users, due to high steps. The AUB and Amsterdam Tourist Board produce brochures listing disabled-friendly accommodation, restaurants and attractions in the city.

Electricity

The Netherlands uses standard European 220V, 50-cycle AC voltage via two-pin continental plugs. Visitors from Britain will need an adaptor; American visitors may need a transformer.

Embassies

American Consulate General

Museumplein 19, (575 5309/http:// amsterdam.usconsulate.gov). Tram 2, 3, 5, 12, 16, 24/bus 170.

Australian Embassy

Carnegielaan 4, the Hague (070 310 8200/0800 0224 794 Australian citizen emergency phone/www. australian-embassy.nl).

British Consulate General

Koningslaan 44 (676 4343/www. britain.nl). Tram 2.

British Embassy

Lange Voorhout 10, the Hague (070 427 0427/www.britain.nl).

Canadian Embassy

Sophialaan 7, the Hague (070 311 1600/www.canada.nl).

Irish Embassy

Dr Kuyperstraat 9, the Hague (070 363 0993/www.irishembassy.nl).

New Zealand Embassy

Eisenhowerlaan 77N, the Hague (070 346 9324/visas 070 365 8037/www. immigration.govt.nz/branch/thehague branchhome).

Gay & lesbian information

COC Amsterdam

Rozenstraat 14, the Jordaan (6263087/ www.cocamsterdam.nl). Tram 13, 17/bus142, 144, 170, 172. **Open** *Telephone enquiries* 10am-4pm Mon-Fri.
The Amsterdam branch of COC deals with the campaigning side of gay life.

Gay & Lesbian Switchboard

Postbus 11573 (623 6565/www.switch board.nl). **Open** noon-10pm Mon-Fri; 4-8pm Sat, Sun.
General information and advice on safe sex, from friendly English-speakers.

Helplines

Alcoholics Anonymous

625 6057 (24hr manned service)/ www.aa-netherlands.org.

A lengthy but informative message in both English and Dutch gives the times and dates of meetings, and contact numbers for counsellors. The website is in English, and you can locate meetings by day or by town.

Narcotics Anonymous

662 6307/www.na-holland.nl.
Offers a 24-hour answerphone service in English and Dutch, with counsellors' phone numbers.

SOS Telephone Helpline

675 7575. **Open** 24hrs daily.
A counselling service – comparable with the Samaritans in the UK and Lifeline in the US – for anyone who is surrering emotional problems. English isn't always understood at first, but keep trying and someone will be able to help.

Internet

All global ISPs have a presence here (check websites for a local number). Most of local hotels are increasingly well equipped, with dataports in the rooms, a terminal in the lobby, or Wi-Fi throughout.

Easy Internet Café

Damrak 33, Old Centre: New Side (no phone/www.easyinternetcafe.com). Tram 4, 9, 16, 24, 25. **Open** 9am-10pm daily. **Rates** vary. **No credit cards.**

Freeworld

Nieuwendijk 30, Old Centre: New Side (620 0902). Tram 1, 2, 5, 13, 17, 20. **Open** 9am-1am Mon-Thur; Sun; 9am-3am Fri, Sat. **Rates** €1/30mins. **No credit cards.**
Also a coffeeshop.

Internet Café

Martelaarsgracht 11, Old Centre: New Side (no phone/www.internetcafe.nl). Tram 4, 9, 16, 20, 24, 25. **Open** 9am-1am Mon-Thur, Sun; 9am-3am Fri, Sat. **Rates** from €1/30mins. **No credit cards.**

Left luggage

There's a staffed left-luggage counter at **Schiphol Airport** (601 2443/www.schiphol.nl) where you can store luggage for up to one month, open daily 6am to 11pm, (€6/item/24hrs, €4/item/each 24hrs after). It also has automated lockers accessible 24 hours daily (from €6/24hrs). There are more lockers in the arrival and departure halls, and central Amsterdam has plenty of lockers over at Centraal Station with 24-hour access (they charge from €4 for 24hrs).

Lost property

Centraal Station

Stationsplein 15, Old Centre: Old Side (0900 321 2100 premium rate/www.ns.nl). Tram 1, 2, 4, 5, 9, 13, 16, 17, 24, 25, 26. **Open** 8am-6pm Mon-Fri; 7am-5pm Sat.
Items found on trains are kept here for three days (it's easiest to just go to any window where tickets are sold and ask), after which time they are forwarded on to Centraal Bureau Gevonden Voorwerpen (Central Lost Property Office), 2e Daalsedijk 4, 3551 EJ Utrecht (030 235 3923, 8am-5pm Mon-Fri), and held for three months. If you pick it up personally it costs €10; having it posted costs €15 and up.

GVB Lost Property

Arlandaweg 100 (0900 8011 premium rate/460 6060). Tram 12. **Open** 9am-4pm Mon-Fri.
Wait at least a day or two before you call, describe what you lost on the bus, metro or tram, and leave a number. They will call you back if it's found. Alternatively, there's also an online form (in Dutch) for lost property at www.gvb.nl.

Police Lost Property

Stephensonstraat 18, Zuid (559 3005). Tram 12/Metro Amstel Station/bus 14.

Open *In person* 9.30am-3.30pm Mon-Fri. *By phone* noon-3.30pm Mon-Fri. Before trying here, check the local police station.

Opening hours

Banks open 9am-5pm, Mon-Fri (Postbank 9.30am-1pm Sat). **Bars** open at various times throughout the day and close at around 1am Mon-Thur, Sun; 2am or 3am Fri, Sat. **Shops** open 1-6pm Mon (although many stay closed on this day); 10am-6pm Tue-Fri (some until 9pm Thur); 9am-5pm Sat.

Pharmacies

Dam Apotheek

Damstraat 2, Old Centre: Old Side (624 4331). Tram 4, 9, 14, 16, 24, 25. **Open** 8.30am-5.30pm Mon-Fri; 10am-5pm Sat.

This central pharmacy has extended opening. Outside these hours, customers can phone Afdeling Inlichtingen Apotheken (694 8709), a 24-hour service that will direct you to your nearest late-opening chemist.

Police stations

For details and contact information on local stations, look under 'Politie' in the *Gouden Gids*.

Amsterdam Tourist Assistance Service (ATAS)

Nieuwezijds Voorburgwal 104-108 (625 3246). Tram 1, 2, 5, 6, 13, 17. **Open** 10am-10pm daily.

Hoofdbureau van Politie (Police Headquarters)

Elandsgracht 117, the Jordaan (0900 8844 premium rate). Tram 13, 17/ bus 170, 172. **Open** 24hrs daily.

Post

Post offices are usually open 9am-5pm Mon-Fri; 9.30am-1pm Sat. The postal information phoneline is 058 233 3333. The main post office is at Singel 250, Old Centre: New Side (0900 767 8526 premium rate). It's open 9am-6pm Mon-Fri; 10am-2pm Sat.

Safety

Amsterdam is a relatively safe city, but do take care. The Red Light District is rife with undesirables who, if not violent, are expert pickpockets; be vigilant, especially on or around bridges; and don't ever make eye contact with anyone who looks like they're up to no good, drug dealers especially.

Be extra careful of thieves on the Schiphol train; if you cycle, lock your bike up well (two locks). Keep valuables in your hotel safe, don't leave bags unattended, and make sure cash and cards are tucked and preferably zipped up in your bag.

Smoking

As of summer 2008, the Netherlands imposed a smoking ban in all public indoor spaces. As for cannabis, locals have a relaxed attitude, but smoking it isn't acceptable everywhere in the city: use discretion, and if in doubt, ask before you spark up.

Telephones

Amsterdam's dialling code is 020; to call within the city, you don't need the code. If you're dialling from outside the Netherlands, dial the country code, 31, then the number; drop the first '0' of the area code; for Amsterdam you would use 20 rather than the full 020.

US mobile phone users should be sure to contact their provider in advance of departure, to check compatibility with GSM bands.

Public phones

Public phones take cards not coins, available from the Tourist Board, tobacconists, stations and post offices. Many also take credit cards.

Time

Amsterdam is one hour ahead of Greenwich Mean Time (GMT). All clocks on Central European Time (CET) now go back and forward on the same dates as GMT.

Tipping

Service charges are included in hotel, taxi, bar, café and restaurant bills, but it's polite to round up to the nearest euro for small bills or the nearest five for larger sums, though tipping ten per cent is becoming more common (leave the extra in change rather than filling in the credit card slip). In taxis, most people tip ten per cent.

Tourist information

Amsterdam Tourist Board (VVV)

Stationsplein 10, Old Centre: New Side (0900 400 4040/www.visitamsterdam. nl). Tram 1, 2, 4, 5, 9, 13, 16, 17, 24, 25, 26. **Open** 9am-5pm daily.
The main office is right outside Centraal Station. English-speaking staff change money and provide info on transport, entertainment, exhibitions and day-trips. They also arrange hotel bookings (for a fee), excursions or car hire for free. Brochures detail walks and cycling tours, plus you'll find cassette tours, maps and a monthly listings mag, Day by Day. The info line has an English-language service (€0.40/min).
Other locations: Leidseplein 1 (9.15am-5pm Mon-Thur, Sun; 9.15am-7pm Fri, Sat); Centraal Station, platform 2B 15 (8am-8pm Mon-Sat;

9am-5pm Sun); Schiphol Airport, arrivals hall 2 (7am-10pm daily).

Translators & interpreters

Amstelveens Vertaalburo

Ouderkerkerlaan 50, Amstelveen (645 6610/www.avb.nl). Tram 51/bus 166, 170, 199, 300. **Open** 9am-5pm Mon-Fri. **No credit cards**.

Mac Bay Consultants

PC Hooftstraat 15, Museum Quarter (24hr phoneline 662 0501/fax 662 6299/www.macbay.nl). Tram 2/bus 170, 172. **Open** 9am-7pm Mon-Fri.

Visas

EU citizens do not require a visa; citizens of the USA, Canada, Australia and New Zealand need a valid passport for stays up to three months. Otherwise, apply for a tourist visa. EU nationals with a resident's permit can work here; for non-EU citizens it's hard to get a visa without a job in place. Either way, jobs are not easy come by.

When to go

Climate

Amsterdam's climate is extremely changeable. January and February are cold, and summer humid. If you know Dutch, call the weather line on 0900 8003 (€0.60/min).

Public holidays

Called 'Nationale Feestdagen' in Dutch: New Year's Day; Good Friday; Easter Sunday and Monday; Koninginnedag (Queen's Day, 30 April); Remembrance Day (4 May); Liberation Day (5 May); Ascension Day; Whit (Pentecost) Sunday and Monday; Christmas Day; and Boxing Day.

ESSENTIALS

Vocabulary

Almost every person you'll come across in Amsterdam will speak good English, and you'll be able to get by without a word of Dutch during your stay. However, a bit of effort goes a long way, and locals are appreciative of those visitors polite enough to take five minutes to learn some basic phrases. Here are a few that might help.

Useful expressions

Hello hallo/dag; **goodbye** tot ziens/dag; **yes** ja; **yes please** ja, graag; **no** nee; **no thanks** nee, dank je; **please** alstublieft; **thank you** dank u; **excuse me** pardon; **do you speak English?** spreekt u Engels?; **sorry, I don't speak Dutch** het spijt me, ik spreek geen Nederlands; **I don't understand** ik begrijp het niet; **I am ill** ik ben ziek; **good** goed; **bad** slecht; **big** groot; **small** klein; **nice** mooi; **tasty** lekker; **open** open; **closed** gesloten/dicht; **entrance** ingang; **exit** uitgang; **the bill** de rekening; **shop** winkel; **hotel room** hotelkamer; **single/twin/double bedroom** eenpersoonskamer/tweepersoonskamer met aparte bedden/tweepersoonskamer; **I want** ik wil graag; **how much is** wat kost

Getting around

Bus bus; **car** auto; **tram** tram; **train** trein; **ticket/s** kaart/kaarten; **street** straat; **square** plein; **canal** gracht; **left** links; **right** rechts; **straight on** rechtdoor; **far** ver; **near** dichtbij; **here** hier; **there** daar; **where is** waar is

Places

Shop winkel; **bank** bank; **post office** postkantoor; **pharmacy** apotheek; **hotel** hotel; **bar** bar; **restaurant** restaurant; **hospital** ziekenhuis; **bus stop** bushalte; **station** station

Time

Now nu; **later** straks; **morning** ochtend; **afternoon** middag; **evening** avond; **night** nacht; **today** vandaag; **yesterday** gisteren; **tomorrow** morgen; **what time is** hoe laat is; **what's the time?** hoe laat is het?; **noon** middag; **midnight** middernacht; **at eight o'clock** om acht uur; **quarter past eight** kwaart over acht; **20 past eight** tien voor half negen; **25 past eight** vijf half negen; **half past eight** half negen; **25 to nine** vijf over half negen; **quarter to nine** kwaart voor negen

Numbers

0 nul; **1** een; **2** twee; **3** drie; **4** vier; **5** vijf; **6** zes; **7** zeven; **8** acht; **9** negen; **10** tien; **11** elf; **12** twaalf; **13** dertien; **14** veertien; **15** vijftien; **16** zestien; **17** zeventien; **18** achttien; **19** negen-tien; **20** twintig; **21** eenentwintig; **22** twee'ntwintig; **30** dertig; **40** veertig; **50** vijftig; **60** zestig; **70** zeventig; **80** tachtig; **90** negentig; **100** honderd; **101** honderd een; **200** tweehonderd; **1,000** duizend; **1,000,000** een miljoen

Days & months

Monday maandag; **Tuesday** dinsdag; **Wednesday** woensdag; **Thursday** donderdag; **Friday** vrijdag; **Saturday** zaterdag; **Sunday** zondag; **January** januari; **February** februari; **March** maart; **April** april; **May** mei; **June** juni; **July** juli; **August** augustus; **September** september; **October** oktober; **November** november; **December** december

Menu Glossary

Basics

Bestek cutlery; **brood** bread; **broodje** bread roll; **glas** glass; **lepel** spoon; **menukaart** menu; **mes** knife; **peper** pepper; **de rekening** the bill; **vork** fork; **wijnkaart** wine list; **zout** salt

Snacks

Bitterballen round, mini-croquettes filled with meat and potato; **borrel/bittergarnituur** sharing platter of snacks to accompany drinks (usually sausage, salami, cheese and *bitterballen*); **borrelnoten** crispy-coated nuts; **frikadel** a very popular deep-fried skinless sausage with ingredients best left a mystery; **kaassouffle** cheese fritter, only tasty when very hot; **kroket** croquette filled with meat and potato; **oliebollen** deep-fried dough balls traditionally served around New Year, either plain or supplemented with raisins, currants and/or diced apples; **pannekoek** pancake; **patat** French fries/chips, also called *frites*; **patat met** French fries/chips with mayonnaise; **pindas** peanuts; **saucijzenbroodje** hot sausage roll made with puff pastry; **snert** a thick pea soup, also called *erwtensoep*; **tostis** grilled ham and/or cheese sandwiches; **uitsmijter** cheese and/or ham on bread topped with three fried eggs

Meat

Bal/gehaktbal meatball; **biefstuk** steak; **bio** organic; **eend** duck; **kalf** veal; **kalkoen** turkey; **kip** chicken; **lam** lamb; **rund** beef; **scharrel** free-range; **spek** bacon; **struisvogel** ostrich; **varkensvlees** pork; **vlees** meat; **worst** sausage

Fish

Ansjovis anchovies; **gambas** prawns; **garnalen** shrimps; **gerookte** smoked; **haring** herring; **maatjesharing** first herring of the season; **makreel** mackerel; **mosselen** mussels; **oesters** oysters; **paling** eel; **tong** sole; **tonijn** tuna; **venusschelpen** clams; **vis** fish; **zalm** salmon; **zeeduivel** monkfish; **zeevruchten/zeebanket** seafood

Fruit & vegetables

Aardappel potato; **aardbei** strawberry; **appel** apple; **bosbes** blueberry; **champignons** mushrooms; **citroen** lemon; **druiven** grapes; **framboos** raspberry; **fruit/vruchten** fruit; **groenten** vegetables; **kersen** cherries; **knoflook** garlic; **kruiden** herbs; **limoen** lime; **rauwkost** coleslaw; **rijst** rice; **sinasappel** orange; **zuurkool** sauerkraut

Puddings & cakes

Flensje crêpe; **gember** ginger; **griesmeel** semolina; **hangop** strained thick yoghurt; **honing** honey; **koek** cake; **koekje** biscuit; **roomijs/ijs** ice-cream; **slagroom** whipped cream; **stroop** syrup; **suiker** sugar; **toetje** dessert; **vla** custard

Dairy

Blauwe kaas blue cheese; **boter** butter; **geitenkaas** goat's cheese; **kaas** cheese; **magere/halfvolle/volle melk** skimmed/semi-skimmed/full milk; **oud/extra belegen** mature; **roomkaas** cream cheese; **schapenkaas** cheese made from sheep's milk

Index

Sights & areas

ESSENTIALS

ESSENTIALS

ESSENTIALS

Notes

ESSENTIALS

ESSENTIALS

ESSENTIALS

ESSENTIALS

ESSENTIALS